Mometrix
TEST PREPARATION

Certified Energy Manager® Exam Secrets Study Guide

Dear Future Exam Success Story

First of all, **THANK YOU** for purchasing Mometrix study materials!

Second, congratulations! You are one of the few determined test-takers who are committed to doing whatever it takes to excel on your exam. **You have come to the right place.** We developed these study materials with one goal in mind: to deliver you the information you need in a format that's concise and easy to use.

In addition to optimizing your guide for the content of the test, we've outlined our recommended steps for breaking down the preparation process into small, attainable goals so you can make sure you stay on track.

We've also analyzed the entire test-taking process, identifying the most common pitfalls and showing how you can overcome them and be ready for any curveball the test throws you.

Standardized testing is one of the biggest obstacles on your road to success, which only increases the importance of doing well in the high-pressure, high-stakes environment of test day. Your results on this test could have a significant impact on your future, and this guide provides the information and practical advice to help you achieve your full potential on test day.

Your success is our success

We would love to hear from you! If you would like to share the story of your exam success or if you have any questions or comments in regard to our products, please contact us at **800-673-8175** or **support@mometrix.com**.

Thanks again for your business and we wish you continued success!

Sincerely,
The Mometrix Test Preparation Team

Need more help? Check out our flashcards at:
http://MometrixFlashcards.com/EnergyManager

Written and edited by the Mometrix Exam Secrets Test Prep Team
Printed in the United States of America

TABLE OF CONTENTS

Introduction

Thank you for purchasing this resource! You have made the choice to prepare yourself for a test that could have a huge impact on your future, and this guide is designed to help you be fully ready for test day. Obviously, it's important to have a solid understanding of the test material, but you also need to be prepared for the unique environment and stressors of the test, so that you can perform to the best of your abilities.

For this purpose, the first section that appears in this guide is the **Secret Keys**. We've devoted countless hours to meticulously researching what works and what doesn't, and we've boiled down our findings to the five most impactful steps you can take to improve your performance on the test. We start at the beginning with study planning and move through the preparation process, all the way to the testing strategies that will help you get the most out of what you know when you're finally sitting in front of the test.

We recommend that you start preparing for your test as far in advance as possible. However, if you've bought this guide as a last-minute study resource and only have a few days before your test, we recommend that you skip over the first two Secret Keys since they address a long-term study plan.

If you struggle with **test anxiety**, we strongly encourage you to check out our recommendations for how you can overcome it. Test anxiety is a formidable foe, but it can be beaten, and we want to make sure you have the tools you need to defeat it.

Secret Key #1 – Plan Big, Study Small

There's a lot riding on your performance. If you want to ace this test, you're going to need to keep your skills sharp and the material fresh in your mind. You need a plan that lets you review everything you need to know while still fitting in your schedule. We'll break this strategy down into three categories.

Information Organization

Start with the information you already have: the official test outline. From this, you can make a complete list of all the concepts you need to cover before the test. Organize these concepts into groups that can be studied together, and create a list of any related vocabulary you need to learn so you can brush up on any difficult terms. You'll want to keep this vocabulary list handy once you actually start studying since you may need to add to it along the way.

Time Management

Once you have your set of study concepts, decide how to spread them out over the time you have left before the test. Break your study plan into small, clear goals so you have a manageable task for each day and know exactly what you're doing. Then just focus on one small step at a time. When you manage your time this way, you don't need to spend hours at a time studying. Studying a small block of content for a short period each day helps you retain information better and avoid stressing over how much you have left to do. You can relax knowing that you have a plan to cover everything in time. In order for this strategy to be effective though, you have to start studying early and stick to your schedule. Avoid the exhaustion and futility that comes from last-minute cramming!

Study Environment

The environment you study in has a big impact on your learning. Studying in a coffee shop, while probably more enjoyable, is not likely to be as fruitful as studying in a quiet room. It's important to keep distractions to a minimum. You're only planning to study for a short block of time, so make the most of it. Don't pause to check your phone or get up to find a snack. It's also important to **avoid multitasking**. Research has consistently shown that multitasking will make your studying dramatically less effective. Your study area should also be comfortable and well-lit so you don't have the distraction of straining your eyes or sitting on an uncomfortable chair.

The time of day you study is also important. You want to be rested and alert. Don't wait until just before bedtime. Study when you'll be most likely to comprehend and remember. Even better, if you know what time of day your test will be, set that time aside for study. That way your brain will be used to working on that subject at that specific time and you'll have a better chance of recalling information.

Finally, it can be helpful to team up with others who are studying for the same test. Your actual studying should be done in as isolated an environment as possible, but the work of organizing the information and setting up the study plan can be divided up. In between study sessions, you can discuss with your teammates the concepts that you're all studying and quiz each other on the details. Just be sure that your teammates are as serious about the test as you are. If you find that your study time is being replaced with social time, you might need to find a new team.

Secret Key #2 – Make Your Studying Count

You're devoting a lot of time and effort to preparing for this test, so you want to be absolutely certain it will pay off. This means doing more than just reading the content and hoping you can remember it on test day. It's important to make every minute of study count. There are two main areas you can focus on to make your studying count.

Retention

It doesn't matter how much time you study if you can't remember the material. You need to make sure you are retaining the concepts. To check your retention of the information you're learning, try recalling it at later times with minimal prompting. Try carrying around flashcards and glance at one or two from time to time or ask a friend who's also studying for the test to quiz you.

To enhance your retention, look for ways to put the information into practice so that you can apply it rather than simply recalling it. If you're using the information in practical ways, it will be much easier to remember. Similarly, it helps to solidify a concept in your mind if you're not only reading it to yourself but also explaining it to someone else. Ask a friend to let you teach them about a concept you're a little shaky on (or speak aloud to an imaginary audience if necessary). As you try to summarize, define, give examples, and answer your friend's questions, you'll understand the concepts better and they will stay with you longer. Finally, step back for a big picture view and ask yourself how each piece of information fits with the whole subject. When you link the different concepts together and see them working together as a whole, it's easier to remember the individual components.

Finally, practice showing your work on any multi-step problems, even if you're just studying. Writing out each step you take to solve a problem will help solidify the process in your mind, and you'll be more likely to remember it during the test.

Modality

Modality simply refers to the means or method by which you study. Choosing a study modality that fits your own individual learning style is crucial. No two people learn best in exactly the same way, so it's important to know your strengths and use them to your advantage.

For example, if you learn best by visualization, focus on visualizing a concept in your mind and draw an image or a diagram. Try color-coding your notes, illustrating them, or creating symbols that will trigger your mind to recall a learned concept. If you learn best by hearing or discussing information, find a study partner who learns the same way or read aloud to yourself. Think about how to put the information in your own words. Imagine that you are giving a lecture on the topic and record yourself so you can listen to it later.

For any learning style, flashcards can be helpful. Organize the information so you can take advantage of spare moments to review. Underline key words or phrases. Use different colors for different categories. Mnemonic devices (such as creating a short list in which every item starts with the same letter) can also help with retention. Find what works best for you and use it to store the information in your mind most effectively and easily.

Secret Key #3 – Practice the Right Way

Your success on test day depends not only on how many hours you put into preparing, but also on whether you prepared the right way. It's good to check along the way to see if your studying is paying off. One of the most effective ways to do this is by taking practice tests to evaluate your progress. Practice tests are useful because they show exactly where you need to improve. Every time you take a practice test, pay special attention to these three groups of questions:

- The questions you got wrong
- The questions you had to guess on, even if you guessed right
- The questions you found difficult or slow to work through

This will show you exactly what your weak areas are, and where you need to devote more study time. Ask yourself why each of these questions gave you trouble. Was it because you didn't understand the material? Was it because you didn't remember the vocabulary? Do you need more repetitions on this type of question to build speed and confidence? Dig into those questions and figure out how you can strengthen your weak areas as you go back to review the material.

Additionally, many practice tests have a section explaining the answer choices. It can be tempting to read the explanation and think that you now have a good understanding of the concept. However, an explanation likely only covers part of the question's broader context. Even if the explanation makes perfect sense, **go back and investigate** every concept related to the question until you're positive you have a thorough understanding.

As you go along, keep in mind that the practice test is just that: practice. Memorizing these questions and answers will not be very helpful on the actual test because it is unlikely to have any of the same exact questions. If you only know the right answers to the sample questions, you won't be prepared for the real thing. **Study the concepts** until you understand them fully, and then you'll be able to answer any question that shows up on the test.

It's important to wait on the practice tests until you're ready. If you take a test on your first day of study, you may be overwhelmed by the amount of material covered and how much you need to learn. Work up to it gradually.

On test day, you'll need to be prepared for answering questions, managing your time, and using the test-taking strategies you've learned. It's a lot to balance, like a mental marathon that will have a big impact on your future. Like training for a marathon, you'll need to start slowly and work your way up. When test day arrives, you'll be ready.

Start with the strategies you've read in the first two Secret Keys—plan your course and study in the way that works best for you. If you have time, consider using multiple study resources to get different approaches to the same concepts. It can be helpful to see difficult concepts from more than one angle. Then find a good source for practice tests. Many times, the test website will suggest potential study resources or provide sample tests.

Practice Test Strategy

If you're able to find at least three practice tests, we recommend this strategy:

Untimed and Open-Book Practice

Take the first test with no time constraints and with your notes and study guide handy. Take your time and focus on applying the strategies you've learned.

Timed and Open-Book Practice

Take the second practice test open-book as well, but set a timer and practice pacing yourself to finish in time.

Timed and Closed-Book Practice

Take any other practice tests as if it were test day. Set a timer and put away your study materials. Sit at a table or desk in a quiet room, imagine yourself at the testing center, and answer questions as quickly and accurately as possible.

Keep repeating timed and closed-book tests on a regular basis until you run out of practice tests or it's time for the actual test. Your mind will be ready for the schedule and stress of test day, and you'll be able to focus on recalling the material you've learned.

Secret Key #4 – Pace Yourself

Once you're fully prepared for the material on the test, your biggest challenge on test day will be managing your time. Just knowing that the clock is ticking can make you panic even if you have plenty of time left. Work on pacing yourself so you can build confidence against the time constraints of the exam. Pacing is a difficult skill to master, especially in a high-pressure environment, so **practice is vital**.

Set time expectations for your pace based on how much time is available. For example, if a section has 60 questions and the time limit is 30 minutes, you know you have to average 30 seconds or less per question in order to answer them all. Although 30 seconds is the hard limit, set 25 seconds per question as your goal, so you reserve extra time to spend on harder questions. When you budget extra time for the harder questions, you no longer have any reason to stress when those questions take longer to answer.

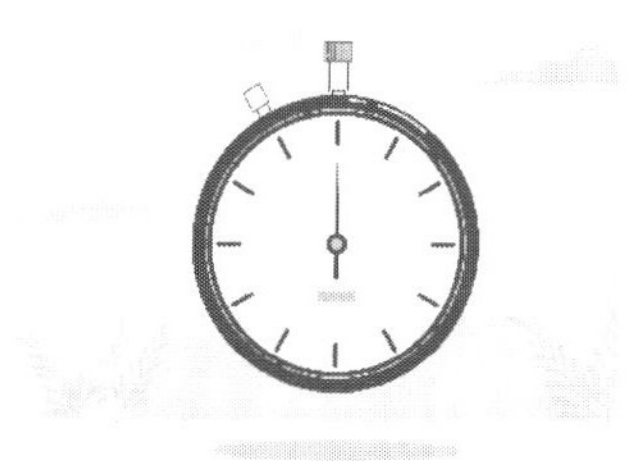

Don't let this time expectation distract you from working through the test at a calm, steady pace, but keep it in mind so you don't spend too much time on any one question. Recognize that taking extra time on one question you don't understand may keep you from answering two that you do understand later in the test. If your time limit for a question is up and you're still not sure of the answer, mark it and move on, and come back to it later if the time and the test format allow. If the testing format doesn't allow you to return to earlier questions, just make an educated guess; then put it out of your mind and move on.

On the easier questions, be careful not to rush. It may seem wise to hurry through them so you have more time for the challenging ones, but it's not worth missing one if you know the concept and just didn't take the time to read the question fully. Work efficiently but make sure you understand the question and have looked at all of the answer choices, since more than one may seem right at first.

Even if you're paying attention to the time, you may find yourself a little behind at some point. You should speed up to get back on track, but do so wisely. Don't panic; just take a few seconds less on each question until you're caught up. Don't guess without thinking, but do look through the answer choices and eliminate any you know are wrong. If you can get down to two choices, it is often worthwhile to guess from those. Once you've chosen an answer, move on and don't dwell on any that you skipped or had to hurry through. If a question was taking too long, chances are it was one of the harder ones, so you weren't as likely to get it right anyway.

On the other hand, if you find yourself getting ahead of schedule, it may be beneficial to slow down a little. The more quickly you work, the more likely you are to make a careless mistake that will affect your score. You've budgeted time for each question, so don't be afraid to spend that time. Practice an efficient but careful pace to get the most out of the time you have.

Secret Key #5 – Have a Plan for Guessing

When you're taking the test, you may find yourself stuck on a question. Some of the answer choices seem better than others, but you don't see the one answer choice that is obviously correct. What do you do?

The scenario described above is very common, yet most test takers have not effectively prepared for it. Developing and practicing a plan for guessing may be one of the single most effective uses of your time as you get ready for the exam.

In developing your plan for guessing, there are three questions to address:

- When should you start the guessing process?
- How should you narrow down the choices?
- Which answer should you choose?

When to Start the Guessing Process

Unless your plan for guessing is to select C every time (which, despite its merits, is not what we recommend), you need to leave yourself enough time to apply your answer elimination strategies. Since you have a limited amount of time for each question, that means that if you're going to give yourself the best shot at guessing correctly, you have to decide quickly whether or not you will guess.

Of course, the best-case scenario is that you don't have to guess at all, so first, see if you can answer the question based on your knowledge of the subject and basic reasoning skills. Focus on the key words in the question and try to jog your memory of related topics. Give yourself a chance to bring the knowledge to mind, but once you realize that you don't have (or you can't access) the knowledge you need to answer the question, it's time to start the guessing process.

It's almost always better to start the guessing process too early than too late. It only takes a few seconds to remember something and answer the question from knowledge. Carefully eliminating wrong answer choices takes longer. Plus, going through the process of eliminating answer choices can actually help jog your memory.

Summary: Start the guessing process as soon as you decide that you can't answer the question based on your knowledge.

How to Narrow Down the Choices

The next chapter in this book (**Test-Taking Strategies**) includes a wide range of strategies for how to approach questions and how to look for answer choices to eliminate. You will definitely want to read those carefully, practice them, and figure out which ones work best for you. Here though, we're going to address a mindset rather than a particular strategy.

Your odds of guessing an answer correctly depend on how many options you are choosing from.

Number of options left	5	4	3	2	1
Odds of guessing correctly	20%	25%	33%	50%	100%

You can see from this chart just how valuable it is to be able to eliminate incorrect answers and make an educated guess, but there are two things that many test takers do that cause them to miss out on the benefits of guessing:

- Accidentally eliminating the correct answer
- Selecting an answer based on an impression

We'll look at the first one here, and the second one in the next section.

To avoid accidentally eliminating the correct answer, we recommend a thought exercise called **the $5 challenge**. In this challenge, you only eliminate an answer choice from contention if you are willing to bet $5 on it being wrong. Why $5? Five dollars is a small but not insignificant amount of money. It's an amount you could afford to lose but wouldn't want to throw away. And while losing $5 once might not hurt too much, doing it twenty times will set you back $100. In the same way, each small decision you make—eliminating a choice here, guessing on a question there—won't by itself impact your score very much, but when you put them all together, they can make a big difference. By holding each answer choice elimination decision to a higher standard, you can reduce the risk of accidentally eliminating the correct answer.

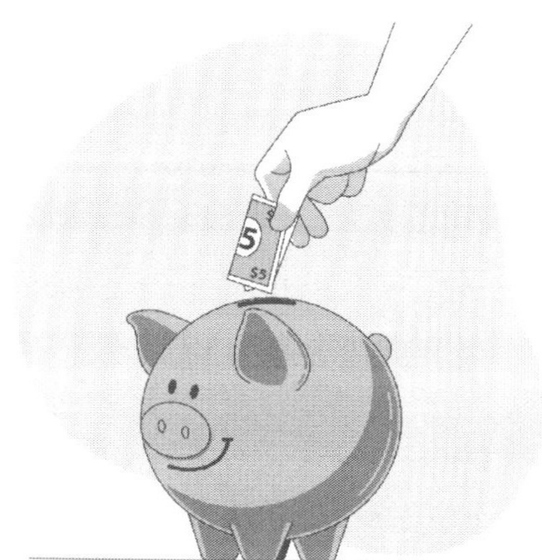

The $5 challenge can also be applied in a positive sense: If you are willing to bet $5 that an answer choice *is* correct, go ahead and mark it as correct.

Summary: Only eliminate an answer choice if you are willing to bet $5 that it is wrong.

Which Answer to Choose

You're taking the test. You've run into a hard question and decided you'll have to guess. You've eliminated all the answer choices you're willing to bet $5 on. Now you have to pick an answer. Why do we even need to talk about this? Why can't you just pick whichever one you feel like when the time comes?

The answer to these questions is that if you don't come into the test with a plan, you'll rely on your impression to select an answer choice, and if you do that, you risk falling into a trap. The test writers know that everyone who takes their test will be guessing on some of the questions, so they intentionally write wrong answer choices to seem plausible. You still have to pick an answer though, and if the wrong answer choices are designed to look right, how can you ever be sure that you're not falling for their trap? The best solution we've found to this dilemma is to take the decision out of your hands entirely. Here is the process we recommend:

Once you've eliminated any choices that you are confident (willing to bet $5) are wrong, select the first remaining choice as your answer.

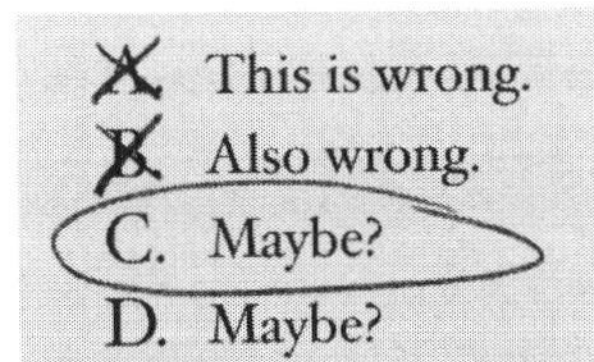

Whether you choose to select the first remaining choice, the second, or the last, the important thing is that you use some preselected standard. Using this approach guarantees that you will not be enticed into selecting an answer choice that looks right, because you are not basing your decision on how the answer choices look.

This is not meant to make you question your knowledge. Instead, it is to help you recognize the difference between your knowledge and your impressions. There's a huge difference between thinking an answer is right because of what you know, and thinking an answer is right because it looks or sounds like it should be right.

Summary: To ensure that your selection is appropriately random, make a predetermined selection from among all answer choices you have not eliminated.

Test-Taking Strategies

This section contains a list of test-taking strategies that you may find helpful as you work through the test. By taking what you know and applying logical thought, you can maximize your chances of answering any question correctly!

It is very important to realize that every question is different and every person is different: no single strategy will work on every question, and no single strategy will work for every person. That's why we've included all of them here, so you can try them out and determine which ones work best for different types of questions and which ones work best for you.

Question Strategies

✓ Read Carefully

Read the question and the answer choices carefully. Don't miss the question because you misread the terms. You have plenty of time to read each question thoroughly and make sure you understand what is being asked. Yet a happy medium must be attained, so don't waste too much time. You must read carefully and efficiently.

✓ Contextual Clues

Look for contextual clues. If the question includes a word you are not familiar with, look at the immediate context for some indication of what the word might mean. Contextual clues can often give you all the information you need to decipher the meaning of an unfamiliar word. Even if you can't determine the meaning, you may be able to narrow down the possibilities enough to make a solid guess at the answer to the question.

✓ Prefixes

If you're having trouble with a word in the question or answer choices, try dissecting it. Take advantage of every clue that the word might include. Prefixes can be a huge help. Usually, they allow you to determine a basic meaning. *Pre-* means before, *post-* means after, *pro-* is positive, *de-* is negative. From prefixes, you can get an idea of the general meaning of the word and try to put it into context.

✓ Hedge Words

Watch out for critical hedge words, such as *likely, may, can, often, almost, mostly, usually, generally, rarely*, and *sometimes*. Question writers insert these hedge phrases to cover every possibility. Often an answer choice will be wrong simply because it leaves no room for exception. Be on guard for answer choices that have definitive words such as *exactly* and *always*.

✓ Switchback Words

Stay alert for *switchbacks*. These are the words and phrases frequently used to alert you to shifts in thought. The most common switchback words are *but, although*, and *however*. Others include *nevertheless, on the other hand, even though, while, in spite of, despite*, and *regardless of*. Switchback words are important to catch because they can change the direction of the question or an answer choice.

✓ Face Value

When in doubt, use common sense. Accept the situation in the problem at face value. Don't read too much into it. These problems will not require you to make wild assumptions. If you have to go beyond creativity and warp time or space in order to have an answer choice fit the question, then you should move on and consider the other answer choices. These are normal problems rooted in reality. The applicable relationship or explanation may not be readily apparent, but it is there for you to figure out. Use your common sense to interpret anything that isn't clear.

Answer Choice Strategies

✓ Answer Selection

The most thorough way to pick an answer choice is to identify and eliminate wrong answers until only one is left, then confirm it is the correct answer. Sometimes an answer choice may immediately seem right, but be careful. The test writers will usually put more than one reasonable answer choice on each question, so take a second to read all of them and make sure that the other choices are not equally obvious. As long as you have time left, it is better to read every answer choice than to pick the first one that looks right without checking the others.

✓ Answer Choice Families

An answer choice family consists of two (in rare cases, three) answer choices that are very similar in construction and cannot all be true at the same time. If you see two answer choices that are direct opposites or parallels, one of them is usually the correct answer. For instance, if one answer choice says that quantity x increases and another either says that quantity x decreases (opposite) or says that quantity y increases (parallel), then those answer choices would fall into the same family. An answer choice that doesn't match the construction of the answer choice family is more likely to be incorrect. Most questions will not have answer choice families, but when they do appear, you should be prepared to recognize them.

✓ Eliminate Answers

Eliminate answer choices as soon as you realize they are wrong, but make sure you consider all possibilities. If you are eliminating answer choices and realize that the last one you are left with is also wrong, don't panic. Start over and consider each choice again. There may be something you missed the first time that you will realize on the second pass.

✓ Avoid Fact Traps

Don't be distracted by an answer choice that is factually true but doesn't answer the question. You are looking for the choice that answers the question. Stay focused on what the question is asking for so you don't accidentally pick an answer that is true but incorrect. Always go back to the question and make sure the answer choice you've selected actually answers the question and is not merely a true statement.

✓ Extreme Statements

In general, you should avoid answers that put forth extreme actions as standard practice or proclaim controversial ideas as established fact. An answer choice that states the "process should be used in certain situations, if..." is much more likely to be correct than one that states the "process should be discontinued completely." The first is a calm rational statement and doesn't even make a definitive, uncompromising stance, using a hedge word *if* to provide wiggle room, whereas the second choice is far more extreme.

⊘ BENCHMARK

As you read through the answer choices and you come across one that seems to answer the question well, mentally select that answer choice. This is not your final answer, but it's the one that will help you evaluate the other answer choices. The one that you selected is your benchmark or standard for judging each of the other answer choices. Every other answer choice must be compared to your benchmark. That choice is correct until proven otherwise by another answer choice beating it. If you find a better answer, then that one becomes your new benchmark. Once you've decided that no other choice answers the question as well as your benchmark, you have your final answer.

⊘ PREDICT THE ANSWER

Before you even start looking at the answer choices, it is often best to try to predict the answer. When you come up with the answer on your own, it is easier to avoid distractions and traps because you will know exactly what to look for. The right answer choice is unlikely to be word-for-word what you came up with, but it should be a close match. Even if you are confident that you have the right answer, you should still take the time to read each option before moving on.

General Strategies

⊘ TOUGH QUESTIONS

If you are stumped on a problem or it appears too hard or too difficult, don't waste time. Move on! Remember though, if you can quickly check for obviously incorrect answer choices, your chances of guessing correctly are greatly improved. Before you completely give up, at least try to knock out a couple of possible answers. Eliminate what you can and then guess at the remaining answer choices before moving on.

⊘ CHECK YOUR WORK

Since you will probably not know every term listed and the answer to every question, it is important that you get credit for the ones that you do know. Don't miss any questions through careless mistakes. If at all possible, try to take a second to look back over your answer selection and make sure you've selected the correct answer choice and haven't made a costly careless mistake (such as marking an answer choice that you didn't mean to mark). This quick double check should more than pay for itself in caught mistakes for the time it costs.

⊘ PACE YOURSELF

It's easy to be overwhelmed when you're looking at a page full of questions; your mind is confused and full of random thoughts, and the clock is ticking down faster than you would like. Calm down and maintain the pace that you have set for yourself. Especially as you get down to the last few minutes of the test, don't let the small numbers on the clock make you panic. As long as you are on track by monitoring your pace, you are guaranteed to have time for each question.

⊘ DON'T RUSH

It is very easy to make errors when you are in a hurry. Maintaining a fast pace in answering questions is pointless if it makes you miss questions that you would have gotten right otherwise. Test writers like to include distracting information and wrong answers that seem right. Taking a little extra time to avoid careless mistakes can make all the difference in your test score. Find a pace that allows you to be confident in the answers that you select.

⊘ Keep Moving

Panicking will not help you pass the test, so do your best to stay calm and keep moving. Taking deep breaths and going through the answer elimination steps you practiced can help to break through a stress barrier and keep your pace.

Final Notes

The combination of a solid foundation of content knowledge and the confidence that comes from practicing your plan for applying that knowledge is the key to maximizing your performance on test day. As your foundation of content knowledge is built up and strengthened, you'll find that the strategies included in this chapter become more and more effective in helping you quickly sift through the distractions and traps of the test to isolate the correct answer.

Now that you're preparing to move forward into the test content chapters of this book, be sure to keep your goal in mind. As you read, think about how you will be able to apply this information on the test. If you've already seen sample questions for the test and you have an idea of the question format and style, try to come up with questions of your own that you can answer based on what you're reading. This will give you valuable practice applying your knowledge in the same ways you can expect to on test day.

Good luck and good studying!

Energy and Sustainability Policies, Codes, and Standards

Climate Change

The terms *climate change* and *global warming* are often used interchangeably. Climate change is defined by the long-term shifts in weather and temperature patterns. The changes can be caused by nature, such as from large volcanic eruptions, or from man. Human activities that affect climate change come largely from the burning of fossil fuels. The combination of human activities and natural changes leads to a rise in greenhouse gas emissions and the earth's average surface temperature.

The US's climate change policy was defined when the US rejoined the Paris Agreement and committed to reducing GHG emissions by 50% by 2030. The policy also sets a goal of becoming net zero by 2050. The climate policy focuses on both adaptation and mitigation. *Adaptation* is defined by building resilience against climate impacts, and *mitigation* is focused primarily on reducing emissions. To meet the targets, the US government is engaged in multiple sectors, including transportation, electricity, land use, and buildings.

Decarbonization Policies

The main goals of decarbonization policies are to transition to a more sustainable, low-carbon future and to reduce greenhouse gases.

Key activities and strategies associated with decarbonization are:

- Power generation shift: Shift away from fossil fuels (oil, coal, natural gas), and move toward renewable energy sources, such as hydro, wind, biomass, or solar.
- Energy efficiency and demand management: Install more efficient equipment (HVAC, boilers, etc.), and use rates or programs to incentivize demand management.
- Circular economy and consumption: Encourage recycling and reuse, and promote sustainable energy consumption.
- Carbon capture, utilization, and storage (CCUS): Deploy technologies that capture and store carbon emissions. This includes carbon pricing and policies such as taxing and cap-and-trade.

United Nations Sustainable Development Goals (SDGs)

Sustainable Development Goals (SDGs) were adopted by the United Nations in 2015. At that time, the United Nations adopted the 2030 Agenda for Sustainable Development. There are 17 SDGs associated with the shared blueprint that call for action by both developing and developed countries.

The SDGs cover three main dimensions: economic, social, and environmental:

1. No poverty
2. Zero hunger
3. Good health and well-being
4. Quality education
5. Gender equality
6. Clean water and sanitation

7. Affordable clean energy
8. Decent work and economic growth
9. Industry, innovation, and infrastructure
10. Reduced inequalities between and among countries
11. Sustainable cities and communities
12. Responsible consumption and production
13. Climate action
14. Life below water
15. Life on land
16. Peace, justice, and strong institutions
17. Partnerships for the goals

Electrification Policies

Electrification policies refer to a set of initiatives and strategies that are designed to promote the adoption of electric strategies. These strategies span various sectors and consist of several defining aspects. The Biden-Harris administration in the US is leading a clean energy transition that has goals to reduce greenhouse gas emissions by 50% by 2030. Further goals aim to achieve a pollution-free grid by 2035 and net zero by 2050.

The clean energy transition is designed to make equitable and efficient electric options available to everyone. The Biden-Harris administration's clean energy transition has an innovation agenda that aims to create new clean technologies produced and deployed in the US. An item on the agenda is to create a network of EV charging stations. Several approaches outlined in the clean energy transition address incentives and mandates to rate design and procurement policies. Local approaches include community-scale electrification and grass roots initiatives. Organizations such as the Electrification Coalition advocate for federal policies to accelerate the adoption of electric vehicles (EVs).

Benefits of Nuclear Energy

Nuclear energy technologies play a significant role in meeting the UN's Sustainable Development Goals. Nuclear energy contributes not only to energy goals but also to environmental protection, clean water, and agriculture goals.

Below are some key benefits of nuclear energy in sustainable development:

- Sustainable energy planning: Nuclear energy is a zero-emission energy source.
- Low carbon footprint: Compared to other energy sources, nuclear energy requires less land and materials.
- Energy intensity: A small pellet of uranium generates as much energy as half a ton of coal, 350 cubic meters of natural gas, or 3 barrels of oil.
- Abundance of nuclear fuel: Uranium is more abundant than gold or platinum, and there is enough uranium for 100 to 150 years based on our current consumption. If we increased our use of nuclear fuel, we would need to look at other options such as thorium or breeder reactors.

Local and National Tax Incentives for Sustainability

The most notable tax incentives for energy efficiency and sustainability projects are included in the Inflation Reduction Act (IRA). Introduced in 2022, this act outlined several new tax incentives for clean energy projects. Eligible projects include carbon capture, nuclear power, clean hydrogen, and renewable electricity production.

State and local governments offer various tax incentives to promote clean energy and sustainability projects. These include property tax exemptions, sales tax exemptions, and state-specific tax credits. Examples of sustainable projects that may receive incentives include installation of solar panels, purchase of energy efficiency appliances, and adoption of electric vehicles.

A comprehensive list of incentives offered across the US can be found in the Database of State Incentives for Renewables & Efficiency (DSIRE).

ADDITIONAL DETAILS ON THE INFLATION REDUCTION ACT

The Inflation Reduction Act (IRA) was signed by President Biden in August 2022. It is a significant piece of legislation that addresses combating inflation, lowering prescription drug prices, investing in domestic energy production, and creating jobs.

The Inflation Reduction Act also addresses sustainability and climate change in a significant way through the following initiatives:

- Emissions reduction: By 2030, the IRA aims to reduce greenhouse gas emissions by 40%. This goal aligns with the Paris Climate Agreement targets.
- Clean energy investment: The IRA allocates $369 billion in subsidies and tax credits for clean energy initiatives. This significant investment supports funding in a variety of projects, such as energy storage, electric vehicles, carbon capture, and renewable energy.
- Job creation: The IRA fosters innovation and creates thousands of jobs through the clean energy boom.

GHG ACCOUNTING AND REPORTING

Greenhouse gas (GHG) reporting is a process where organizations and industries track, report, and measure their GHG emissions to quantify the GHG produced by their processes or activities. GHG accounting helps organizations set reduction targets and supports climate action and stakeholder engagement. There are three key points associated with GNG accounting and carbon footprint calculations.

- Scope or emissions: There are three scopes of emissions. Scope 1 is the direct emissions from sources in the process or organization, such as fuel combustion. Scope 2 is the indirect emissions from purchased steam, electricity, or heat. Scope 3 is other indirect emissions, such as those from waste disposal or employees commuting to work.
- Carbon footprint calculation: This is calculated by following the GHG protocol. The steps involved are identifying the emission sources, collecting the relevant data, applying emission factors, and calculating the emissions for Scopes 1, 2 and 3. The sum of these items equals the total carbon footprint.
- Reporting and verification: Organizations will report their emissions data in annual reports to regulatory bodies or in sustainability reports. Independent verification is recommended. Two common reporting frameworks are the Carbon Disclosure Project (CDP) and Global Reporting Initiative (GRI).

ESG AND CSR REPORTING

ESG (environmental, social, and governance) reporting refers to the disclosure of a corporation's ESG data. The purpose of ESG reporting is to share a company's ESG activities in a positive light to improve investor transparency and stakeholder engagement. CSR (corporate social responsibility) reporting refers to a company's initiatives related to social and environmental responsibility. Both

ESG and CSR reporting are essential in promoting accountability and sustainable practices within an organization.

In ESG reporting, environmental aspects focus on items such as carbon emissions, climate change initiatives, waste management, and resource usage. Social factors take into account a corporation's relationships with its employees, customers, and communities. Governance refers to the corporation's internal policies, structure, and decision-making processes. This includes executive-compensation reports, ethics, and board composition.

CSR can be further defined by breaking the main components of the company's voluntary actions that contribute positively to the environment and society. These efforts include those related to philanthropy, ethical practices, community involvement, and sustainability initiatives.

Net Zero Buildings

Net zero buildings (NZEB) are also known as zero energy buildings (ZEB). NZEBs are buildings that achieve net zero energy consumption. The total energy used by an NZEB over a year equals the amount of renewable energy generated (either on- or off-site). Common equipment used to achieve net zero energy are high-efficiency windows, insulation, heat pumps, and solar panels.

Net zero energy buildings achieve super-efficient energy consumption by special design, construction, and operation. By incorporating renewable energy sources, they minimize their dependence on fossil fuels. Owners benefit from reduced energy costs and contribute significantly to climate change mitigation. NZEBs also have increased resiliency and reduced dependence on the grid. The states with the most NZEBs are California, New York, Oregon, and Massachusetts.

Smart Cities

Smart cities are urban environments that use technology and data to drive sustainability, improve infrastructure, and modernize government services. Smart cities use the Internet of Things (IoT), digital technology, and communication technologies to manage resources, services, and assets across the city. Examples of smart city technologies are autonomous vehicles, AI-driven traffic management, and AI-powered smart parking solutions. Smart cities offer numerous benefits that enhance quality of life.

Smart cities face some challenges:

- They require public engagement to ensure participation.
- There are privacy and security concerns due to the collection and management of data from numerous sensors. The large amount of data will require robust data management and analytics systems.
- The initiatives need to be equitable and benefit all residents, not just those who can afford the latest technology.
- Upgrading infrastructure can be disruptive and costly, especially in older cities. A robust and dependable network is required.

Transition to Clean Energy

The transition to clean energy is defined by the shifting of energy production from fossil fuels and sources that release a significant amount of greenhouse gases (GHG) to sources that emit little or no GHG. These "clean" solutions may be solar, nuclear, hydro, or wind energy. Clean solutions are renewable and sustainable and emit significantly less GHG. The US has a goal to achieve 100% carbon-free electricity by 2035.

The transition to clean energy provides numerous benefits:

- Economic growth is driven by job creation, innovation, and research and development of sustainable technologies.
- Health benefits are gained from cleaner air and water and a reduction of pollution-related illnesses.
- Benefits to the environment are derived from shifting away from fossil fuels to mitigate climate change and protect the planet.
- Energy independence is gained from relying on domestic clean energy resources rather than foreign oil.

Climate Change Risk, Climate Resilience, and Climate Adaptation

Climate change risk refers to the negative effects of climate change on the environment, people, ecosystem, and economy. Negative effects have been seen in extreme weather events (floods, fires, hurricanes, heat waves), shifts in rain/snow patterns, and sea level rises.

Climate resilience refers to building and designing communities, systems, and infrastructure in order to withstand negative climate-related stresses. Examples can be found in the adaptation of new building codes designed to withstand extreme weather events.

Climate adaptation refers to actions taken to enhance resiliency and actions taken to adjust to changing climate conditions. Natural solutions include wetland restoration, sustainable land use, and reforestation. Social adaptation activities include community engagement and education. Technical solutions include planting of drought-resistant crops and desalination.

Approaches to Green Hydrogen

Green hydrogen is produced using renewable energy sources such as wind or solar power, unlike conventional hydrogen, which often uses fossil fuels for production. Green hydrogen can be used to replace coal as a heat source in refineries, in fuel cell hydrogen for EVs, and in powering container ships using liquid ammonia made from hydrogen.

The approaches to green hydrogen are:

- Electrolysis: Water (H_2O) is split into hydrogen (H_2) and oxygen (O_2) using electricity powered by a renewable source.
- Biomass: Fermentation or biomass gasification can produce hydrogen. Agricultural waste or algae is broken down to release hydrogen.
- Solar, hydro, or wind hydrogen: Solar panels, hydro turbines, or wind turbines generate electricity for electrolysis.

Circular Economy in Energy

A circular economy seeks to maximize the use of materials, keeps products and materials in circulation, and designs for reuse and recycling. The goal of a circular economy in energy is to minimize waste generation and energy use. A circular economy supports energy transition by promoting and defining sustainable practices, recycling programs, and resource-efficiency guidelines.

A circular economy encourages increased recycling, which helps conserve valuable materials like lithium, cobalt, and rare earth elements that are needed for clean energy technologies. These materials are critical for storage batteries.

A circular economy aims to reduce waste and emissions and fosters a positive environmental impact. Mining-related waste, biodiversity waste, and ecological degradation are reduced, contributing to a sustainable energy system.

Intersection of Cybersecurity Issues with Sustainability and ESG

Recent research suggests that cybersecurity should be treated as an environmental, social, and governance (ESG) issue. Cybersecurity needs to be integrated into an organization's ESG strategy as failing to do so can make the organization less sustainable and less resilient. Cybersecurity breaches can negatively impact the organization's value because a large percentage of the organization's values are in intangible assets, like data.

Cybersecurity intersects with ESG goals/aspects:

- Environmental aspect: Responsible storage of large amounts of data must eliminate e-waste.
- Social aspect: Protecting personal data is critical. Processes must ensure privacy to align with social responsibility.
- Governance aspect: Cybersecurity governance must commit to addressing risk management and transparency. This aspect must evaluate board oversight and cybersecurity policies.

Energy Standard vs. Energy Code

An energy standard describes how a building or system should be designed. A standard is not mandatory, but the recommendations in standards provide expert guidance on how to meet industry agreed best practices in terms of energy efficiency and performance. Standards are written by respected organizations within the industry such as American Society of Heating, Refrigerating and Air-Conditioning Engineers (ASHRAE). An energy code specifies mandatory minimum performance levels for construction or specific building services that are legally enforceable at a local, state, or national level. Energy codes are often based wholly or in part upon standards such as ASHRAE 90. The International Energy Conservation Code (IECC) has been widely adopted by local governments and incorporated into the building codes to specify minimum energy performance requirements.

ASHRAE Standard 55

ASHRAE Standard 55 specifies the ideal thermal environmental conditions in buildings for comfortable human occupancy. The conditions specified are temperature, thermal radiation, humidity, and air movement within normal indoor environments in both summer and winter. The type of seasonal clothing that occupants may be wearing is also considered. Combinations of conditions are specified so that the indoor thermal conditions will be acceptable to 80% or more of occupants. Allowances are made to the specified conditions depending upon the activity levels of occupants. To comply with the standard, the requirements should be met when weather conditions do not exceed the design weather conditions.

ASHRAE Standard 90.1

ASHRAE Standard 90.1 specifies minimum energy efficiency requirements for the design and construction of buildings and building systems. The standard applies to all new buildings as well as renovations to existing buildings, except for single-family homes and multifamily buildings of three stories or less. The standard has mandatory requirements that must be met unless there is a specific exception and prescriptive requirements that must be met unless there is an approved trade-off allowed or a specific exception. Compliance with the standard can be demonstrated by either of the following:

18. Meeting the mandatory and prescriptive performance requirements.
19. Satisfying all mandatory requirements and using the energy cost budget (ECB) method.

The ECB is the annual energy costs of a building that meets the minimum requirements of the standard, which must be calculated using an approved simulation tool. The same simulation tool is then used to calculate the design energy cost of the proposed building design, which has trade-offs whereby some systems do not meet the minimum requirements but others exceed the minimum requirements. If the design energy cost does not exceed the ECB, then the building is compliant with the standard.

ASHRAE Standard 90.2

ASHRAE Standard 90.2 specifies minimum energy efficiency requirements for the design and construction of low-rise residential buildings. The standard covers all new buildings as well as specifically stated new portions or systems in existing dwellings. The residential dwellings included are single-family homes, multifamily buildings of three stories or less, and modular homes. The standard applies to the building fabric and heating, cooling, and domestic hot water equipment. Compliance can be demonstrated by following a prescriptive path or performance path for each building system or using an annual energy cost (AEC) method. The prescriptive path states minimum requirements that must be met for each system, and the performance path for a system allows some trade-offs if the overall performance at least meets the prescriptive path performance. The AEC method compares the expected energy cost of a proposed design with that of a design that meets the prescriptive method. If the proposed AEC is less than the AEC of the prescriptive design, then the design is compliant with the standard.

ASHRAE Standard 62.1

ASHRAE Standard 62.1 specifies minimum ventilation rates to provide acceptable indoor air quality and to minimize the potential for adverse health effects. The standard applies to new buildings and additions or alterations to existing buildings, except individual dwellings. Acceptable indoor air quality is defined in the standard as there being no known contaminants at harmful concentrations and 80% or more of occupants do not express dissatisfaction. The three procedures that may be used to meet the requirements of the standard follow:

1. The Ventilation Rate Procedure—A prescriptive design procedure to calculate minimum outdoor air flow rates based on the type of space, occupancy, and floor area. Minimum outdoor air rates are provided in tables within the standard.
2. The Indoor Air Quality Procedure—A performance-based procedure to determine outdoor air flow rates based on analysis of contaminant sources, contaminant concentrations, and perceived air quality.
3. The Natural Ventilation Procedure—A prescriptive design procedure that allows natural ventilation via openings directly to the outside, with or without mechanical ventilation.

Indoor Environmental Quality and Its Key Factors

Indoor environmental quality (IEQ), also referred to as indoor air quality, measures the conditions inside a building that directly affect the occupant's comfort and well-being. Poor IEQ can cause health issues and discomfort and affect productivity. IEQ is critical in most building types but is especially critical in office spaces, school buildings, healthcare facilities, and R&D facilities.

The key factors associated with IEQ are:

- Air quality: Proper ventilation, proper humidity levels, and low levels of pollutants are essential for good quality air.
- Lighting: While it does not directly affect air quality, lighting levels and the balance of artificial and natural light affect mood and productivity.
- Thermal comfort: It is critical to maintain a comfortable temperature range (i.e., not too hot or too cold) and make sure the level of air being blown on the occupant is appropriate.
- Acoustic: While not directly associated with air quality, controlling noise levels leads to a comfortable, peaceful, and productive environment.
- Materials and finishes: The building must be designed with safe, odor-free, non-toxic materials.

ASHRAE Standard 135

ASHRAE Standard 135 is the BACnet standard, which is a data communication protocol for building automation and control systems. BACnet is intended to improve the interoperability of equipment from different manufacturers. It provides a means for the exchange of information among building services equipment regardless of their function within the building and the internal, and often proprietary, communication languages that these systems may use. Examples of the building services that may use BACnet include heating, ventilation, air-conditioning, lighting, fire and safety systems, elevators, and access control systems.

ASHRAE Standard 189.1

ASHRAE Standard 189.1 is the standard for the design of high-performance green buildings, except for low-rise residential buildings. It applies to new buildings and systems as well as new systems and parts of existing buildings. It specifies minimum requirements for site sustainability, water use efficiency, energy efficiency, indoor environmental quality, the impact on the atmosphere, materials and resources, and construction and plans for operation. Like other green building standards, ASHRAE Standard 189.1 is intended to improve the sustainability of buildings by balancing their environmental impact and demand for resources with occupant comfort and well-being. The standard is not a design guide or green building rating system, but it is intended to be incorporated into codes as a baseline model for green buildings.

ASHRAE Guideline 14-20XX

ASHRAE Guideline 14-20XX is important to facility managers, energy managers, and building operators because it provides guidance on measurement, verification, and reporting of energy savings gained from energy efficiency projects. Specifically, ASHRAE Guideline 14-20XX provides procedures for using pre-retrofit and post-retrofit billing data to calculate energy savings.

The guidelines cover the following sections:

- Purpose and scope (sections 1 – 3): purpose, scope, and definitions
- Requirements and common elements (section 4): measurement approaches, compliance requirements, and savings process design
- Specific measurement approaches (section 5): retrofit isolation, whole building, and calibrated simulation approaches
- Instrumentation and data management (section 6): addresses instrumentation and data handling

- Additional topics (Sections 7 – 10): added in 2014 and covers water, electric demand, renewables, and references
- Appendices: covers topics such as regression techniques and retrofit isolation calculations

ASHRAE Standard 211-2018

ASHRAE Standard 211-2018 defines the practices for conducting a consistent energy audit and for writing the energy audit report. This standard is for commercial buildings and is an important guideline for energy professionals and facility managers. It plays a vital role in achieving net zero and sustainability goals.

The key components of ASHRAE Standard 211-2018 are:

- Energy audits: The standard provides the steps for conducting an energy audit in a commercial building. The audits identify energy savings opportunities, assess existing equipment and processes, and recommend improvements. It defines the standards for ASHRAE level 1, 2, and 3 energy audits.
- Consistent approach: The standard outlines the process to audit, collect data, and analyze and report findings. This ensures a consistent approach to energy audits that allows for benchmarking and comparison.
- Compliance and certification: Many energy efficiency programs, regulations, and certifications require adherence to ASHRAE 211-2018. These are LEED certification, Energy Star, and utility rebate programs.

IEEE PQ Standard 519

IEEE standard 519 has a major role in defining the management of electric power quality. The standard was introduced in 1981 to address harmonics that were introduced by static power converters and nonlinear loads. It was revised in 1992 to address compatibility between the grid and connected equipment. The most recent version is IEEE 519-2022, which continues to address harmonic control.

IEEE standard 519 can be further broken down into the following components:

- Goals for electrical system design: IEEE standard 519 addresses goals for designing electrical systems that include both linear and nonlinear loads. The standard also sets waveform distortion goals for system designers.
- Point of Common Coupling (PCC): IEEE 519 defines the interface between the grid and loads (motors, electronic devices) as the PCC. The design goals help reduce interference between the grid and load.
- Quality of power: The standard addresses steady state limitations and the limits of transient conditions that can occur.
- Harmonic distortion limits: The standard defines limits for current distortion and total harmonic voltage that aim to maintain acceptable power quality and prevent excessive harmonics.

International Energy Conservation Code (IECC)

The International Energy Conservation Code (IECC) is a model code published by the International Code Council (ICC) that sets minimum energy efficiency standards for new and renovated commercial and residential buildings. The IECC was first published in 1998 and is updated every three years. It has mandatory requirements as well as prescriptive requirements that have some allowances for trade-offs within limits. The IECC is written in language that is legally enforceable so that states and local governments can easily adopt it as part of their building codes. Adopting a model code ensures buildings are being designed and constructed to meet industry standards. After each update to the IECC, the US Department of Energy reviews the new code and make an official assessment as to whether the energy efficiency standards have been improved. If the code does have more stringent requirements, then states must review their building codes and decide if they need to be revised.

ISO 50001

ISO 50001 is an international standard for establishing an energy management system that is aimed at continually improving the energy performance of an organization. It specifies requirements for systems and processes that should be put in place to achieve improved energy performance, including preparing an energy policy, carrying out an energy review to identify significant energy end uses, determining an energy baseline, setting objectives and targets, developing action plans, documenting the energy management system, and monitoring and reviewing performance. The standard was developed by the International Organization for Standardization and is based on upon the plan-do-check-act continual improvement framework that is the foundation for many other standards, such as ISO 9001. It also emphasizes the need for top management commitment toward implementing an energy management system and communication throughout the organization.

Sustainable Design

Sustainable design is designing a building to reduce negative impacts on the environment and to improve the well-being of the occupants. Sustainable design integrates environmental, social, and governance (ESG) factors into the design phase of buildings, products, and services. Sustainable design creates positive and lasting solutions.

The key elements of sustainable design are:

- Environmental impacts: Sustainable designs aim to reduce negative environmental impacts. The designs are built to reduce consumption, waste, and pollution.
- ESG alliance: Sustainable designs aim to lower carbon emissions, work to achieve net zero, and align with the United Nations Sustainable Development Goals (UNSDGs).
- Health and well-being: Sustainable designs focus on providing a positive quality of life for the occupants and community. This is achieved by promoting a healthy indoor environment, good indoor air and water quality, and overall well-being.
- Sustainable architecture: Sustainable designs feature architecture that optimizes energy efficiency, considers building life cycle, and conserves water. This requires collaboration among the engineers, architects, and building designers.

International Electrotechnical Commission (IEC)

The IEC is the International Electrotechnical Commission. It sets international standards for all electrical, electronic, and related technologies. The IEC develops consensus-based standards and has more than 200 technical committees and subcommittees that develop standards. The committees include TC2 Rotating Machinery, TC13 Electrical Energy Measurement and Control, and SC23K Electrical Energy Efficiency Products, for example. IEC standards are in a series beginning from 60000. The IEC develops some standards jointly with the International Organization for

Standardization (ISO), and these standards are numbered from 80000. Example IEC standards include the following:

- IEC 60034: Rotating electrical machines—standard for energy efficiency classes of motors
- IEC 60068: Environmental testing—standard for tests such as vibrations
- IEC 60364: Low-voltage electrical installations—standard for electrical installations in buildings
- IEC 60598: Luminaires—standard for light fixture requirements
- IEC 60904: Photovoltaic devices
- IEC 61000: Electromagnetic compatibility—standard for power quality
- IEC 61800: Adjustable speed electric power drive systems—standard for VFDs
- IEC 62717: Light-emitting diode (LED) modules for general lighting—performance requirements

Energy Independence and Security Act of 2007

The stated purpose of the Energy Independence and Security Act 2007 is to move the United States toward greater energy independence and security; increase the production of renewable fuels; increase the efficiency of products, buildings, and vehicles; and improve the energy performance of the federal government among other purposes. The act comprises 13 titles, the first of which sets a target of 35 miles per gallon for the combined fleet of passenger and non-passenger vehicles by 2020. Title II requires that 36 billion gallons of renewable fuels are used in vehicles in 2022. Title IV includes provisions that energy use in federal buildings in 2015 be 30% lower than in 2005, fossil fuel use in federal buildings is eliminated by 2030, and the period allowed for life cycle costing be increased from 25 years to 40 years.

Energy Policy Act of 2005

The Energy Policy Act 2005 is primarily concerned with energy production but includes several energy efficiency and renewable energy provisions. Some of the specific targets for federal facilities include the following:

1. The baseline year was changed to 2003 and an annual energy reduction goal of 2% per year from 2006 to 2015 was set for a total energy reduction of 20%.
2. Electric metering was to be installed in all federal buildings by 2012.
3. New federal buildings will be evaluated using life cycle costing and will be designed 30% below the ASHRAE or IECC standard if it is cost-effective.
4. Renewable electricity consumption by the federal government will be at least 7.5% from 2013.

Energy Star Building Rating System

Energy Star is a voluntary building energy performance rating program operated by the Environmental Protection Agency (EPA). Existing buildings can become Energy Star certified to demonstrate a commitment to energy-efficient management of the building. Energy Star utilizes an online tool called Portfolio Manager to determine building energy performance. The Energy Star rating process in Portfolio Manager is as follows:

1. The building type is selected from 80 options in 18 general categories.
2. Energy and water data are entered.
3. Building benchmark performance indicators are calculated.
4. Energy Star rating is determined.

Portfolio Manager normalizes energy data, so comparisons can be made between buildings in different climate zones. Performance benchmarks are calculated from the 2003 Commercial Buildings Energy Consumption Survey (CBECS). The Energy Star rating ranges from 1 to 100 and indicates the percentage of similar buildings that it performs better than. For example, a building with an Energy Star rating of 80 performs better than 80% of all similar buildings. Buildings are eligible for Energy Star certification if they have an Energy Star rating of 75 or higher. An Energy Star label is available for display in Energy Star-certified buildings so the achievement can be communicated to building occupants.

BROAD PRINCIPLES OF GREEN BUILDING DESIGN AND CONSTRUCTION

There is no single definition of a green building. It is generally accepted that the planning, design, construction, and operation of a green building will be carried out with an understanding that buildings have a significant impact on their environment and occupants. The five broad principles for the sustainable design of green buildings are as follows:

1. Minimize negative impacts on the local environment, and develop sites sustainably.
2. Use water efficiently to reduce consumption.
3. Use energy efficiently, utilize renewable resources, and minimize emissions.
4. Use materials and resources sustainably.
5. Maximize indoor environmental air quality.

Green building rating systems such as LEED and Green Globes include these elements to assess the sustainability of a building. The ASHRAE Green Guide describes how buildings may be designed, constructed, and operated sustainably using an integrated building systems approach. Many building codes incorporate the International Energy Conservation Code (IECC) or ASHRAE 90.1, which set minimum energy performance requirements.

GREEN GLOBES AND LEED BUILDING RATING SYSTEMS

There are numerous green building rating systems in use around the world. The most popular in North America are Leadership in Energy and Environmental Design (LEED) and Green Globes. LEED was developed by the United States Green Building Council (USGBC) and first launched in 2000. LEED is applicable to all buildings in all phases of development. A total of 110 points are available for implementing specific sustainable actions in nine categories including location and transport, sustainable sites, energy and atmosphere, water efficiency, resources and materials, and indoor environmental quality. Information is submitted for third-party verification via online templates.

Green Globes is an online green building rating tool. It was developed by Energy and Environment Canada and began in 2000. It was first launched in the United States in 2004 and is managed by the Green Building Initiative. Green Globes is a questionnaire-based self-assessment tool that is designed to be easy to use and has guides to implement an integrative design process. It has modules for new construction, existing buildings, and commercial interiors. Up to 1,000 points can be earned in seven categories: project management, site, energy, water, resources, emissions, and indoor environment.

LEED RATING SYSTEMS

- LEED BD+C—The LEED rating system for buildings undergoing a major renovation is the Building Design + Construction system. It applies to new construction, schools, core and shell, retail, health care, data centers, warehouses and distribution centers, and hospitality.

- LEED O+M—For buildings that are undergoing improvements but with little or no construction, the LEED Building Operations + Maintenance rating system is used. It applies to existing buildings, data centers, warehouses and distribution centers, schools, retail, and hospitality.
- LEED ID+C—Projects that are a complete interior fit-out utilize the LEED Interior Design + Construction rating system. It applies to commercial interiors, retail, and hospitality.
- LEED ND—Projects involving new land development or redevelopment containing residential, nonresidential, or a mix of uses will utilize the LEED Neighborhood Development rating system. It applies to projects at any stage up to 75% constructed.
- LEED Homes—Single-family homes, low-rise (one to three stories) multi-family homes, and mid-rise (four to six stories) multi-family homes can use the LEED Homes rating system.

Minimum Program Requirements LEED Certification

Projects must have specific characteristics or conditions to be eligible for LEED certification. These are known as minimum program requirements (MPRs). A summary of the MPRs is as follows:

1. The project must be in a permanent location and be on existing land. The location is an important aspect for many LEED credits, so buildings cannot be moveable, and existing land must be used so artificial land masses that could disrupt ecosystems are avoided.
2. The LEED boundary must be reasonable. A project must contain all contiguous land that supports the development and cannot unreasonably exclude portions of a building or space to improve the points awarded.
3. The project must meet the size requirements. Each rating system has specific minimum building or development sizes. Both LEED Building Design + Construction and LEED Operations + Maintenance require a minimum floor area of 1,000 square feet.

The rating system to be used for a project should be selected based on published guidance. Only one rating system can be used for an entire project. In the case of mixed-use buildings deciding upon which rating system to use is not always obvious. In this case each unit of floor area is assigned an appropriate rating system. The total area for each rating system being considered is calculated. If the total area for an applicable rating system is less than 40% of the overall area, then it is not suitable. If it is more than 60% of the overall area, it should be selected. When appropriate rating systems are between 40% and 60% of the overall area, the project teams must choose the system they believe to be most appropriate.

Prerequisites, Credits, and Points in the LEED Rating System

The LEED rating system has three fundamental components: prerequisites, credits, and points. Prerequisites are the minimum requirements that all projects must meet to achieve LEED certification within a particular rating system. Credits are the specific sustainable features that a project can incorporate. Each credit has certain requirements and possibly options for achieving the credit. Each credit is allocated a specific number of points. It is the total number of points earned from all credits that will determine the final LEED rating. LEED has a credit library for each rating system, and project teams will select the most appropriate credits for their project to earn points and achieve the desired LEED rating level. The different LEED rating systems can have the same credits, but the number of points allocated and the requirements may be different. Prerequisites do not earn points for a project. The certification levels and points required are as follows:

- LEED Certified = 40 to 49 points
- LEED Silver = 50 to 59 points

- LEED Gold = 60 to 79 points
- LEED Platinum = 80 or more points

Credit Categories in LEED v3-2009 and LEED v4

LEED is revised and updated periodically with changes to the prerequisites, categories, credits, and points available. LEED v3 was launched in April 2009. In November 2013, LEED v4 was launched, and since October 2016 it has become the only LEED rating system available for new projects. The credit categories in the two versions of LEED Building Design + Construction are as follows:

LEED v3		LEED v4	
Sustainable Sites	26 pts	Sustainable Sites	10 pts
Water Efficiency	10 pts	Water Efficiency	11 pts
Energy and Environment	35 pts	Energy and Environment	33 pts
Material and Resources	14 pts	Material and Resources	13 pts
Indoor Environmental Quality	15 pts	Indoor Environmental Quality	16 pts
Innovation	6 pts	Innovation	6 pts
Regional Priority	4 pts	Regional Priority	4 pts
		Location and Transportation	16 pts
		Integrative Process	1 pt

The major differences in LEED v4 include new categories for location and transportation, which were previously included in sustainable sites, and a new credit worth one point for an integrative process, which promotes the consideration of synergies between credit options for energy and water systems to improve the overall design. The maximum number of points possible within each category has also changed slightly.

LEED Credentials Awarded by the GBCI

Green Business Certification Inc. (GBCI) administers the LEED credential programs as well as the LEED certification programs. LEED credentials are awarded to individuals who have demonstrated their knowledge of LEED by passing an examination. This is different from LEED certification, which is awarded to projects. The LEED credentials available are the LEED Green Associate and the LEED Accredited Professional (LEED AP). The LEED Green Associate credential demonstrates an awareness and understanding of green building principles and practices. It is also the prerequisite for achieving the LEED AP credential. The LEED AP is awarded to individuals who have passed an exam in one of the five specialized rating systems: Building Design + Construction (BD+C), Building Operations + Maintenance (O+M), Interior Design + Construction (ID+C), Neighborhood Development (ND), or Homes. Having a LEED AP involved in a project earns one point from the innovation category for that project.

Energy Rates, Tariffs, and Supply Options

Basic Energy Units and Their Conversions

Energy is a conserved quantity that can be accumulated and transferred as heat, work, and matter. Energy cannot be created or destroyed, but some forms can be depleted.

Listed below are the basic energy units and their conversions:

The kilowatt-hour (kWh) is a unit of electrical energy commonly used for billing purposes. One kWh equals 3.6 megajoules (MJ).

The joule (J) is the SI unit of energy. It's equivalent to 1 newton-meter (N*m). For example, lifting a 1 kg weight requires 9.8 joules of energy.

A calorie (cal) is the energy required to raise the temperature of 1 gram of water by 1 degree Celsius. It is approximately 4.18 joules.

A British thermal unit (BTU) is equal to 1055 joules or 778 foot-pounds.

Fuel Price Risk Management

Fuel price risk management is a process that helps organizations address the volatility of fuel prices. Fuel price risk management is designed to assess when and how to hedge against exposure to fuel price fluctuations. In trucking, fuel price risk management is often referred to as "fuel hedging." It's referred to as "bunker hedging" in the marine and shipping industries. Factors such as international conflicts, natural disasters, and oil disruptions may affect fuel prices and are hard to predict.

The three main areas of fuel price risk management are:

- Risk assessment: An organization will calculate fuel costs, identify risks, and analyze its exposure to price fluctuations.
- Risk treatment: The organization will implement the fuel risk strategy, which is normally some type of hedging or another mitigation measure.
- Real investments and risk reduction: The organization may implement energy efficiency improvements, operational improvements, or cutbacks and reductions.

Fuel Price Risks Associated with Supply Options

Rising fuel prices create risks for the global supply chain. Supply chain options are affected by volatility in fuel prices in several ways.

Political instability in key oil-producing regions impacts the supply of fuel and affects the cost. A recent example of this is with the ongoing conflict between Russia and Ukraine. Volatility in fuel prices (primarily rising fuel prices) causes supply chain disruptions and delays. Many companies rely on a "just in time" fuel-delivery method and may experience downtime and outages if their fuel is delayed.

Customers may experience higher than average heating, gasoline, and cooling bills due to rising fuel prices. Escalated fuel prices will also cause an increase in food prices, which could lead to food insecurity issues in poorer countries.

The search for alternative fuel solutions will increase as fuel prices rise. Liquefied natural gas (LNG) from fracking, solar, and wind are viable alternative fuel solutions.

Rate Structure and Rate Analysis

Rate structure is how a utility charges its customers for water and sewer services. The rate structure determines how the costs are allocated across the different customer classes. Rate analysis describes the process of assessing the revenue requirements, allocating costs, and designing an appropriate rate structure.

Common rate structures:

- Uniform rates: All customers pay the same rate per unit of water consumed ($/gallon). This approach is the most straightforward.
- Decreasing block rates: In this structure, the rate per unit decreases as consumption increases.

Rate analysis considerations:

- Revenue requirements: The organization must determine the total revenue needed to cover operating expenses, capital costs, and debt service. They must also factor in inflation, population growth, and infrastructure improvements.
- Cost allocation: The costs must be allocated across operations, maintenance, and capital and be distributed among customer classes.
- Rate design: A rate is designed that considers equity, affordability, and conservation goals.

Primary vs. Secondary Power Supply Options

Primary power supplies deliver electricity directly from the grid to distribution substations. Primary power supplies consist of feeders, main trunks, and lateral taps. These systems can be configured several ways:

- Radial: A fault on a radial interrupts all downstream customers until repaired.
- Primary loop: Two feeders are connected with a normally open switch.
- Radially operated networks: These are highly interconnected systems controlled with multiple switches and offer high reliability.

Secondary power supply options convert DC electricity from one voltage to another. Electronic products often require a secondary power supply to operate. Secondary power supplies involve distribution transformers and metering and will adjust voltage levels as required by the load.

Demand-Side Management

Demand-side management, often referred to as DSM, is a strategy used by electric utilities to control demand. DSM emerged in the 1970s, largely as a response to the 1970s energy crisis. DSM programs have evolved over the years but still offer incentives, programs, and education to customers to encourage them to conserve energy and to use it more efficiently.

Demand-side management is important and offers the following benefits:

- Infrastructure efficiency: Implementing DSM initiatives allows a utility to avoid the cost of adding new generation and transmission lines. Utilities offer incentives for customers to install more efficient equipment and to shift consumption away from peak demand hours.

- Cost savings: DSM helps reduce market prices for electricity and can pass these savings on to customers in the form of lower rates or incentives for participating in programs.
- Environmental benefits: DSM impacts the environment in a positive manner as lower demand for electricity will lead to fewer emissions from power plants.

Energy Efficiency in Transportation

Energy efficiency in transportation is typically measured by the useful traveled distance divided by the total energy input into the propulsion system. It refers to how effectively energy is utilized for moving passengers, goods, or any type of load. Improving energy efficiency in transportation contributes to energy independence, resilience, and reduced emissions. Sustainable transportation such as electric and alternative-fuel vehicles provide environmental benefits.

The units of measurement in transportation efficiency are:

- Liters or gallons are used for liquid fuels.
- The energy unit used for electric propulsion is the kWh.
- Calories are the unit of measurement for human-propelled vehicles.
- Passenger transport efficiency is measured by the formula (passengers x distance)/joule.
- Cargo transport efficiency is measured by the formula (kg x distance)/joule.

Natural Gas Market in the United States

The transportation and sale of natural gas between states is regulated by the Federal Regulatory Energy Commission (FERC); its regulatory activities include approving tariffs for transportation, approving new interstate pipelines and storage facilities, and overseeing environmental matters. Natural gas is extracted and sent to processing plants and transported through pipelines to LNG terminals, storage facilities, or gas-fired electricity generators. Local distribution companies (LDCs) provide natural gas to electricity generators, industrial facilities, and commercial and residential customers. The main natural gas pricing hub in the United States is the Henry Hub in Louisiana. Natural gas purchases from an LDC may be at a firm rate (uninterruptible) to guarantee supply, or a cheaper interruptible rate, but they agree subject to supply restrictions. Natural gas may be bought at an index price that varies constantly depending upon supply and demand factors. Customers may also choose to purchase at an index rate with a capped maximum price to mitigate some higher price risk but enable the benefits of lower prices to be realized. A fixed price may also be selected, which eliminates all price risk for the term of the contract.

Oil Market in the United States

The oil market is a worldwide market that is heavily influenced by world supply, demand, and events. In the United States, the interstate transportation tariffs for oil are monitored by the Federal Regulatory Energy Commission (FERC). Safety issues are monitored by the Department of Transportation, and environmental issues are the responsibility of the Environmental Protection Agency. Extracted oil is transported via pipeline, ship, or rail to terminals or hubs where it is stored. The largest hub in the United States is at Cushing and is the price settlement point for West Texas Intermediate (WTI) crude oil. Oil is purchased at trading hubs on the spot market. From storage facilities, the oil goes to refineries, then to bulk storage facilities, then finally to consumers.

Factors Affecting Fuel Prices

The price of fuels such as natural gas and oil are affected by many factors that include the following:

- Supply—Exploration and drilling activities, and the amount of fuel extracted are significant price-driving factors.
- Weather—If the weather is colder than expected, then this can increase prices for heating fuels because there will be more demand. Severe storms can interrupt the energy supply chain and cause sharp price increases. Hotter weather can increase electricity demand for air-conditioning, so power plants will require more fuel and cause price increases.
- Storage—Fuels are stored in hub facilities and the amount of stored fuel is announced regularly. Market prices will change depending on the storage reserves and the expected demand and replenishment of the stored fuel.
- Economy—The state of the national and world economy will affect the demand for energy and therefore the price of fuels.
- World events—Conflicts will tend to increase energy prices, especially when they occur in fuel-producing regions. Government elections and policies will also affect prices.

Electricity Deregulation

The electricity industry was initially a natural monopoly of vertically integrated generators, transmission, and distribution companies with no retail choice for consumers. A series of legislative changes beginning in the 1970s began to change the structure of the industry.

- Public Utilities Regulatory Policy Act (PURPA)—PURPA was enacted in 1978 to allow independent qualifying facilities to sell electricity into the market if they met certain energy conservation standards.
- Energy Policy Act—The EPACT of 1992 allowed exempt wholesale generators (EWGs) to produce power any way they wanted. These generators exerted competitive pressures on the traditional generators. EPACT removed the obstacles to wholesale and retail electricity competition.
- FERC Orders 888 and 889—The Federal Regulatory Energy Commission (FERC) directed the establishment of independent system operators (ISOs) to enable competition in the industry and set standards for how market participants should interact.
- FERC Order 2000—In 1999 FERC issued Order No. 2000 to establish regional transmission organizations (RTOs) to improve the efficiency and reliability of transmission and electricity markets. The electricity market in the United States currently has seven RTOs/ISOs as well as three other reginal transmission networks with more federal control.

Electricity Market Purchasing Options

Electricity customers may have options as to who they purchase their electricity from in markets with wholesale and retail competition. Larger consumers can also choose how they purchase their electricity. Small consumers generally pay a fixed rate for all of their electricity because this is simpler and they do not have the ability or need to negotiate more complicated contracts. Large industrial consumers such as manufacturers can end up paying more under a fixed price contract, but it has less risk and helps with budgeting. Alternative pricing strategies include index pricing or block and index. Index pricing is a strategy whereby electricity is purchased at the prevailing wholesale price for each hour of the day. There is a high degree of price risk using this strategy but also the possibility for substantial benefits when prices are low. In a block and index pricing strategy, the majority of electricity is purchased in blocks at a fixed price based on historical demand, and the remainder is purchased at the spot market index price.

Electricity Demand Response

Electricity transmission and distribution infrastructure requires long-term planning to build and is expensive. Infrastructure developments can sometimes not keep pace with demand on the grid network due to rapid population growth, and seasonal demand variations may mean there is an excess of supply capacity during some periods of the year, and at others the grid nears capacity. Demand response programs are promoted by utilities so they can defer the decision to invest in infrastructure upgrades just to meet short-term peak demands. They offer incentives to customers to reduce their electricity demand for a few hours of the year when the grid nears its capacity. This is a more cost effective and quicker means of response to seasonal demand variability within the grid transmission and distribution network.

Components of Electric Rate Structures

Electricity tariffs are different depending upon the utility, but there are many elements that are common to most suppliers. Tariffs typically include the following:

- Unit rate—This is the basic charge for each kilowatt-hour of electricity used. The unit rate could be the same for every hour of the day, or it may be split into peak and off-peak rates for different times of the day. Some suppliers also use block rates that apply a different rate to increasing amounts of electricity use; for example, $0.03/kWh for the first 1,000kWh, $0.05/kWh for the next 1,000kWh, and $0.09/kWh for any additional kWh.
- Fuel cost adjustment—This is an additional cost applied to each kilowatt-hour of electricity depending on the utilities fuel costs. It may vary seasonally or change as the fuel mix a utility uses varies, or a customer may choose tariffs with a different rate, for example, an extra charge for using renewable energy.
- Demand rate—Larger commercial customers will often have a monthly demand charge applied to the highest peak kilowatt demand for the month.
- Power factor charges—This charge will apply to larger commercial customers that have a low power factor, typically under 0.9.

Demand Ratchet

A demand ratchet is a type of charging structure that a utility uses to cover their cost of maintaining the capacity needed to meet seasonal peaks. Many of a utility's generation assets will have a low capacity factor during some periods of the year because they are only used to meet peak demand times. However, there is a cost associated with building and maintaining these units that the utility needs to recover. Customers that have a very seasonal demand will often pay a demand ratchet so that they pay their share of these costs and not just for the energy they use. The demand ratchet means a customer pays a minimum amount each month regardless of actual demand. The minimum amount is usually set to be a percentage of the customer's highest peak demand for the year. For example, 60% of the peak demand for a tourist resort that is only open for a few months per year may be charged every month of the year, even if they use no electricity when closed.

Real-Time Pricing of Electricity

The real cost of electricity varies every hour of the day depending on fuel mix and demand, which are influenced by the weather, time of day, and other events that may or not be easily predicted and cause volatility in the price of electricity. For simplicity, utilities set tariffs with average unit rates per kilowatt-hour with only some variations such as peak and off-peak rates, seasonal fuel cost adjustments, and demand charges. For most customers, this is the best way to purchase their electricity because it is easier to predict the cost and they have limited ability to change their hourly demand. However, customers that have the ability to significantly shift loads throughout the day can consider real-time purchasing, so they can take advantage of much lower costs at certain times of the day or use day-ahead pricing. This is likely to be industrial facilities that operate various production shifts that can be scheduled accordingly. Customers using real-time pricing can sometimes have negative electricity costs and are actually paid for using electricity because demand is low but particular generators do not want to shut down for relatively short periods of time.

Energy Audits and Instrumentation

Energy Audit

An energy audit is the process of identifying opportunities for energy efficiency within a facility. An energy audit will begin with data collection. Information about all energy supplies should be gathered as well as operating details for the facility such as floor area, occupied hours, and occupancy. Analysis of energy bills is important to understand the daily and seasonal load profiles for each energy supply. Once a basic understanding of the facility is gained, a survey needs to be carried out. The aim of the survey is to identify all the energy end-use services in the facility and determine if there are opportunities to eliminate wastage or install more efficient equipment. The level of detail of the survey depends upon the goals of the audit: the survey may be a quick walk-through to identify as many potential opportunities as possible for more detailed investigation in the future, or it may be detailed and focused on a few of the more energy-intensive end-use services. The potential energy efficiency savings will then be described or calculated and a report prepared explaining recommendations and next steps.

ASHRAE Level 1 Energy Audit

ASHRAE has defined three levels of energy audits. A Level 1 audit is a high-level assessment of building energy performance. A preliminary analysis of bills is conducted, and basic site information is gathered. A brief walk-through survey of the building is carried out to identify no-cost or low-cost opportunities, and more complex energy efficiency opportunities are identified that would be worthwhile investigating in more detail. Only basic, approximate calculations are possible to provide an indication of likely costs and benefits. A Level 1 audit is useful for smaller buildings and for understanding the likely scale and scope of energy efficiency improvements that may be appropriate within the building. The output of a Level 1 audit would be a brief report with descriptions of potential energy efficiency improvements and an explanation of next steps.

ASHRAE Level 2 Energy Audit

ASHRAE has defined three levels of energy audits. A Level 2 audit is an in-depth assessment of building energy performance including detailed energy data analysis, apportionment of energy consumption to each end-use service, a thorough building survey, calculated energy savings for energy efficiency opportunities (EEO) identified during the survey, and predicted costs for each EEO. The building survey will often require measurements and monitoring of equipment and indoor environmental conditions and may require data logging over an extended period. The output of a Level 2 audit should be a comprehensive report detailing the existing systems and performance, prioritized EEOs with associated costs and savings, and an explanation of next steps and recommendations for any operational and maintenance actions. The output could possibly include a building simulation model. A Level 2 audit may build on the results of a Level 1 survey, or it may be the first audit undertaken.

ASHRAE Level 3 Energy Audit

ASHRAE has defined three levels of energy audits. A Level 3 audit is a detailed analysis of capital-intensive modifications. The Level 3 assessment focuses on the energy efficiency potential of specific building end-use services identified in a Level 2 audit. A Level 3 audit enables an accurate prediction of energy savings and costs to assist with decision-making before a significant investment is made. A computer simulation model of the building is often used to assess energy consumption before and after an intended modification for each hour of the year. Equipment suppliers will be involved to provide detailed costs. Additional data gathering and building inspections are likely to be required to improve the accuracy of the analysis.

Investigating Building Systems

Each facility is unique, and yet there are many common building services that should be assessed during an energy audit. Here is a general list of the typical systems and points to consider:

- Building fabric—The walls, roof, windows, doors, and orientation of the building have a major impact on the energy performance of a building. The air tightness and thermal conductivity of the building envelope should be investigated.
- Electrical system—The voltage, power factor, and power quality within the building should be evaluated.
- Heating ventilation and air-conditioning (HVAC) system—One of the largest end uses of energy is likely to be the HVAC system. Equipment such as chillers, fans, motors, controls and set points, and system configuration need to be checked.
- Boilers—Boilers and steam systems can use large amounts of energy, but their efficiency can be easily improved by optimizing the combustion process, recovering waste heat and ensuring pipes are insulated.
- Lighting—Check for energy-efficient retrofit opportunities and improved controls.
- Domestic hot water—The temperature set points, operating hours, and insulation should be checked.
- Process equipment—Many facilities will have large motors, compressed air systems, or other special process equipment that can be optimized.

Gathering Data and Information

A useful energy audit requires data and details regarding the facility. Much of the information should be collected prior to the site survey because it may become clear that some areas will need extra attention during the inspection. The data that are most useful to an auditor include:

- Energy data—At least 12 months of data should be used to determine seasonal demand profiles, but more data may indicate longer-term trends. Interval data is preferable.
- Facility specifications—The floor area, building fabric elements, occupancy, and hours of operation are key. Having plans of the building is useful for the facility survey.
- Weather data—Energy demand for heating and cooling should be weather dependent, so degree-day data for the location should be retrieved.
- Installed building services equipment—If an asset list is available, this will be helpful in identifying all the energy-consuming equipment. The significant energy-using equipment should be investigated during the survey.
- Operating set points—The control systems and equipment schedules need to be assessed to determine if these are appropriate or if equipment could be turned off at during some periods, or indoor environmental settings adjusted.

Using Degree Days for Data Analysis

Degree days are calculated for specific geographical locations based on the amount of time (in days) the local outdoor temperature is above or below a base temperature, normally chosen to be 65°F. Heating degree days are calculated for the time that the average temperature over the period was below the base temperature, and similarly cooling degree days are calculated for the time the average temperature was above the base temperature. The energy consumption for space heating and cooling should be mostly dependent upon the outdoor temperature if the controls are set appropriately. With regression analysis of energy consumption versus degree days, an energy performance equation for the building can be found which can be used to predict monthly consumption. Deviations from the predicted performance could indicate an issue or that savings have been made. If the correlation between energy consumption and degree days is not strong, then this may indicate equipment is operating when it should be turned off, or the temperature set points need to be adjusted.

Benchmarking Audit

Benchmarking is the procedure whereby building energy performance is compared to buildings of a similar type within an organization or to other similar buildings nationally. This enables an understanding of relative performance to be gained so that buildings with significantly higher or lower energy consumption than average can be identified so the reasons for their performance can be investigated in detail. The comparison is usually made by looking at the Energy Use Index (EUI), which is the total energy consumption divided by the floor area (Btu/ft^2). This allows buildings of different sizes to be compared directly because energy consumption is usually heavily dependent on building area. Energy consumption is also dependent on many other factors such as number of occupants and operating hours, but these can be assumed to also be largely determined by building type and size. One other significant contributing factor to energy performance is the weather, so weather normalization of energy data is required when comparing buildings in different regions. Benchmarking can also be conducted using EUIs other than Btu/ft^2, such as Btu/person, Btu/unit of production, or the Energy Cost Index (ECI) in \$/ft^2.

Key Performance Indicators Derived from Energy Audits

The key performance indicators (KPIs) calculated from an energy audit are crucial and should be standardized among audits. They serve to assess the energy efficiency and sustainability of a building.

The common KPIs are:

- Carbon footprint reduction: This KPI measures the environmental impact of the reduction in carbon dioxide emissions.
- Energy cost index: This measures the total energy costs (electric, water, gas, steam) of the building. It is usually expressed as a percentage of total revenues or as a delta compared to previous periods.
- Energy efficiency index: This index represents energy usage per unit of production.
- Site energy use intensity (EUI): EUI quantifies consumption by air-conditioned footage and is usually expressed in BTUs or converted to kWh/square foot per year. Lower EUI generally indicates better energy performance.
- Cost savings in energy consumption: This measures the financial impact of the energy saving initiatives and is essential in calculating the return on investment (ROI) of the energy project.

Using Energy Simulation and Energy Modeling in Energy Audits

Energy simulation provides accurate information to decision-makers to help them make informed and cost-effective choices in implementing energy efficiency projects. Energy simulation involves solving mathematical equations to understand system behavior. Energy simulation also helps to answer "what if" scenarios and provides insight into load profiles, energy consumption, and efficiency measures. Load simulation programs are commercially available to assist with this step.

Energy modeling involves creating a mathematical representation of a system to predict its energy performance. These systems may include an industrial process, a building, or the energy grid. There are significant data inputs needed to build the model. Some examples of the inputs are utility bills, building drawings, equipment schedules, building hours, and occupancy patterns. The model will assess the impact of various factors such as climate, materials, and systems to estimate energy consumption and evaluate design decisions. Numerous software systems are available to assist with modeling.

Digital Tools and Apps Available to Assist with Energy Audits

There are numerous physical tools such as thermometers, gas leak detectors, and cameras used when doing energy audits. More and more digital tools and apps have become available to assist with conducting and reporting energy audits. These apps and digital tools can be available on mobile (IOS and Android), be web-based, or both. Some popular digital tools/apps are:

- Safety Culture (formerly iAuditor): This digital tool features energy-audit checklists and inspection templates to follow during the actual audit.
- EnergyCAP: This tool is designed to manage utility bills and consumption. It features utility bill auditing capabilities, data reporting, and greenhouse gas tracking.
- EnergyElephant: This digital tool tracks energy-consumption rates and features carbon footprint tracking, data collection capabilities, data reporting, and visualization.
- Enerit: This tool is a comprehensive energy-management software with features designed for energy auditing. The software features audit management, energy sensor connections, and corrective-action reporting.
- OptiMiser: This energy auditing software features mobile data entry, automated utility bill calibration, and CRM modules.

Load Factor

The load factor of a facility is the ratio of actual electrical energy used (kWh) during a specified period to the amount that would have been used if the facility used the peak demand (in kW) for the entire period:

$$Load\ Factor = \frac{Actual\ kWh\ used\ in\ period}{Peak\ Demand\ x\ hours\ in\ period}$$

The load factor is a useful measure of how electricity is utilized. A low load factor of less than about 70% indicates that there is relatively high demand for short periods of time, and there may be an opportunity to reduce costs incurred by demand charges. A load factor of less than about 50% indicates very high peak demand, and some form of demand management would be beneficial. Interval data will show when the periods of high demand occur and the loads that are on at those times should be identified. Some loads could be shifted to different times, or other nonessential loads can be switched off or cycled to minimize the peak by installing automatic load-shedding equipment.

Conducting an Energy Balance for a Facility

A facility energy balance is an important step in the energy auditing process. It provides an overview of the total energy supplied to the facility from all sources and where this energy is being used. This will help indicate areas of high priority where the most significant energy and cost savings may be available. Energy bills are the usual source of energy supply information, but meter data could also be used solely or in conjunction with bills. The total energy consumption is then apportioned to each end-use service in the facility based on a combination of sub-metered data, building surveys, estimation through techniques such as regression analysis, and engineering calculations. Reasonable estimates typically need to be made for calculated consumption using assumed equipment load factors and efficiencies, operating hours, and total numbers of some equipment such as lights, for example. Total estimated consumption from all electrical end uses must match total electricity supply, and similarly calculated demand must match supply for other fuels. This will ensure that predicted energy savings will not be unrealistic, and end-use services with relatively high energy demand can be prioritized.

Equipment Used During Energy Audits

Temperature Measurements

Systems that should have temperatures measured to identify potential energy efficiency improvements include air within heating ventilation and air-conditioning (HVAC) and combustion systems, hot water in boiler and steam systems, and some surfaces such as pipes. Temperature measurements should be made using the appropriate device:

- Thermometer—There are a variety of thermometers for different applications and temperature ranges beyond the typical glass thermometer. Electronic thermometers have interchangeable probes, so they can be used for liquid, air, or surface temperatures. Infrared thermometers can measure temperatures from a distance.
- Surface pyrometer—Used to measure surface temperatures, the probe of a surface pyrometer must be in close contact with the surface. Optical pyrometers are used for high-temperature measurements.
- Thermocouple probe—High-temperature measurement of exhaust gases is suited to the use of a thermocouple probe.

Electrical System Measurements

Electrical current is measured by an ammeter. A portable, clamp ammeter is best for an energy audit. Voltage is measured by a voltmeter. A portable multimeter will be able to measure both voltage and current. It is important to make sure the correct measurement range is selected on these portable meters. If a low power factor is an issue, and there are penalty charges from the utility, a permanent power factor meter may be worthwhile. In other cases, particularly for energy audits, a portable power factor meter can be used. With separate current, voltage, and power factor measurements, the power can be calculated; however, a portable wattmeter will provide the instantaneous power directly. Clamp power quality meters are available that will measure the real power, apparent power, reactive power, and power factor in the same device.

Air Velocity Measurements

Air velocity measurements may be required to check the performance of heating ventilation and air-conditioning (HVAC) systems or combustion air flows to a boiler. Instruments that may be used for these measurements include the following:

- Anemometer—There are numerous types of anemometers that may be utilized during an energy audit. The simplest and cheapest types are velometer, deflecting vane, and revolving vane anemometers. A hot-wire anemometer and a heated thermocouple measure air flow based on the cooling of a heated wire in an air steam.
- Pitot tubes—Pitot tubes are reliable air speed measurement devices that can be used when using an anemometer would be difficult, such as in ducts.
- Air flow capture hood—Measurement of flow rates and velocity of air through vents and grills can be accomplished with air flow hoods. This is a useful device for testing and balancing of HVAC systems.

Humidity Measurements

Hygrometers are instruments used to measure the amount of water vapor in air. The measurement is made indirectly from measurements of temperature, pressure, or an electrical change in a material. Humidity measurement is more difficult than other environmental parameters, and the accuracy of hygrometers can be poor due to calibration errors and their operating principle, which relies on consistent air temperatures.

- Psychrometer—Relative humidity may be measured using a psychrometer. This comprises a dry-bulb thermometer and a wet-bulb thermometer. The temperature readings are used in conjunction with a psychrometric chart to determine the relative humidity. A sling psychrometer is swung in the air until the temperature of the wet-bulb thermometer stops decreasing.
- Electronic hygrometers—A variety of electronic instruments are available for measuring humidity that operate based on a change in electrical resistance or capacitance of a material. Another type of instrument measures the change in thermal conductivity.

Air Pressure Measurements

There are three types of pressure measurements that are typically made by instruments: Gauge pressure is measured relative to atmospheric pressure; absolute pressure is measured against a perfect vacuum and is equal to gauge pressure plus atmospheric pressure; differential pressure is the difference in pressure between any two points. Measuring the pressure within a system can be used to indicate operational issues. For example, measuring the static pressure within a heating ventilation and air-conditioning (HVAC) system duct will help determine if flow rates are appropriate. Equipment commonly used for pressure measurements includes the following:

- Manometer—Portable manometers for energy audits can be digital or a tube containing a fluid, and they measure a differential pressure. They may be used over a wide range of pressures and are relatively low cost.
- Draft gauge—Draft gauges are portable, low-differential pressure measurement devices to check for correct flue gas venting. They are low cost and reasonably accurate.
- Bourdon tube—Bourdon tubes measure gauge pressure. They are widely used and useful for medium- to high-pressure measurements.

Combustion Measurements

Combustion processes need to be regularly monitored to ensure they are operating efficiently and safely. Combustion testing is done by analyzing the constituents of the flue gas. Expected values are 0 to 20% carbon dioxide, 0 to 21% oxygen, and 0 to 0.5% carbon monoxide. Orsat gas analyzers are traditionally used to measure combustion gases. This apparatus uses chemical solutions to absorb flue gases. The amount of each gas is determined by comparing the volume of gas remaining after the gas being tested is removed by the chemical solution. However, the apparatus is not easily portable and takes a long time to set up, so it is not suitable for energy audits. More portable solutions are combustion test kits and electronic combustion analyzers.

- Combustion test kit—A combustion test kit includes a Fyrite chemical solution to absorb either carbon dioxide or oxygen in various ranges of concentration. This works on the same principle as an Orsat apparatus but is simpler and cheaper.
- Electronic combustion analyzer—An electronic gas analyzer uses a probe inserted into the flue gas to measure the constituents of the exhaust. These units will typically measure the amount of carbon dioxide and carbon monoxide and calculate the percentage of oxygen.

Lighting Measurements

Lighting in a building is one of the most common energy-efficiency opportunities, so taking measurements of illumination levels is important during an energy audit. The correct amount of illumination is required in each area, and often areas are over-lit. A light meter is used to measure illumination in foot-candles or lux. There are a variety of light meters available with different features depending on the application. A standard light meter will not provide accurate measurements under different types of lights due to the different wavelengths they emit and the response of the eye; therefore, for measuring the illuminance from high-intensity discharge (HID) or LED lamps; for example, the light meter should have filters or adjustments to color correct for different light sources. A cosine corrected light meter is also better because it will account for light entering the meter at an angle. Some light meters also incorporate data logging for long-term measurements of illuminance.

Infrared (IR) Cameras

Infrared (IR) cameras are useful for a variety of tasks during an energy audit. Some of these include the following:

- Heat losses from building fabric—An infrared scan of the outside of a building will indicate where heat is being lost. Problem areas could be insulated further or made more airtight.
- Finding electrical hot spots—Infrared scans of electrical conductors will show where there are loose connections or damaged components because increased heating is a sign of failure.
- Heating ventilation and air-conditioning (HVAC) system testing—Infrared images of different HVAC system components will indicate a range of issues, for example, leakage from duct connections, poor air distribution from diffusers, a non-laminar air flow pattern across coils, and equipment maintenance issues.

Energy Management vs. Energy Efficiency Measures

The purpose of an energy audit is to understand how energy is being used in a facility and to identify opportunities to reduce the total energy consumption. This can be achieved by finding and implementing energy management or energy-efficiency measures. These terms may be considered equivalent and can be used interchangeably, but it is helpful to think of energy management measures as improvements to the operation of existing facility equipment and energy-efficiency measures as requiring retrofitting of systems. Examples of energy management opportunities are adjusting temperature set points, reducing equipment operating hours, or shifting loads to different times to reduce demand charges. Energy-efficiency measures include replacement of motors, chillers, or lamps with more efficient versions, recovering waste heat, or adding additional insulation. Energy management measures can often be found by analysis of energy consumption data and bills and looking at existing policies, procedures, and controls. Inspection of installed equipment during the energy audit building survey will enable inefficient equipment to be identified so recommendations for retrofit opportunities can be made.

Energy Use Index (EUI)

The Energy Use Index (EUI) is a simple metric used to evaluate the energy performance of a facility. Calculating the EUI for a facility enables comparisons with other similar facilities or standard energy performance benchmarks to help understand if a facility is using energy efficiently. The most widely used EUI is Btu per square foot (Btu/ft^2). The total energy consumption for all supplies to a facility are converted to an equivalent Btu value and divided by the total floor area. Other EUIs that may be used are Btu/person or Btu/unit of production. The use of an EUI for facility energy performance evaluation has some limitations that need to be considered. Buildings are categorized for comparison purposes based on the main activity they were designed for, but buildings have different uses and occupancy schedules that don't enable fair comparisons in all cases. The mix of fuels used in a facility can also have a significant impact on the apparent efficiency of a facility due to the way different fuel sources are delivered from their source and then used on site. Also, to compare similar facilities in different climate zones, the energy consumption needs to be weather normalized.

Energy Cost Index ECI (ECI)

The Energy Cost Index (ECI) is a simple metric used to evaluate the energy performance of a facility. The most widely used ECI is dollars per square foot ($\$/ft^2$). To calculate the ECI the total cost for all energy supplies to a facility is added together and divided by the total floor area. The ECI is a useful performance indicator because some energy sources, particularly electricity, have a much higher cost per unit of energy consumed. Therefore, a facility that uses a lot of energy may have a lower ECI than a building using less energy; if reducing costs is the priority, then assessing the performance of a facility's $\$/ft^2$ may be more useful than looking at the Btu/ft^2. There are issues to be aware of when using ECI as a measure of energy performance. Energy costs can depend on the time of day that energy is used or what the peak energy consumption is and are not just dependent on overall facility efficiency. Also, a more efficient building may have higher energy costs than a less efficient building, so in some cases ECI could be misleading.

Calculating Point of Use (POU) Costs

Point of Use (POU) costs are the calculated actual costs of an energy end-use service after the efficiency of equipment utilizing the supply of energy has been considered. The prices of energy supplies are known based on the contracted rates from the supplier; however, different energy supplies have various units of measurement, and their end uses also have different efficiencies. Electricity is usually measured in kilowatt-hours (kWh), natural gas in cubic feet or therms, and heating oil in gallons. To determine what the POU costs for end-use services are, the purchase prices should be converted to a common unit of measurement and then divided by the efficiency of the equipment:

$$POU\ Cost = \frac{Purchase\ Price\ Per\ Common\ Unit}{Efficiency\ of\ Use}$$

For example, if a heating system could use a natural gas boiler at \$7/Mcf and 85% efficiency, heating oil at \$1.60/gallon and 80% efficiency, or electricity at \$0.11/kWh and 300% efficiency (heat pump), which has the lowest POU cost? If the common unit of measurement is chosen to be MMBtu, the POU is calculated as follows:

$$\text{Natural Gas} = \frac{\$7.00}{\text{Mcf}} \times \frac{1\ \text{Mcf}}{1{,}000{,}000\ \text{Btu}} \times \frac{1{,}000{,}000\ \text{Btu}}{\text{MMBtu}} \times \frac{1}{0.85} = \$8.24/\text{MMBtu}$$

$$\text{Heating Oil} = \frac{\$1.60}{\text{gallon}} \times \frac{1\ \text{gallon}}{138{,}000\ \text{Btu}} \times \frac{1{,}000{,}000\ \text{Btu}}{\text{MMBtu}} \times \frac{1}{0.80} = \$14.49/\text{MMBtu}$$

$$\text{Electricity} = \frac{\$0.11}{\text{kWh}} \times \frac{1\ \text{kWh}}{3412\ \text{Btu}} \times \frac{1{,}000{,}000\ \text{Btu}}{\text{MMBtu}} \times \frac{1}{3.00} = \$10.75/\text{MMBtu}$$

Energy Accounting and Economics

Evaluating a Project Using Simple Payback Period

Simple Payback Period is the number of years it takes for the initial investment in a project to be recovered from the annual savings generated.

$$Payback = \frac{Initial\ Investment}{Annual\ Savings}$$

This method is straightforward to calculate and is easy to understand, so it is widely used. Simple Payback is a useful first assessment, especially for small, simple projects, and a short payback may encourage further analysis. The drawbacks to this method are that it doesn't consider the changing value of money over time or full life cycle costs. It doesn't provide an indication of the actual profitability of a project, so it isn't useful to compare project alternatives.

Time Value of Money as It Relates to Energy Accounting and Economics

The time value of money (TVM) refers to the concept that money available today is worth more than the same amount of money in the future. This is due primarily to the fact that it can earn interest or generate returns over time. Key terms associated with TVM are investment opportunity (money invested grows over time) and erosion of value (if money isn't invested, it erodes). There are variations of TVM calculations. Future value (FV) gives you the future value of the cash that you have now. Present discount value (PDV) gives you the current worth of a future sum of money. The calculations are explained below.

The TVM formula calculates the future value (FV) of money based on present value (PV), interest rate (i), number of compounding periods(n), and number of years (t).

$FV = PV\ (1 + (i/n))^{(n \times t)}$

Present Discount Value (PDV) is derived by a mathematical formula to determine how much future money is worth today.

$PDV = a/(1 + R)^{n}$

a = future amount

R = interest rate

n = number of years over which the payment is due

When evaluating energy projects, the time horizon (n) significantly impacts the PDV. The time value of money is a major consideration in the largest of projects, like building a nuclear plant versus a natural gas plant, and the smallest, such as changing out a large heat pump and choosing which efficiency rating to purchase.

Impact of Escalation Rates in Energy Accounting

Escalating rates will have an impact on cost estimates and financial projections related to energy projects. *Inflation* is the general increase in prices over time, and escalation refers to the increase in costs of specific goods or services, such as labor and energy prices. Real price change considers both inflation and escalation.

Escalation is analyzed by considering key factors such as the overall economy, market prices, and government effects. Educated, long-term assumptions about fuel prices and interest rates increase the accuracy of estimating future costs. Energy savings performance contracts (ESPC) are particularly sensitive to escalation rates as these rates directly influence the upper limit of the project scope. High escalation rates allow for larger payments in the ESPC and result in a shorter payback period.

LIFE CYCLE COST METHOD FOR PROJECT EVALUATION

The Life Cycle Cost (LCC) of a project includes all the costs for the entire life of a project. For an energy conservation project, this will usually begin with an initial investment at the beginning of the project. There will be ongoing or one-off costs for maintenance throughout the life of the project, and there may be a decommissioning cost once equipment reaches the end of its useful life. LCC analysis enables a better evaluation of the profitability of an individual project as well as comparing multiple project alternatives. Because costs may occur at different times throughout the lives of different projects, and they may have different expected lives, costs must be discounted to an equivalent period, which may be the present worth, or an annual cost. For a present worth analysis, all future cash flows are converted to an equivalent present worth using a selected discount rate. The project with the lowest cost will be the best option. In the annual cost method, the initial investment is converted to an annual cost, as are all other costs, and the project with the lowest annual cost is then considered to be the most favorable option.

COMPOUND INTEREST FACTOR $F/P_{I,N}$

The compound interest factor F/P is used to calculate the single payment compound amount. This is the future worth *F* of a payment *P* made today after *n* periods at an interest rate *i*. This can be illustrated on a cash flow diagram as follows:

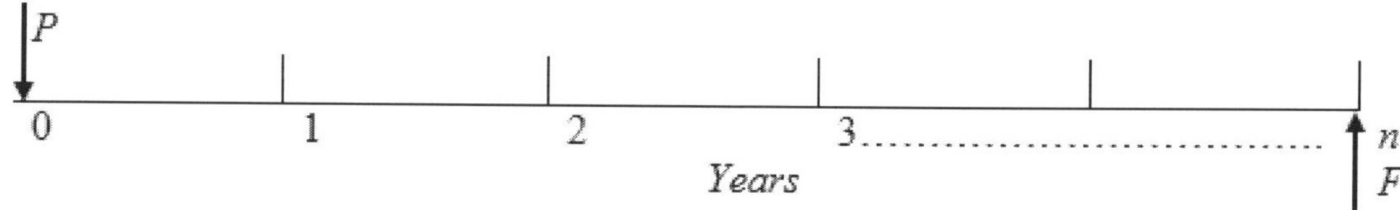

You use the compound interest factor $F/P_{i,n}$ when the present worth of a payment, the interest rate, and life of the project are known and the future worth must be calculated. It is read as follows: "What is *F* given *P*?" Compound interest factors are arranged in tables according to the interest rate. The rows of the table are ordered by the period *n*. The columns of the table correspond to the various interest factors. The present worth of the payment is simply multiplied by the appropriate factor to determine its future worth:

$$F = P \times \left(\frac{F}{P}\right)_{i,n}$$

For example, the future worth of $1,000 after 5 years at 10% interest is $1,000 x 1.6105 = $1,610.50.

Compound Interest Factor $P/F_{i,n}$

The compound interest factor P/F is used to calculate the single payment present worth. This is the present worth *P* of a future payment *F* made *n* periods from now when the interest rate over the period is *i*. This can be illustrated on a cash flow diagram as follows:

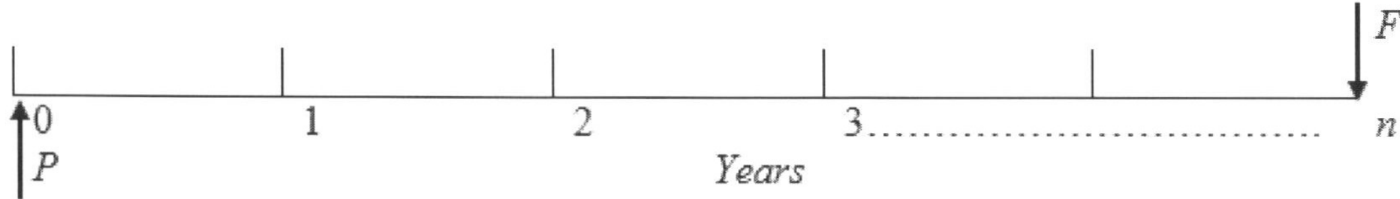

You use the compound interest factor $P/F_{i,n}$ when the future worth of a payment, the interest rate, and life of the project are known, and the present worth of the payment must be calculated. It is read as follows: "What is *P* given *F*?" Compound interest factors are arranged in tables according to the interest rate. The rows of the table are ordered by the period *n*. The columns of the table correspond to the interest factors. The future worth of the payment is simply multiplied by the appropriate factor to determine its present worth:

$$P = F \times \left(\frac{P}{F}\right)_{i,n}$$

For example, the present worth of receiving $1,000 five years from now when the interest is 10% is $1,000 x 0.6209 = $620.90.

Compound Interest Factor $F/A_{i,n}$

The compound interest factor F/A is used to calculate the uniform series compound amount. This is the future worth *F* of a series of payments *A* made for *n* periods at an interest rate *i*. This can be illustrated on a cash flow diagram as follows:

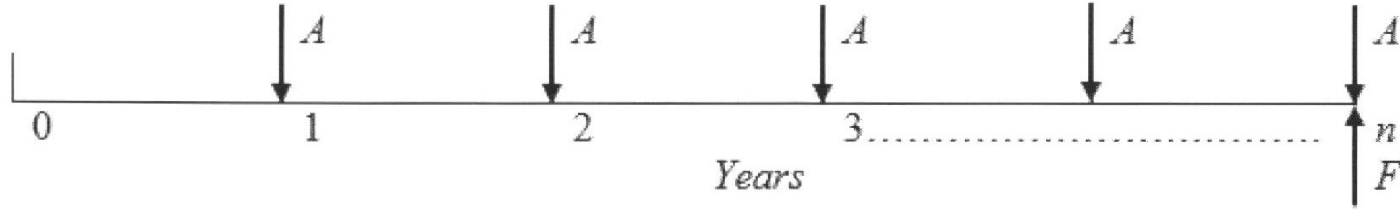

You use the compound interest factor $F/A_{i,n}$ when the annual payment, the interest rate, and life of the project are known and the future worth must be calculated. It is read as follows: "What is *F* given *A*?" Compound interest factors are arranged in tables according to the interest rate. The rows of the table are ordered by the period *n*. The columns of the table correspond to the interest factors. The annual payment is simply multiplied by the appropriate factor to determine its future worth:

$$F = A \times \left(\frac{F}{A}\right)_{i,n}$$

For example, the future worth of receiving $200 every year at 10% interest for 5 years is $200 x 6.1051 = $1,221.02.

Compound Interest Factor $A/F_{i,n}$

The compound interest factor A/F is used to calculate the sinking fund payment amount. This is the annual worth *A* of a future payment *F* after *n* periods at an interest rate *i*. This can be illustrated on a cash flow diagram as follows:

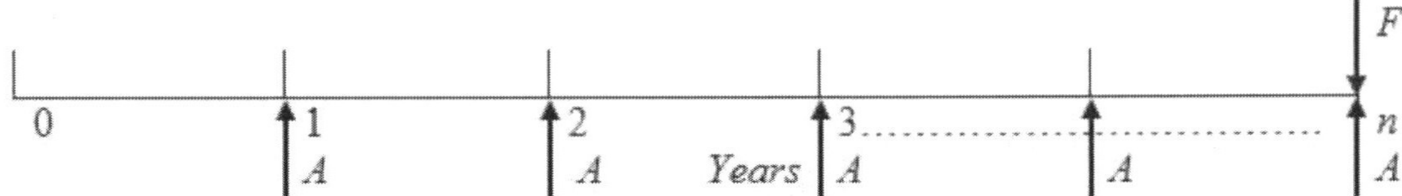

You use the compound interest factor $A/F_{i,n}$ when the future worth of a payment, the interest rate, and life of the project are known, and the equivalent annual worth must be calculated. It is read as follows: "What is *A* given *F*?" Compound interest factors are arranged in tables according to the interest rate. The rows of the table are ordered by the period *n*. The columns of the table correspond to the interest factors. The future worth is simply multiplied by the appropriate factor to determine the annual worth:

$$A = F \times \left(\frac{A}{F}\right)_{i,n}$$

For example, the annual worth of $1,000 at 10% interest 5 years from now is $1,000 x 0.1638 = $163.80.

Compound Interest Factor $A/P_{i,n}$

The compound interest factor A/P is used to calculate the capital recovery amount. This is the series of annual amounts *A* for *n* periods at an interest rate *i* equal to a payment having a present worth *P*. This can be illustrated on a cash flow diagram as follows:

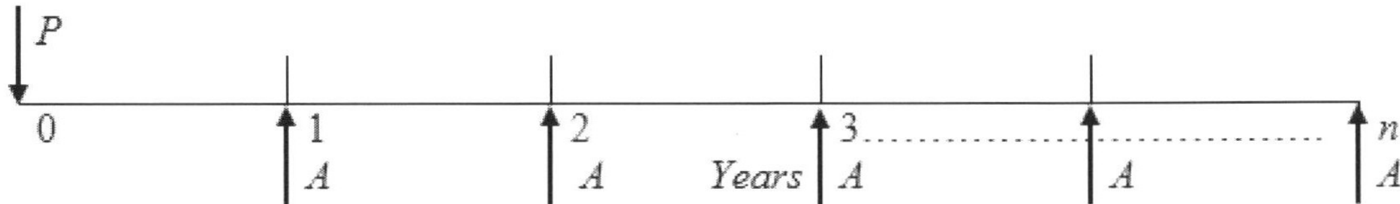

You use the compound interest factor $A/P_{i,n}$ when the present worth of a payment, the interest rate, and life of the project are known and an equivalent annual amount must be calculated. It is read as follows: "What is *A* given *P*?" Compound interest factors are arranged in tables according to the interest rate. The rows of the table are ordered by the period *n*. The columns of the table correspond to the interest factors. The present worth of a payment is simply multiplied by the appropriate factor to determine the equivalent annual worth:

$$A = P \times \left(\frac{A}{P}\right)_{i,n}$$

For example, the annual worth over 5 years of $1,000 now at 10% interest is $1,000 x 0.2638 = $263.80.

Compound Interest Factor $P/A_{i,n}$

The compound interest factor P/A is used to calculate the uniform series present worth. This is the present worth *P* of a series of payments *A* made for *n* periods at an interest rate *i*. This can be illustrated on a cash flow diagram as follows:

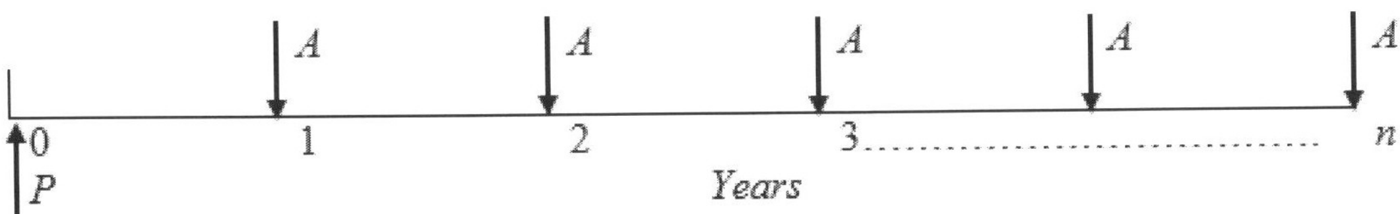

You use the compound interest factor $P/A_{i,n}$ when the annual payment, interest rate, and life of the project are known and the present worth must be calculated. It is read as follows: "What is *P* given *A*?" Compound interest factors are arranged in tables according to the interest rate. The rows of the table are ordered by the period *n*. The columns of the table correspond to the interest factors. The annual payment is simply multiplied by the appropriate factor to determine its present worth:

$$P = A \times \left(\frac{P}{A}\right)_{i,n}$$

For example, the present worth of $200 every year at 10% interest for 5 years is $200 x 3.7908 = $758.16.

Compound Interest Factor $P/G_{i,n}$

The compound interest factor P/G is used to calculate the gradient present worth. This is the present worth *P* of a series of linearly increasing payments *G* made for *n* periods at an interest rate *i*. This can be illustrated on a cash flow diagram as follows:

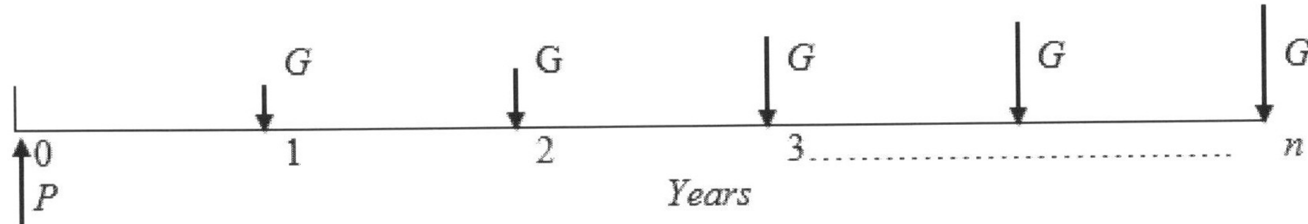

To find the present worth, it is necessary to consider this series of payments *G* as having two separate components. The first component is the present worth of the payment at the end of the first year. The second component is the amount each payment increases from the second year onward. For example, if payments of $1,000, $1,200, $1,400, $1,600, and $1,800 are received, then we have a uniform series of $1,000 and a gradient series increasing by $200 (stating in Year 2). The total period *n* is 5 years, and with an interest rate over the period of 10%, the present worth is calculated as such:

$$P = 1{,}000 \times \left(\frac{P}{A}\right)_{10,5} + 200 \times \left(\frac{P}{G}\right)_{10,5} = 1{,}000 \times 3.7908 + 200 \times 6.8618 = \$5{,}163.16$$

Compound Interest Factor $A/G_{i,n}$

The compound interest factor A/G is used to calculate the gradient annual worth. This is the annual worth *A* of a series of linearly increasing payments *G* made for *n* periods at an interest rate *i*. This can be illustrated on a cash flow diagram as follows:

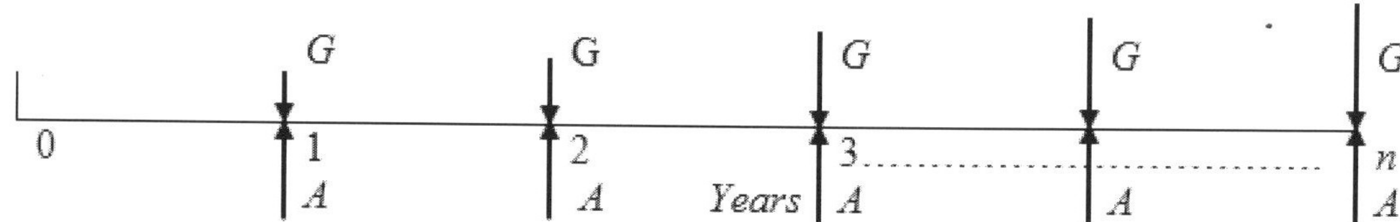

To find the annual worth it is necessary to consider this series of payments *G* as having two separate components. The first component is the annual worth of the payment at the end of the first year. The second component is the amount each payment increases from the second year onward. For example, if payments of $1,000, $1,200, $1,400, $1,600, and $1,800 are received, then we have a uniform series of $1,000 and a gradient series increasing by $200 (starting in Year 2). The total period *n* is 5 years, and with an interest rate over the period of 10%, the annual worth is calculated as such:

$$A = 1{,}000 + 200 \times \left(\frac{A}{G}\right)_{10,5} = 1{,}000 + 200 \times 1.8101 = \$1{,}362.02$$

Comparing Two or More Projects Using the Present Worth Economic Analysis Method

It can be difficult to compare alternative project options when the cash flows within each project occur at different points in time and have different values. Because the value of money changes over time, all cash flows within project alternatives must be converted to a common point in time so an accurate determination of the real value of a project can be made. The present worth method converts all cash flows to the present time. The project with the greatest present worth should be implemented if the present worth is greater than $0. For example, the cash flows for two alternative projects with an interest rate of 10% are as follows:

	Year 0	Year 1	Year 2	Year 3	Year 4	Year 5
Project 1	-$5,000	$2,000	$2,000	$1,000	$1,000	$1,000
Project 2	-$5,000	$2,000	$1,500	$1,500	$1,000	$1,000

The present worth of Project 1 is calculated by converting the future worth of all cash flows using the single payment present worth interest factors at 10%, which are found in tables:

$$-5{,}000 + 2{,}000 \times \left(\frac{P}{F}\right)_{10,1} + 2{,}000 \times \left(\frac{P}{F}\right)_{10,2} + 1{,}000 \times \left(\frac{P}{F}\right)_{10,3} + 1{,}000 \times \left(\frac{P}{F}\right)_{10,4} + 1{,}000 \times \left(\frac{P}{F}\right)_{10,5}$$

$$= -\$5{,}000 + \$1{,}818 + \$1{,}653 + \$751 + \$683 + \$621 = \$526$$

Similarly, the present worth of Project 2 is calculated as such:

$$-5{,}000 + 2{,}000 \times \left(\frac{P}{F}\right)_{10,1} + 1{,}500 \times \left(\frac{P}{F}\right)_{10,2} + 1{,}500 \times \left(\frac{P}{F}\right)_{10,3} + 1{,}000 \times \left(\frac{P}{F}\right)_{10,4} + 1{,}000 \times \left(\frac{P}{F}\right)_{10,5}$$

$$= -\$5{,}000 + \$1{,}818 + \$1{,}240 + \$1{,}127 + \$683 + \$621 = \$489$$

Project 1 should be chosen because it has the greatest present worth and the present worth is more than $0, indicating it provides a positive return on the investment.

Principle of Depreciation

Depreciation allows an organization to reduce its tax liability in recognition of the fact that the value of equipment decreases over time. The rate at which the equipment value can be decreased each year is specified by the Internal Revenue Service. Different methods of depreciating assets have been used in the past, but the current method allowed by the IRS is the *Modified Accelerated Cost Recovery System (MACRS)*. Under the MACRS, the annual percentage of depreciation allowed is specified, and this depends upon the property class and cost basis of the equipment.

The simplest method of depreciation is *straight-line* depreciation. The annual straight-line depreciation rate is constant over the life of the equipment and is calculated as follows:

$$Depreciation = \frac{Initial\ Cost\ -\ Salvage\ Value}{Equipment\ Life}$$

The *sum-of-years digits* depreciation rate changes each year as a function of the amount of useful life remaining out of the total useful life, *n*, and is calculated according to the formula:

$$Depreciation = \frac{useful\ life\ remaining}{n \times \frac{n+1}{2}} \times (Initial\ Cost\ -\ Salvage\ Value)$$

Declining balance depreciation allows faster depreciation at the beginning of the equipment's life. Up to twice the straight-line depreciation rate is allowed, and this constant rate is multiplied by the remaining undepreciated value of the equipment each year. It is calculated as follows:

$$Depreciation = \frac{2}{Useful\ Life} \times (Undepreciated\ Value)$$

Evaluating Life Cycle Costs

Using an Equivalent Annual Annuity (EAA)

When mutually exclusive projects with different project lives are being considered, it is not possible to directly compare them using present worth analysis. This is because the present worth does not take into consideration how quickly a project will provide a return on investment, which is important because a faster return will allow for further reinvestment sooner. One method of evaluating projects with different lives is to convert the present worth to an Equivalent Annual Annuity (EAA). The EAA is the series of annual cash flows for the life of the project equal to the present worth. The EAA is calculated by the formula:

$$EAA = \frac{i \times Present\ Worth}{1 - (1+i)^{-n}}$$

In this equation *i* is the interest rate and *n* is the project life.

For example, if one project has a present worth of $100,000 with a life of 5 years and another project has a present worth of $150,000 with a life of 12 years, then based on the present worth alone, the second project with the higher present worth would be selected. However, if the first project provides a higher return on investment each year, then it may be a more beneficial option. Assuming an interest rate of 10%, the EAA for the first project (*n* = 5, present worth = $100,000) would be $26,380, and the EAA for the second project (n = 12, present worth = $150,000) would be $22,014. In this case the first project may be preferred because it provides a higher annual return.

Using the Replacement Chain Methodology

When mutually exclusive projects with different project lives are being considered, it is not possible to directly compare them using present worth analysis. This is because the present worth does not take into consideration how quickly a project will provide a return on investment, which is important because a faster return will allow for further reinvestment sooner. One method of evaluating projects with different lives is the replacement chain method. This is useful for projects that are repeatable and when the projects have a convenient common time period for comparison. For example, if one project has a life of 5 years and another has a life of 10 years, then you could assume the first project is repeatable once and use a common life of 10 years for a standard present worth analysis. This method becomes less useful if the lowest common life is unrealistic; for example, if one project will last 5 years and the second 6 years, then the earliest common project life is 30 years.

Tax Credit vs. Tax Deduction

Many energy efficiency projects are eligible for either a tax credit or a tax deduction. The Energy Policy Act of 2005 introduced a tax deduction of up to $1.80 per square foot for heating ventilation and air-conditioning (HVAC), lighting, hot water systems, and building envelope of commercial buildings; tax credits for some Energy Star appliances; tax credits for solar equipment; and a 30% tax credit for residential solar hot water and solar present value, among others. A tax credit is more valuable than a tax deduction because it reduces the tax liability by the amount of the credit. A tax deduction reduces the taxable amount, so its value depends upon the applicable tax bracket. For example, if a company received a 30% tax credit on the purchase of equipment worth $100,000, the value of the credit would be $30,000. However, if an organization must pay taxes on $100,000, then a 30% tax deduction would reduce the taxable amount to $70,000; therefore, the value of the deduction at a 39% tax rate would be 39% x (100,000–70,000) = $11,700.

Importance of Interest Rate, Discount Rate, or Minimum Attractive Rate of Return in Discounted Cash Flow Analysis

Economic analysis of projects that occur over many years should take into account the changing value of money over time. Cash flows that occur in the future will have less value than an equivalent amount today. One of the reasons for this is interest. This is the return that can be earned over a period of time by investing the money you have today. The interest earned will depend upon how the money is invested, but historical returns are known for a variety of investment options. When evaluating a project, the interest rate chosen should be at least equal to the weighted average cost of capital, which is a company's overall cost of raising more money. This interest rate is also called a discount rate, or the minimum attractive rate of return. The net present value of a series of cash flows is very sensitive to the interest rate chosen. A higher interest rate means that cash flows further into the future have less effect on the net present value.

Internal Rate of Return (IRR)

The Internal Rate of Return (IRR) is the interest rate that makes the net present value (NPV) of a series of cash flows equal to zero. The IRR of a project is therefore the interest rate at which the NPV of the investment is equal to the NPV of the savings. The IRR can also be called the return on investment. If the IRR of a project is greater than a company's cost of capital, then the investment is worthwhile considering. Generally, the higher the IRR the more attractive a project should be. However, a project with a high IRR may also have a low NPV, and a project with a high NPV may have a low IRR. This may occur when a high IRR is used to compare a project with a shorter life and a project with a longer life. The shorter project may return the investment more quickly, but the longer project may add more overall value.

Net Present Value (NPV)

The net present value (NPV), or net present worth, of a project is the difference between the discounted cash flow of all savings and the discounted cash flow of all costs, including the initial investment. The NPV of a project is a useful metric for deciding if it is a worthwhile investment. A project with a larger NPV will add more value to an organization than a project with a smaller NPV, so for mutually exclusive projects, this is a commonly used method of analysis. One of the biggest drawbacks to using the NPV is it relies on the accuracy of a number of assumptions, including the choice of discount rate and the predicted cash flows throughout the life of the project.

Benefit/Cost Ratio (BCR)

The benefit/cost ratio (BCR), also called the savings to investment Ratio (SIR), is a decision-making metric using discounted cash flows. It is the present worth of all benefits divided by the present worth of all costs. When comparing project alternatives, a higher BCR is desirable because this would mean greater benefits or lower costs. Also, the BCR must be greater than 1 for a project to be cost-effective. This approach also considers nonfinancial benefits or costs, for example, better employee or customer well-being or improved corporate image. These subjective qualities must be assessed in financial terms before the BCR can be calculated, and they can sometimes be difficult to quantify.

Effects of Inflation on a Series of Cash Flows

Economic analysis of projects that occur over many years should consider the changing value of money over time. Cash flows that occur in the future will have less value than an equivalent amount today. One of the reasons for this is inflation. Inflation is caused by rising prices over time, resulting in a loss of purchasing power in the future of an equivalent amount of money today. The need to consider inflation when calculating life cycle costs when making a decision between alternative project options is important because energy costs, labor costs, and material and equipment costs are all rising over the long term. A discounted cash flow analysis using life cycle costing should be used to evaluate projects so that the changing value of money over time is included in a financial evaluation.

Calculating after-Tax Savings Cash Flows

Tax can be an important consideration when making decisions about competing project alternatives. The impact of tax credits or deductions can significantly improve a project's financial viability. When the after-tax savings need to be calculated the following formula can be used:

$$After\text{-}Tax\ Savings = Savings - [(Savings - Depreciation) \times Tax\ Rate]$$

This is a simplified calculation ignoring any costs of financing. Depreciation reduces the amount of tax paid and is a dollar amount for the year. Depreciation can include deductible expenses such as maintenance costs, operating costs, and insurance.

Electrical Power Systems and Motors

Demand and Energy in Electrical Power Systems

Demand is measured in kilowatts (kW) and refers to the maximum amount of electrical power being consumed at a given instant. Knowing demand is critical for the grid operators and utilities as they must ensure they can meet the peak demand and avoid blackouts or power disruptions. Utilities often offer programs that incentivize customers to reduce demand during on-peak hours and to consume energy during off-peak hours.

Energy is measured in kilowatt-hours (kWh). Energy represents the total amount of power used over a period of time and reflects cumulative consumption. Energy is measured by multiplying watts by hours. For example, a 50-watt bulb operating for 20 hours would consume 1 kilowatt-hour.

A utility bill is typically set up with a line item of charges for demand (kW) and a line item for energy (kWh) charges.

Calculating the Power of a Balanced Single-Phase Load in an AC System

In resistive DC circuits the relationship among voltage, current, and resistance is described by Ohm's law: $V = I \times R$. The power in a circuit is described by Joule's Law: $P = I^2 \times R$. Combining these two relationships results in a useful equation for calculating the power in a simple resistive DC circuit when the voltage and current are known: $P = V \times I$. In AC circuits the instantaneous voltage and current are not constant, and the power is calculated this way:

$$P = V \times I \times Power\ Factor$$

The unit of electrical power is the Watt and is a measure of the instantaneous rate of doing work. The energy consumed is a measure of the work done over a period of time and is measured in Watt-hours. The same amount of energy is used by a 100W lamp in 1 hour as a 50W lamp in 2 hours.

Calculating the Power of a Balanced Three-Phase Load in an AC System

The power in a three-phase AC system is calculated by the formula:

$$P = \sqrt{3} \times V \times I \times Power\ Factor$$

Three-phase systems are most commonly either a four-wire wye connection or a three-wire delta connection. The four-wire connection has three live lines and a neutral line; the phase voltage is the voltage level from a line to the neutral wire. The three-wire delta connection has three live lines and no neutral; therefore, the phase and line voltages are the same. The relationships between the line and phase currents and voltages and the typical voltages in the US are as follows:

Configuration	Line and Phase Currents	Line and Phase Voltages	Typical Voltage Levels
4-Wire Wye	$I_L = I_P$	$V_L = \sqrt{3} \times V_P$	120/208V 277/480V
3-Wire Delta	$I_L = \sqrt{3} \times I_P$	$V_L = V_P$	240V 400V 480V

Real, Apparent, and Reactive Power in an AC Electrical System

The AC electrical systems in facilities have inductive and capacitive loads that create a non-resistive impedance called reactance. This reactance results in reactive power within the system that does no useful work and results in the voltage and current being out of phase with each other. Reactive power is measured in volt-amps and does not transfer any net power to the load but is necessary for the delivery of real power. Real power is the power that is paid for at the meter, measured in kW, and is used by equipment for useful work. The total power that must be supplied by the utility is the apparent power, measured in volt-amps. The apparent, real, and reactive powers can be added vectorially to be represented by a power triangle:

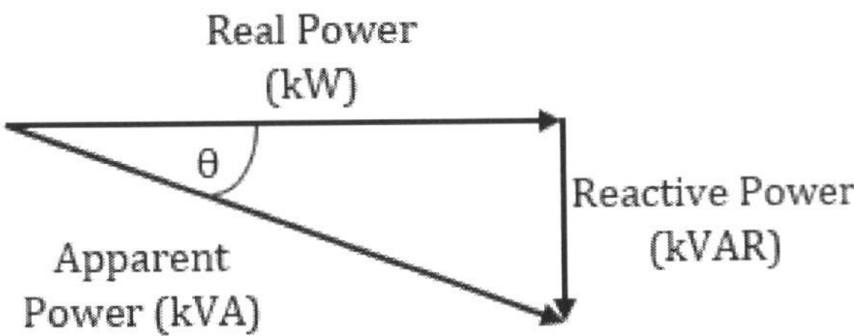

The cosine of the angle, θ, which is the phase angle between the voltage and current, is the ratio of the real power to the apparent power and is called the power factor. The calculation of power may be carried out as for any Pythagorean triangle:

$$Apparent\ Power^2 = Real\ Power^2 + Reactive\ Power^2$$

Power Factor in an AC Electrical System

The displacement power factor of an AC electrical system is a result of the difference in phase between the voltage and current in the system due to inductive and capacitive loads. In inductive loads, the current lags the voltage resulting in a "lagging power factor." The current leads the voltage in capacitive loads, so this creates a "leading power factor." Looking at a power triangle, the angle, θ, between the real and apparent power is the phase angle between the voltage and current. The power factor is the cosine of this angle:

$$Power\ Factor = \cos\theta$$

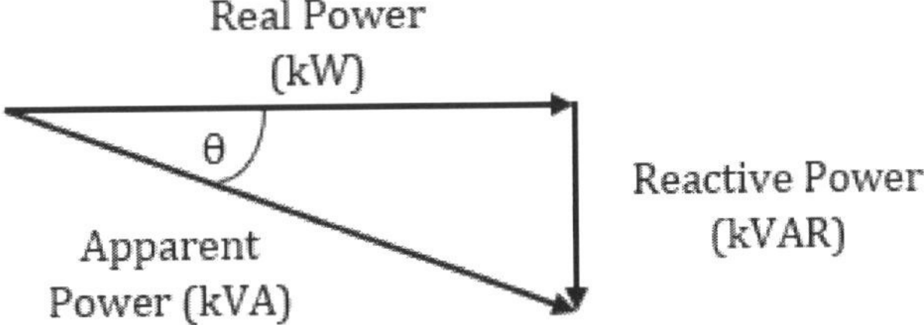

The power factor is also the ratio of the real power (measured in Watts) to the apparent power, which is the product of the rms voltage and current and measured in volt-amps:

$$Power\ Factor = \frac{Real\ Power\ (W)}{Apparent\ Power\ (VA)}$$

A low power factor, which may typically be considered to be a value less than 0.9, will result in increased current flowing through the circuit, which may shorten the life of equipment due to more heat being generated. Utilities often charge a power factor penalty, which can be substantial and makes power factor correction worthwhile.

Correcting a Low (Lagging) Power Factor Using Capacitors

Inductive loads in AC electrical systems require some current to maintain a magnetic field for them to operate. This additional magnetizing current reduces the efficiency of power consumption and lowers the power factor of the system. The solution is to install capacitors because they act as reactive current generators and therefore decrease the amount of reactive current needed from the grid. Capacitors may be installed anywhere within the system, and there are four general locations that may be considered:

- At the load—The best location is at the inductive load because the capacity can be closely matched to the current requirement and losses are minimized.
- At the main busbar—Capacitors may be connected on the load side of the main distribution feeder via a breaker or switch. This is useful when the reactive current required is continuous and stable throughout the electrical system.
- Within local distribution areas—If the electrical system is extensive, and the reactive current requirements vary within distribution areas, then capacitors may be installed at local distribution boards.
- Utility side of incoming transformer—Installing capacitors on the utility side of the transformer will not improve the power factor within your electrical system but will reduce the reactive power supplied by the utility so power factor penalty charges are still reduced.

A lagging power factor is typically an issue in AC electrical systems, which is corrected by installing capacitors. When correcting the power factor, the real power demand will remain constant, but the apparent power and reactive power will change. The amount of capacitance required to reduce the reactive power is the typical problem that must be solved. For example, in a system with a power demand of 1,000kW and a power factor of 0.75, what should the kVAR of the capacitor bank be to improve the power factor to 0.90?

Power factor correction problems are best solved by looking at a power triangle to visualize the system, so the first step should be to illustrate the situation.

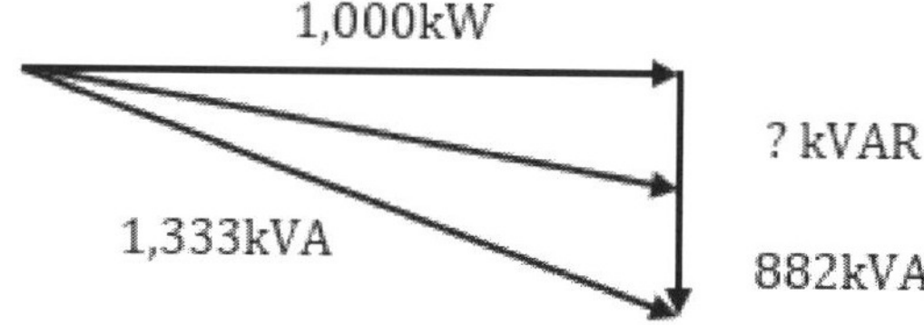

The existing apparent power is:

$$\frac{1000}{0.75} = 1{,}333 \text{ kVA}$$

Therefore, the reactive power is:

$$\sqrt{1333^2 - 1000^2} = 882 \text{ kVAR}$$

For a power factor of 0.9, the new apparent power will be:

$$\frac{1000}{0.9} = 1{,}111 \text{ kVA}$$

And the reactive power will be:

$$\sqrt{1111^2 - 1000^2} = 484 \text{ kVAR}$$

So, the amount of reactive power needed is 882 – 484 = 398kVAR. This result can also be found using a power factor correction table. The table has multipliers for a range of original and desired power factors that are multiplied by the real power (kW) to find the required capacitor kVAR. The multiplier for improving the power factor from 0.75 to 0.90 is 0.398. In the example here the kVAR needed is therefore 1,000 x 0.398 = 398kVAR, which is the same result.

HARMONICS

Harmonics are multiples of the fundamental frequency of the power system. In a system with a fundamental frequency of 60Hz, the second harmonic is 120Hz, the third is 180Hz, and so on. Harmonics are caused by nonlinear loads, which means they draw a current in pulses instead of in a consistent sinusoidal manner. Examples of nonlinear loads are computers, uninterruptible power supplies, electronic lighting ballasts, and variable frequency drives. Harmonic distortion results in various issues such as circuit breakers tripping, transformers and neutral conductors overheating, excessive heat in motors, and capacitor failure. When harmonics are created in a system, the current waveform becomes less sinusoidal, and this also decreases the power factor of the system. Harmonic filters are used to limit the effects of harmonics in a power system. Passive filters use a combination of capacitors, inductors, and resistors to remove harmonics through low impedance paths to ground. Active filters try to condition the current waveform by sensing harmonics and producing waveforms that cancel them out. IEEE Standard 519 describes recommended practice and requirements for harmonic control in power systems.

GROUNDING

Proper grounding is important for three main reasons: The first is safety because high voltages from lightning or a power surge, or shock hazards from equipment failure, are dangerous; the second reason is it protects equipment from faults and high voltages; it also enables all sensitive electrical equipment to have the same reference voltage. Grounding is critical in ensuring acceptable power quality. About 75% to 80% of power quality issues are the result of poor grounding. Noise or electromagnetic interference is a common power quality problem in systems with poor grounding. Grounding helps prevent currents being generated in communication lines. Grounding problems can be the result of loose connections, or from older installations that no longer meet the modern standard for grounding, and does not provide adequate protection for new electronic equipment. Grounding standards are specified by the National Electrical Code.

VOLTAGE IMBALANCE

Voltage imbalance is caused when the loads on the three phases of an electrical system are not equal. This is especially a problem for motors. Voltage imbalance in a motor can cause it to overheat, or the motor controller may shut down. The percentage of voltage imbalance is calculated as the largest voltage difference from the average divided by the average voltage:

$$\%\, Imbalance = \frac{|V_{Max\ Diff} - V_{Average}|}{V_{Average}}$$

For example, if the voltages on each phase are 234V, 240V, and 243V, then the average voltage is 239V and the percent imbalance is calculated as follows:

$$\frac{|234V - 239V|}{239V} = \frac{5V}{239V} = 2.1\%$$

NEMA Standard MG1-14.35 states that motors are operating correctly when the voltage imbalance is less than 1%, and a voltage imbalance of more than 5% is likely to result in damage to the motor.

Power Quality

Power quality refers to the reliability of the voltage level, frequency, and waveform in an electrical system. Voltage problems include short-term voltage increase "swells," short-term voltage decrease "sags," brief voltage increase "spikes," and longer-term overvoltage or undervoltage. The frequency may vary from the ideal 60Hz when standby generators are operated or poor electrical infrastructure, which can cause motors to run faster or slower. Waveform issues are generally the result of harmonics in the power system caused by nonlinear loads. Factors leading to poor power quality include faults in the distribution network, when large loads are connected, during switching of lines, faults in power factor correction capacitors, when large loads are disconnected, frequent starting and stopping of motors, nonlinear loads, improper grounding, and voltage imbalance among the three phases. IEEE publishes many standards regarding power quality, including IEEE 519 (harmonic control), IEEE 1159 (monitoring power quality), and IEEE 1564 (voltage sag). Solutions to poor power quality include power conditioners and uninterruptible power supplies.

DC Motor Applications

DC motors are not widely used in buildings but are still commonly used in industrial applications. They are best for when precise speed control is important because the speed of DC motors is easily controlled or remains very constant. There are many types of DC motors, such as permanent magnet, series, shunt, and compound motors. Series motors have a high starting torque and slow down as the load increases. Shunt motors have an almost constant speed regardless of the torque but are not suitable for high torque loads when starting. The construction of DC motors may be with a brush or brushless. Electrically commutated (EC) DC motors are brushless and are now becoming very popular in heating ventilation and air-conditioning (HVAC) applications. They are very energy efficient, low maintenance, and enable precise speed control for fans in air handling units, fan coil units, and chiller condensers instead of using AC motor fans with variable frequency drives.

Types of AC Motors

AC motors are able to operate over a wide range of loads, typically down to 50% of maximum load, and maintain their efficiency. Peak efficiency of AC motors is often around 75% of rated load. Larger motors tend to be more efficient and have a better power factor. AC motors may be synchronous or asynchronous:

- Synchronous motors—These motors operate at a precise, constant speed that matches the frequency of the AC supply current. They can run at leading power factor and therefore generate or absorb reactive power, which improves the overall power factor. They are best for low-speed and high-torque applications.
- Asynchronous motors—These are also called induction motors, and they operate at a speed slightly slower than the frequency of the AC current due to slippage caused by the torque of an applied load. Asynchronous motors are the type most commonly used today due to their lower cost and better ability to operate at higher speeds and with speed variation possible.

Types of Losses Occurring in Motors

There are five types of losses in electric motors:

1. Friction losses—These losses are due to bearing or brush friction.
2. Windage losses—This is loss due to the air resistance and drag on the rotor's motion.
3. Core losses—This is mostly present in the stator and is due to both hysteresis loss and eddy current loss caused by the constantly changing magnetic field.
4. Resistive losses—The stator and rotor circuits have resistive losses that are equal to the square of the current flowing through them multiplied by their resistance (I^2R). The largest losses in AC motors are the stator resistance loss and then the rotor resistance loss.
5. Stray load losses—These are other losses that are not easily determined, for example, harmonic losses in the core and current flow through the core. These losses tend to increase as motor load increases.

The following chart shows how these losses typically vary as the load on a motor changes:

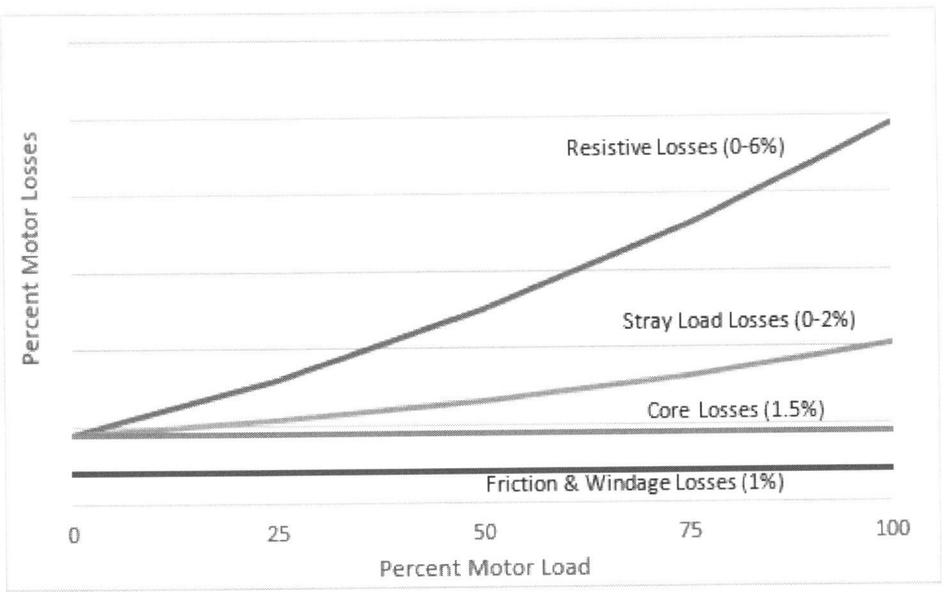

No Load RPM (NLRPM), Full Load RPM (FLRPM), and Slip

No Load RPM—This is the synchronous speed of the motor based on the frequency of the supply current and the number of motor poles:

$$No\ Load\ RPM = \frac{f \times 60}{number\ of\ pole\ pairs}$$

For 60Hz power supplies the NLRPM is either 3600, 1800, 1200, 900, and so on.

Full Load RPM—This is the nameplate speed when the motor is operating at 100% load.

Slip—Slip is the difference between NLRPM and FLRPM due to the torque from an applied load. The percent load on a motor is:

$$\%\ Load = \frac{True\ Slip}{Design\ Slip} = \frac{NLRPM - Measured\ RPM}{NLRPM - FLRPM}$$

It can be difficult to measure the actual RPM accurately in practice, so measuring the actual power input to the motor and dividing by the power at rated load is another method to calculate the motor load:

$$\% \, Load = \frac{Power_{measured\ input}}{Power_{rated\ input}} = \frac{V \times I \times PF \times \sqrt{3}}{\frac{hp}{\eta} \times 745.7 \left(\frac{W}{hp}\right)}$$

In this equation *V* is the mean line-to-line RMS voltage of the three phases, *I* is the mean of the RMS current in the three phases, *PF* is the power factor, *hp* is the rated horsepower, and η is the motor efficiency at 100% rated load.

AC Motor Efficiency and Power Factor

AC motor efficiency remains high from 100% of rated load down to about 50% of rated load. The peak motor efficiency is generally around 75% of rated load. Motor efficiency is the mechanical power output divided by the electrical power input:

$$Efficiency = \frac{Output}{Input} = \frac{Speed \times Torque}{Voltage \times Current \times PF}$$

Motor speed is at its maximum when there is no load, and at this point the efficiency is zero. As the torque begins to increase, the efficiency starts to increase, but the speed also slows slightly (slip). When there is no load, the magnetizing component of the input current is high, so the current lags the voltage by up to 90°. This causes a low power factor because the power factor is the cosine of the angle between the current and voltage. As the load increases the magnetizing current stays constant, but it is less of the total current in the motor, so power factor improves. Motor efficiency is classified by the National Electrical Manufacturers Association (NEMA) based on test standards according to IEEE 112.

Advantages of Using Higher-Efficiency Motors

The efficiency of a motor is calculated by dividing the mechanical power output by the electrical power input:

$$Efficiency = \frac{Output}{Input} = \frac{Input - Losses}{Input} = \frac{Output}{Output + Losses}$$

High-efficiency motors have improved construction that reduces the losses in motors. Motor losses include constant losses that do not vary considerably as the load on the motor changes (friction, windage, and core) and variable losses that increase as motor load increases (resistive and stray losses). High-efficiency motors can provide significant energy savings for motors that operate for many hours of the year because motor operating costs over their lifetimes are many times their initial purchase price. Motors should be changed if they are significantly oversized (loading is only about 25%), and higher-efficiency motors should be purchased to replace failed motors. Motor rewinds are an option for larger motors over about 24 HP. Rewinds can cost 60% of the price of a new motor, and efficiency decreases after a motor rewind.

Calculating the Electrical Power Input of a Motor

Motor power in kilowatts is calculated this way:

$$P\ (kW) = \frac{HP \times\ 0.746 \left(\frac{kW}{HP}\right)\ \times LF}{\eta}$$

In this equation *HP* is the motor horsepower, *LF* is the load factor on the motor, and η is the motor efficiency. The power savings that can be achieved by replacing a standard-efficiency motor with an energy-efficient motor is:

$$P_{saved}\ (kW) = \left[\frac{HP \times\ 0.746 \left(\frac{kW}{HP}\right)\ \times LF}{\eta}\right]_{Standard} - \left[\frac{HP \times\ 0.746 \left(\frac{kW}{HP}\right)\ \times LF}{\eta}\right]_{High\ Efficiency}$$

The energy savings are then calculated by multiplying the power savings by the hours of operation. For example, if a 50HP motor with an efficiency of 91% and a load factor of 80% is replaced with a motor having an efficiency of 95%, the power savings are:

$$P_{saved}\ (kW) = \frac{50\ \times 0.746\ \times 0.8}{0.91} - \frac{50\ \times 0.746\ \times 0.8}{0.95} = 32.8 - 31.4 = 1.4\ \text{kW}$$

If the motor operates for 8,760 hours per year, then the energy savings are 1.4 x 8760 = 12,264kWh.

Variable Frequency Drives (VFD)

A variable frequency drive (VFD) is used to control the speed of an AC motor. It works by rectifying the AC supply to a DC supply and then creating an approximate AC signal at the desired frequency in an inverter by chopping the DC supply into short pulses. They are often used to control the speed of pump and fan motors that operate in systems with variable demands, for example, variable air volume air-handling unit fans and primary chilled water pumps. When fan and pump demands are variable and a constant speed motor is used, the flow of air or liquid must be controlled by mechanical throttling and this is not energy efficient. When demands are variable it is beneficial to control motor speed with a VFD because the power of a fan or pump motor is proportional to the cube of the speed. Therefore, reducing motor speed by 20% reduces power demand by 51.2% (0.83). In practice the motor speed will likely change over a range of speeds from 100% to maybe 40%. In this case the difference in power input is multiplied by the fraction of the time it occurs, so the energy savings from a VFD are calculated by:

$$Savings\ (kWh) = HP \times 0.746 \left(\frac{kW}{HP}\right) \times\ \Delta Power\ Input\ Ratio\ \ \times \%\ Duty\ Cycle\ \ \times Total\ Run\ Hours$$

Affinity Laws for Centrifugal Fans and Pumps

The affinity laws for centrifugal fans and pumps enable the flow, pressure, and power to be calculated when motor speed is altered. When the speed of the motor is RPM_1 and then the speed changes to RPM_2, then the system changes as follows:

The flow rate, *Q*, of a pump or fan is proportional to its speed:

$$\frac{Q_2}{Q_1} = \frac{RPM_2}{RPM_1}$$

The pressure, *P*, in a system is proportional to the square of the motor speed:

$$\frac{P_2}{P_1} = \frac{(RPM_2)^2}{(RPM_1)^2}$$

The motor power, *HP*, is proportional to the cube of the motor speed:

$$\frac{HP_2}{HP_1} = \frac{(RPM_2)^3}{(RPM_1)^3}$$

For example, if the power demand of a fan at full speed is 10kW, then slowing the speed to 80% would reduce the power demand this way:

$$\frac{HP_2}{10} = \frac{0.8^3}{1} = 10 \times 0.512 = 5.12kW$$

Motor Speed Control Options for Variable Volume Systems

A variable volume system can be achieved by restricting the flow or varying the motor speed.

The speed of motors in variable volume systems are now most commonly controlled by variable frequency drives (VFDs). These drives adjust the speed of the motor by rectifying the AC supply to a DC supply and then creating an approximate AC signal at the desired frequency in an inverter by chopping the DC supply into short pulses. Eddy current drives are a type of magnetic clutch and have similar performance to VFDs without causing problems with harmonics, but they are bulky and heat generation can be an issue. Another speed control option is variable pitched sheaves. A less efficient method of varying the flow volume in a system is to restrict the flow with valves or guide vanes. Restricting the flow to reduce the flow volume when less than the peak flow is required requires the motor to work harder and increases energy consumption.

Motor Selection and Motor Management Software

Motor selection will depend upon the expected loads, operating characteristics, and physical size. The National Electrical Manufacturers Association (NEMA) publishes a Motors and Generators Standard, MG 1-16, to assist with the proper selection of motors and contains practical performance data and specifications. Motor efficiency is classified by NEMA based on test standards according to IEEE 112. NEMA motor efficiency classes are standard, high, premium, and super premium. There are four different NEMA designs that designate the relationship among speed, torque, and slip. For example, NEMA Design B has a maximum of 5% slip, low staring current, and high locked rotor torque. The physical motor size also needs to be considered when retrofitting motors. MotorMaster+ is a motor management software tool provided by the Department of Energy. It helps with motor selection based on life cycle cost analysis using a database of motors that are available as well as enabling the tracking of maintenance tasks and savings.

Considerations for New vs. Rewound Motors

There are several factors to consider when deciding between a new motor and a rewound motor.

- Cost/economics: Rewinding is significantly cheaper than buying a new motor. It is approximately 40% cheaper, so when budget is a big concern, rewinding is an economical choice.
- Motor condition: Are the critical components like the stator core and rotor in good shape? If so, rewinding is a good option. If the critical components are damaged and not repairable, buying new is a better option.

- Efficiency: It used to be believed that rewinding a motor reduces efficiency by several percent each time it is done. New research has shown that there is no change in efficiency after a rewind, so this has become less of a factor in making the choice.
- Environmental impact: Rewinding is more environmentally friendly. Buying a new motor will likely mean that the old motor parts end up in a landfill.

Lighting Systems

Color Rendering Index (CRI) and Color Temperature

The Color Rendering Index (CRI) of a light source is a measure of how well it enables colors to be perceived when compared to a reference light source, usually daylight. The CRI is a numerical value from 0 to 100, with 100 indicating that color perception under a light source is equivalent to daylight, and zero being monochromatic light with poor color perception, such as light from low-pressure sodium lamps. The color temperature of a light source describes the color appearance of a light source and affects the mood of a space. Color temperature is given in units of Kelvin. A reddish-yellow or "warm" light has a color temperature less than 3,000K. A neutral white light has a color temperature between 3000K and 5000K. A bluish "cool" light has a color temperature greater than 5000K. The CRI is independent of color temperature, so some lamps will have a better CRI at a color temperature of 2,000 to 3,000K than at higher color temperatures around 5,000K. The typical CRI and color temperature range for common lamp types is as follows:

Lamp Type	Color Rendering Index (CRI)	Color Temperature (K)
High-pressure sodium	65	2100–2700
Metal halide	70	3000–5500
Fluorescent	75–85	3000–5000
Compact fluorescent	80–85	2700–5000
Incandescent	100	2800
Halogen	100	3000
LED	80–90	3000-5000

Visual Comfort

Visual comfort is an important consideration when assessing overall lighting quality and occupant satisfaction. Visual comfort is subjective, but it generally means that people can carry out their tasks without any discomfort. The factors that usually contribute to poor visual comfort include the following:

- Glare—Glare from light sources or reflections will cause discomfort from excessive contrast as our eyes try to adapt to two levels of brightness at the same time.
- Non-uniform lighting—It is preferable to have uniform lighting because it will avoid excessive contrast and will be less distracting to occupants.
- Surface reflectance—If the walls of a room are dark, they will reflect less light so higher levels of task lighting may be required, which will increase the contrast between the work area and the other parts of a room. Light-colored surfaces reflect more light so will reduce glare and increase uniformity of light.

The visual comfort probability (VCP) is a rating from 0 to 100 for light fixtures that indicates how likely they are to be acceptable to occupants with regard to glare. A VCP of 80% means that 80% of people would not feel affected by glare.

Human Centric Lighting Design

Human centric lighting is a lighting design technique that takes into account the human circadian rhythm and the natural cycles of daylight and darkness. It is a relatively new design practice that aims to elevate mood, productivity, and social interaction. Color temperature and intensity can be controlled and varied to impact the occupants' mood. For example, warmer temperatures (2500k - 3000k) often create a more relaxed mood and thus spur collaboration, creativity, and socialization. Cooler temperatures (5000k and above) create alertness and will foster concentration, focus, and a serious environment.

Human centric lighting design can be adjusted to accommodate the specific building occupants or business need. For example, the retail and hospitality industries will look to provide a relaxed and inviting environment, while a healthcare facility may need a combination of warm and cool environments. A school or office building would look for a lighting design that could fluctuate throughout the day or evening to create a mixture of serious concentration or work periods and periods of social engagement or collaboration. Human centric lighting designs can be applied to both new and retrofit applications and can be obtained by incorporating tunable LED fixtures, natural lighting concepts, and a lighting control system.

Pupil Lumens in Lighting Systems

Pupil lumens measure the amount of usable light emitted by a given light source based on how effectively the eye can perceive the produced light. Some terms related to pupil lumens are:

- Luminous flux/light output: This is measured in lumens but does not take into account the direction the light is sent.
- Illuminance/light level: This is the amount of light on a surface and is measured in footcandles (FC) or lumens per square foot.
- Luminance/brightness: This is the amount of light reflected by a surface and is measured in footlamberts. Our eyes "see" luminance.

Pupil lumens consider both the low-light (scotopic) response of the eye and the correction factors applied to conventional daylight (photopic) lumen readings. To calculate pupil lumens, multiply the photopic lumens by the scotopic/photopic ratio: pupil lumens = photopic lumens × (photopic lumens ÷ scotopic lumens)

Spectral Power Distribution in Lighting Systems

Spectral power distribution (SPD) is the power per unit area per unit wavelength of an illumination. SPD quantifies how much optical radiation exists at different wavelengths reflected from a surface or within a light source.

Mathematically, the SPD for a radiant exitance (or irradiance) can be expressed as:

$M(\lambda)=\mathrm{d}\Phi / (\mathrm{d}A \cdot \mathrm{d}\lambda)$

$M(\lambda)$ = spectral radiance of the light (SI units: W/m^2)

$\mathrm{d}\Phi$ = radiant flux of the source (SI units: watt)

$\mathrm{d}A$ = the area in square meters

$\mathrm{d}\lambda$ = wavelength in meters

The relative SPD compares the concentration of radiance at a given wavelength to that at a reference wavelength. SPDs are often normalized at 555 or 560 nanometers. SPDs also help determine the response of a sensor at specific wavelengths. SPDs play a critical role in color perception, sensor design, and many optical applications.

Efficacies of Common Lamp Types

The efficacy of a lamp is a measure of how efficiently it provides light by comparing the light output to power demand. Efficacy is calculated by dividing the luminous flux by the power demand. Luminous flux is the amount of light output from a lamp and is measured in lumens, and the power demand is measured in Watts.

$$Efficacy = \frac{lumens}{Watts}$$

The efficacy should include power losses in the ballast. The typical efficacy range for common lamp types is as follows:

Lamp Type	Typical Efficacy Range
Incandescent	10–20
Halogen	15–30
Fluorescent	65–110
Compact fluorescent	60–80
High-pressure sodium	50–140
Low-pressure sodium	120–200
Metal halide	70–115
LED	70–140

Light Sources in Lighting Systems Design

Light sources can be natural, artificial, or a combination. Natural light sources include sunlight and skylight. Artificial light sources consist primarily of electric lamps and luminaires.

The primary function of a light source is to ensure that there is adequate visibility in the space. Proper lighting enhances functionality and allows for tasks to be performed comfortably and safely in the space. The quantity and quality of the light must also be accounted for.

The light source will also have a big impact on the mood and atmosphere of the space. Color temperature (measured in kelvin) plays a large role. For example, warmer lights (lower kelvin temperatures) create a quiet and intimate atmosphere. These could be used in a residential environment or a restaurant. Cooler lights (higher kelvin temperatures) foster a productive and alert environment. These would be common in a classroom, hospital, and office environment.

Illuminance

The candela (cd) is the fundamental measure of luminous intensity and is measured in lumens per steradian (lm/sr). A 1 cd light source will produce 1 lumen per square foot at a distance of 1 foot. Illuminance is a measure of the amount of light provided per unit of area and is measured in footcandles (lumens per square foot) or lux (lumens per square meter). As a surface moves away from a light source, it gets dimmer, and the inverse square law describes the relationship between luminous intensity and illuminance as follows:

$$E = \frac{I}{d^2}$$

In this equation, E is the illuminance, I is the luminous intensity, and d is the distance of a surface to the light source. For example, if high bay lamps are mounted at 30 feet and the floor illuminance is 30 footcandles, then lowering the lamps to 20 feet would increase the illuminance like this:

$$30\ FC = \frac{I}{30^2} \therefore \frac{(30\ FC \times 30^2)}{20^2} = 67.5\ FC$$

Components of Lighting Systems

A typical lighting system is generally comprised of the lamp, ballast or driver, and a fixture (or luminaire) with a reflector and a lens or louver.

- Lamp—The type of lamp chosen will depend upon the required illuminance and light quality for the specific area and application. Other considerations may be the average rated life of a lamp, which is the median age at which 50% of lamps have failed when operated for a specified number of hours each day, and the strike and restrike times, which are how long it takes for a lamp to start or restart after it has been switched off and return to full brightness.
- Ballast—The ballast controls the voltage and current supplied to the lamp. Ballasts may be electronic or magnetic. Electronic ballasts are more efficient and can be dimmable so the light output from a lamp is variable depending upon occupancy or natural daylight. Some lamps do not require a ballast, for example, incandescent, halogen, and LED lamps.
- Fixture—The lamp and ballast are housed in a fixture that will also have a reflector and lens or louver. A reflector is used to direct the light out of the fixture, and a lens or louver will reduce glare.

Light Levels

Light is measured in footcandles (FC), which is the lumens per square foot; or in lux, which is lumens per square meter. FC or lux levels are the illuminance on a surface, and this can be measured directly with a light meter. The Illuminating Engineering Society (IES) publishes *The Lighting Handbook*, and this guide covers all lighting fundamentals, technologies, and system design principles. The recommended lighting levels for different rooms and activities in the United States are set by the IES, and these have been incorporated into ASHRAE standards, such as ASHRAE 90.1.

Typical lighting levels for different spaces and activities are as follows:

Activity/Space	Footcandles	Example Locations/Activities
Public space	3	parking lot, concourse
Simple orientation only for short visits	5	Waiting room, corridor
Work space with only simple visual tasks occasionally performed	10	Lobby, platforms
Tasks with high contrast or large size	30	Library, stockroom, factory floor
Tasks with medium contrast or small size	50	Schools, offices, service repairs
Tasks with low contrast or very small size	100	Finishing and inspection, display case
Tasks with low contrast or very small size for prolonged periods	300–1000	Cutting, sewing, operating room

Light Loss Factors (LLF)

The light loss factor (LLF) of a lighting system is used to account for the degradation of light output over time. Light loss factors may be due to any part of the lighting system, and the overall LLF is calculated by multiplying the individual loss factors. There are two general categories of light loss factors: recoverable and non-recoverable. Recoverable factors can be mitigated by regular maintenance, but non-recoverable loss factors are a result of the characteristics of the system components and environment and cannot be improved by maintenance.

Some typical examples of recoverable loss factors include these:

- Lamp lumen depreciation (LLD)—All lamps gradually reduce their lumen output as they age, and some allowance is also often made for lamp burnouts that are not immediately replaced.
- Luminaire dirt depreciation (LDD)—Light output from fixtures will decrease as dirt accumulates on them.
- Typical non-recoverable loss factors include these:
  - Ballast factor (BF)—The ballast factor is the ratio of actual lumen output when using the chosen ballast to its rated lumen output.
  - Luminaire surface depreciation (LSD)—The surface of luminaires (fixtures) will deteriorate over time due to exposure to heat and blemishes that occur that absorb light instead of reflecting it.
  - Ambient fixture temperature (AFT)—The ambient temperature the system operates in will affect lumen output.
  - Supply voltage factor (SVF)—The building supply voltage will affect the actual lumen output.

The overall LLF for a system having the loss factors described would be calculated this way:

$$LLF = LLD \times LDD \times BF \times LSD \times AFT \times SVF$$

Lamp Life in Lighting Systems

Lamp life is also known as *rated life*. Lamp life is the duration in hours that a lamp (light bulb) will last before a certain percentage of the lamp burns out. Lamp life is generally the number of hours it takes for half of a large sample of lamps to burn out. Lamp life will vary depending on the type of light source. Because the definition and testing criteria are different for different light sources, comparisons are challenging.

Lamp life is impacted by the type of lighting system—specifically, how the lamp is started. Instant start systems have shorter lives, whereas rapid start systems have longer lives due to their use of a lower initial voltage during start up. Programmed start electronic ballasts offer an even longer lamp life due to the use of specialized ballasts.

Lamp life can be increased several ways:

- Evaluating starting parameters
- Using higher quality components (lamps and ballasts)
- Maintenance practices, such as regular cleaning and proper handling
- Operating conditions such as voltage fluctuations, switching frequency, and temperature

Zonal Cavity Design Method (Lumen Method)

The zonal cavity method of lighting design is a simple procedure for determining the number of lamps required in a room, assuming an equal level of illuminance throughout the area. The formula is:

$$N = \frac{F \times A}{L \times LLF \times CU}$$

N is the number of lamps required.

F is the required level of illuminance in footcandles.

A is the area of the room in square feet.

L is the lumen output per lamp.

LLF is the light loss factor.

CU is the Coefficient of Utilization

The LLF takes into consideration various factors that reduce light output over time from the rated lamp output. The CU is the percentage of the light output from a lamp that reaches a work surface. The CU is a function of room size and shape, mounting height, and the reflectance of the ceiling and walls.

Obtaining Glare Control Using Reflectors, Diffusers, and Uplighting

A well-lit environment with glare control is necessary to achieve a safe and productive space. The use of reflectors, diffusers, or uplighting can effectively control and manage glare.

Reflectors can be white, silver, gold, or black. Reflectors act like mirrors and redirect light to specific areas. White reflectors provide even illumination and fill in shadows, while black reflectors deepen shadows for dramatic effect. Silver reflectors create intense reflected light and brighten shadows, while gold reflectors reflect light with a soft yellow cast.

Diffusers scatter light to reduce glare. Diffusers are used to control LED glare, to reflect lighting off ceilings or walls, and to enhance water features by bouncing light off the water.

Uplighting directs light upward to minimize glare. Indirect light sources direct more light upward than downward, and parabolic louvers are used on fixtures to scatter the light output.

IES Lighting Standard

The Illuminating Engineering Society (IES) provides guidelines for lighting levels in numerous applications to ensure proper illumination and safety. The recommendations are based on foot candles (fc) and measure illuminance in lumens/square foot. The guidelines are housed in the IES handbook. The most recent version is the 10th edition. Below are some key points that are addressed by the standard in the handbook:

- Lighting application standards collection: This section provides detailed design criteria for various applications, such as industrial, healthcare, and commercial spaces.
- Lighting measurement and testing standards collection: Testing and measurement standards are addressed in this section.

- Lighting practice standards: This section covers lighting design principles for indoor and outdoor lighting.
- Lighting science standards: This section covers the physics of lighting, vision, and color science.
- Lighting roadway and parking facilities standards: This section addresses roadway lighting, parking lot lighting, and environmental concerns with lighting.

Coefficient of Utilization

The Coefficient of Utilization (CU) is an indication of how effectively light is used and is the percentage of the light output from a lamp that reaches a work surface. The CU is a function of room size and shape, mounting height, and the reflectance of the ceiling and walls. The CU is a factor used in the lumen method of calculating the number of lamps required in an area.

A photometric chart can be used to find the CU of a lamp, which is an indication of how well a lamp's light output contributes to the useful light at the work surface. Each lamp has a unique photometric chart, and the CU depends upon the reflectance of the ceiling (RC) and reflectance of the wall (RW), which may be found in tables as well as the room cavity ratio (RCR). The RCR for a rectangular room is calculated this way:

$$RCR = \frac{5 \times h \times (l + w)}{(l \times w)}$$

In this equation *h* is the height from the lamp to the surface of interest, *l* is the room length, and *w* is the room width. The RCR for a general room is calculated this way:

$$RCR = \frac{2.5 \times h \times perimeter}{area}$$

Lighting Retrofit Energy Conservation Measures

There are generally two types of energy efficiency lighting retrofit projects: reducing the power demand of lamps or reducing the number of hours they operate.

- Power reduction—Total power can be reduced by retrofitting lamps with lower power equivalent lamps, for example, replacing incandescent bulbs with compact fluorescent lamps or LEDs. The light quality and illuminance should be maintained.
- Operating hour reduction—Ensuring lights are switched off when they are not needed may be achieved by adding automatic lighting controls. Daylight or occupancy sensors can be cost-effective when there is the potential for lights to be left switched on when they are not needed.

When lighting retrofit opportunities are being considered during an energy audit, it is important to collect information regarding the numbers and types of lamps, including the individual lamp power and ballast factors and the approximate daily operating hours. The costs per unit of energy throughout the day and demand charges should be determined when calculating cost savings. The dimensions of some rooms should be measured if it is suspected they are over lit, so the lumen method can be used to calculate the number of lamps required.

Metal Halide Lamps

Metal halide lamps are high-intensity discharge (HID) lamps. It is essentially a mercury vapor lamp but has had halides added to improve the efficacy and color rendition. Light is produced due to an electrical discharge through gaseous mercury. A ballast is needed for ignition and to limit the current. It can take up to 15 minutes for these lamps to warm up and reach their full light output. Once they are switched off, they must cool down before they can be restarted; this restrike time is about 15 minutes. Metal halide lamps are often used for high bay lighting in factories and warehouses, outdoor parking lots, sports facility lighting, and general outdoor lighting in public spaces or commercial buildings. The typical characteristics of metal halide lamps are summarized below:

Typical power demand (Watts)	20–1,000
Typical efficacy range	70–115
Average rated life (hours)	5,000–30,000
Color rendering index (CRI)	70
Color temperature (K)	3000–5500

High-Pressure Sodium Lamps

High-pressure sodium (HPS) lamps are high-intensity discharge (HID) lamps. Light is produced due to an electrical discharge through gaseous mercury and sodium. A ballast is needed for ignition and to limit the current. It can take up to 5 minutes for these lamps to warm up and reach their full light output. Once they are switched off, they must cool down before they can be restarted; this restrike time is about 5 minutes. HPS lamps are often used for outdoor parking lots, general outdoor lighting in public spaces or commercial buildings and inside some industrial facilities where color rendition is not critical. The typical characteristics of HPS lamps are summarized below:

Typical power demand (Watts)	35–1,000
Typical efficacy range	50–140
Average rated life (hours)	16,000–40,000
Color rendering index (CRI)	65
Color temperature (K)	2100–2700

Halogen Lamps

Halogen lamps are a type of incandescent lamp. Light is produced when current flows through a tungsten filament and heats it, as also occurs in a traditional incandescent lamp, but the addition of a halogen improves the efficacy. The presence of a halogen causes tungsten that has evaporated from the filament to be deposited back onto the filament, which extends the life of the lamp over other incandescent bulbs and improves light quality throughout its life. There is a wide variety of halogen lamp sizes and shapes depending upon the application. Halogen lamps are often used for decorative lighting, downlights, spot lamps, and perimeter lighting. The typical characteristics of halogen lamps are summarized below:

Typical power demand (Watts)	10–500
Typical efficacy range	15–30
Average rated life (hours)	1,000–4,000
Color rendering index (CRI)	100
Color temperature (K)	3000

Fluorescent Lamps

Fluorescent lamps contain mercury at low pressure and an inert gas needed for starting. When an arc is established, the mercury emits ultraviolet radiation. The inside of the lamp is coated with a phosphor powder that emits visible light when the ultraviolet light hits it. Fluorescent lamps need a ballast to ignite the low-pressure gases and to limit the current. Fluorescent lamps are used in a variety of applications including general lighting in commercial buildings and high-bay lighting of industrial facilities. Fluorescent lamps are available in two main varieties:

- Fluorescent tubes—Fluorescent tubes are very common in commercial buildings. They are generally identified by their diameter, which is measured in eighths of an inch. For example, T12 lamps are twelve-eighths of an inch. Other common sizes are T8 and T5. Newer high-efficiency lamps use an electronic ballast.
- Compact fluorescent lamps (CFL)—CFLs are smaller and can replace incandescent lamps while using about 70% less energy. They have an internal ballast.

The typical characteristics of fluorescent lamps are summarized below:

	Fluorescent Tube	Compact Fluorescent
Typical power demand (Watts)	14–110	9–50
Typical efficacy range	65–110	60–80
Average rated life (hours)	20,000–40,000	10,000
Color rendering index (CRI)	70	80–85
Color temperature (K)	3000–5000	2700–5000

LED Lamps

Light-emitting diode (LED) lamps are solid-state semiconductor devices. Light is produced when current flows across the junction of two different materials. LEDs are very efficient with a long service life and are now being used in all types of commercial lighting applications. Typical LED lighting applications include general interior lighting in place of incandescent and fluorescent lamps as well as high-bay lighting in industrial buildings, outdoor lighting, and parking lots as replacements for metal halide and high-pressure sodium lamps. A 100W LED will replace a 400W high intensity discharge lamp, so they provide significant energy savings. The typical characteristics of LED lamps are summarized below:

Typical power demand (Watts)	3–100
Typical efficacy range	70–140
Average rated life (hours)	50,000
Color rendering index (CRI)	80–90
Color temperature (K)	3000–5000

Lighting Control Methods and Technologies

Lighting may be controlled manually or automatically. The various technologies commonly employed to control lighting include the following:

- Switch—Manual lighting control using a switch is the simplest method, but there is a lot of potential for lights to be left switched on when they are not needed.
- Timer—Timers are a basic form of automatic lighting control to turn lights on and off according to a set schedule. These can be very useful for outdoor lighting but need to be seasonally adjusted as sunrise and sunset times change throughout the year.
- Daylight sensors—Daylight sensors use a photocell to detect the amount of ambient light. These are also very useful for outdoor lighting, and they do not need to be adjusted throughout the year as daylight hours change. Photocells can also be used in buildings to switch off perimeter lights when there is sufficient daylight.

- Occupancy sensors—Occupancy sensors are used to turn off lamps in unoccupied areas. They can be adjusted to set the time that lamps remain on after no motion has been detected. The two most common occupancy sensor types are passive infrared (PIR) and microwave sensors.
- Dimming ballasts—Electronic ballasts can be dimmable, so when daylight and/or occupancy sensors are used, the light output can be increased or decreased depending upon the occupancy or ambient daylight levels. The ballast factor is the ratio of lamplight output using the ballast to what the output would be using a reference ballast under test conditions. Ballasts generally have a ballast factor of 0.85 to 0.95.

Luminaire Level Lighting Controls

Luminaire level lighting controls (LLLC) are lighting control systems in which sensors and controls are integrated directly into the individual luminaire. LLLCs are also referred to as embedded controls. The DesignLights Consortium (DLC) defines LLLCs as having ambient light sensors and networked occupancy sensors installed for each kit directly through manufacturing. The International Energy Conservation Code (IECC) defines LLLC as a system of luminaires that have embedded control logic, occupancy sensors, wireless networking, and local override capabilities.

The components of an LLLC are:

- Sensors: occupancy and light sensors
- Controller: programable microprocessors that sense dimming signals and send the signals to the LED drivers
- Connectivity: achieved by onboard radio transmitters and receivers, allowing the luminaires to communicate within the LLLC network

Studies have shown several benefits associated with LLLCs. The systems show an average energy savings of greater than 50%. The systems are highly flexible, responsive, and provide detailed space-use data.

Using Natural Lighting in Lighting Systems

Natural lighting is also known as daylighting. Natural lighting plays a key role in architectural and decorative design. Natural lighting has been shown to deliver numerous benefits, including improved mood and well-being, enhanced productivity, and energy efficiency. These benefits can be maximized by strategic orientation of buildings and windows, window placement and design, and the use of light shelves and skylights. It is necessary to balance the natural light with thermal comfort. Shading and glazing can be utilized to reduce heat gain.

The main types of natural light are:

- Soft/diffused light: occurs on overcast or cloudy days
- Hard/direct light: sharp direct sunlight
- Twilight: occurs before sunrise and after sunset
- Dappled light: filters through leaves, branches, or other objects

HVAC Systems and Building Envelope

HVAC Systems

Primary HVAC equipment is used to heat or cool a fluid, which is then distributed by secondary HVAC systems to provide space heating and cooling. Equipment commonly used includes the following:

- Chillers—Chillers use the vapor compression refrigeration cycle or an absorption cycle to produce a chilled liquid, usually water or a water/glycol mixture. The chilled liquid is then distributed to air handling or terminal units for space cooling.
- Direct expansion (DX) system—DX systems use a refrigeration cycle to cool air directly, unlike a chiller, which cools a liquid.
- Heat pump—Heat pumps use a refrigeration cycle to move the heat energy available in the environment to the inside to provide space heating or cooling.
- Boiler—Boilers burn a fuel such as natural gas, oil, or biomass to heat water. The hot water can then be used for space heating or domestic hot water.
- Furnace—Furnaces burn a fuel such as natural gas or oil to heat air, which is then distributed through ductwork to areas that require heating.

Supply Air Temperature Control Strategies

HVAC systems that provide space heating and cooling with air are most suited to buildings requiring a lot of comfort cooling because the movement of air is the most important factor for thermal comfort in a hot environment. The supply air temperature control strategies are generally as follows:

- Constant air volume (CAV) system—In a constant air volume system, the temperature of the supply air is variable, and the volume of air supplied to each zone is constant. These systems are generally only suitable for smaller buildings with few zones because the fan must always be operating regardless of the demand for heating or cooling, so they are inefficient for large buildings.
- Variable air volume (VAV) system—In a VAV system the supply air temperature is constant, and the volume of air to each space is varied to control the temperature to the zone set point. This is the most common type of system installed in new, large buildings. The temperature of the supply air is usually about 55°F, and the fan speed is controlled by a variable frequency drive to adjust the volume of air that needs to be delivered. VAV systems are most efficient when system control is optimized by supply air temperature reset based on actual demand and other strategies, such as optimum start and stop and static pressure reset.

Single-Duct HVAC Configurations

Single-duct HVAC systems are the most common type of system. A single-duct system has one supply air duct for all zones. Fresh air and return air are mixed in a chamber and then heated and cooled as required to reach a set supply air temperature. The typical single-duct HVAC system configurations are as follows:

- Single zone—A single zone system has one thermostat to control the temperature in the building. Because air is supplied at the same volume and temperature throughout the building, they are most suited to open areas with uniform heating or cooling loads.

- Variable air volume (VAV)—VAV systems allow different areas of a building to have different temperatures by varying the amount of constant temperature air supplied to each zone.
- Constant air volume (CAV)—CAV systems also enable temperature control in different areas by reheating the supply air as necessary to reach the zone set point.
- Multizone—Multizone systems mix conditioned air in separate zones within the air handling unit to match individual zone temperature requirements.

Dual-Duct HVAC Configurations

A dual-duct HVAC system has separate heating and cooling ducts. Hot and cold air are distributed throughout the building and then mixed in terminal units within each zone. This configuration requires a lot of space for ducts, and fan energy is more than for single-duct systems. Dual-duct systems can be constant air volume (CAV) or variable air volume (VAV) systems. CAV dual-duct systems are the most energy intensive all-air HVAC system and are not widely used. This is because hot and cold air are mixed even when there is little demand for heating or cooling, and a large amount of energy is used by the distribution fans. VAV dual-duct systems are more efficient because less mixing is required and the temperature is mostly controlled by changing the amount of air delivered to each zone.

All-Water HVAC Systems

All-water HVAC systems provide heating and cooling by distributing hot and chilled water throughout a facility. The specific heat capacity of air is about 0.24 Btu/lb°F, but the specific heat capacity of water is about 1 Btu/lb°F, so water can transport about 4.2 times as much heat per pound. The density of air is about $0.074 lb/ft^3$, whereas the water has a density of about $62.3 lb/ft^3$. Therefore, air requires about 840 times more space than water while carrying four times less heat; this is the main advantage of all-water HVAC systems over all-air systems. The disadvantage of all-water systems is that they do not provide fresh air and a separate ventilation system is required. Hot and chilled water is distributed to terminal units, for example, a fan coil unit, in each zone. The distribution systems used are these:

- One-pipe system—All terminal units are connected in series so heating and cooling capacity decreases throughout the system as terminal units are further from the central plant.
- Two-pipe systems—Each terminal unit has a supply and return pipe, and units are connected in parallel. Simultaneous heating and cooling is not possible.
- Three-pipe systems—There are separate supply pipes for heating and cooling, and the return is mixed.
- Four-pipe systems—There are separate supply and return pipes for both heating and cooling. This is the most efficient configuration and has the best thermal control.

Refrigerants and Global Warming Potential Factors in HVAC Systems

Refrigerants possess a global warming potential (GWP) factor. GWP measures how much a substance contributes to global warming over a specific period of time (usually 100 years) compared to CO_2, which has a GWP of 1. Some refrigerants have GWPs a thousand times greater than CO_2, making them potential greenhouse gases (GHG). Mitigation and transition to low-GWP refrigerants is a critical factor in meeting climate change goals.

Below is a list of common refrigerants and their GWPs. Hydrofluorocarbons are the most common and are used as the refrigerant in air-conditioning.

Hydrofluorocarbons (HFCs):

HFC-134a: GWP = 1300

HFC - 410A: GWP = 2090

Chlorofluorocarbons (CFCs):

CFC-12: GWP = 10,200

CFC-11: GWP = 4660

Perfluorinated compounds:

Sulfur hexafluoride (SF6): GWP = 23,900

Nitrogen trifluoride (NF3): GWP = 6500

Cooling Towers

A cooling tower is a type of heat exchanger used to reject heat to the environment from an industrial process or heating ventilation and air-conditioning (HVAC) system. In HVAC systems, cooling towers are used in conjunction with water-cooled chillers and condensers. The condenser water circuit takes the heat removed from inside a building and then ejects this heat to the atmosphere via a cooling tower. The condenser water is sprayed over a fill inside the cooling tower to increase the wetted surface area. Ambient air is then blown over the water, and heat is removed due to some of the condenser water evaporating. The condenser water is then collected at the bottom of the cooling tower and returns to the condenser. The efficiency of cooling towers can be improved by using variable speed fans so that fan energy matched load conditions. Cooling tower operation needs to be considered when implementing condenser water reset strategies because increased cooling tower energy can offset improved chiller efficiency.

Vapor Compression Cycle in Chillers

Many chillers utilize the vapor compression cycle, and it is important to understand the temperature and phase of the refrigerant at each stage of the cycle. Because thermal energy can only move from a hotter object to a cooler object, the refrigerant must go from being cool enough to absorb heat from a room at, for example, 75°F to being hot enough to release the heat to the outside, which may be 100°F or more on a hot summer's day. This is achieved via the four stages of the vapor compression cycle: evaporation, compression, condensation, and expansion. When the refrigerant enters the evaporator, it is a low-temperature, low-pressure liquid. Heat is absorbed from the room, and the refrigerant becomes a low-temperature, low-pressure vapor. To remove this absorbed heat to the outside, the refrigerant must become hotter than the outside, so it is compressed to a high-temperature, high-pressure vapor. The refrigerant then enters the condenser, where the absorbed heat is transferred to outside and the refrigerant becomes a high-temperature, high-pressure liquid. The refrigerant must then return to its initial state, so the temperature and pressure must be reduced, and this is achieved by an expansion valve. Reducing the condensing temperature produces energy savings because the compressor does not have to work as hard to increase the pressure and temperature of the refrigerant to create the required temperature differential.

Variable Refrigerant Flow

Variable refrigerant flow (VRF) is an HVAC technology that precisely controls the amount of refrigerant flowing to multiple areas or zones within a building. VRF allows for a single compressor to serve multiple indoor units. The refrigerant circulates between the indoor and outdoor units, and each indoor unit can operate independently.

The are multiple advantages to VRF, with the primary benefit being energy efficiency. The system will adjust the refrigerant flow based on demand, thus minimizing energy consumption. These systems are also quieter than traditional HVAC systems and offer design flexibility. VRF systems can be either heat pump or heat recovery systems. Heat recovery VRF can simultaneously heat and cool different zones within a building. VRF systems are commonly used in commercial buildings, hotels, hospitals, and residential complexes.

Absorption Chillers

Absorption chillers utilize heat instead of electricity to power the refrigeration cycle. The refrigeration cycle is based on two fluids with high affinity for each other, meaning one fluid dissolves easily in the other. The refrigerant is usually water and the absorbent a lithium bromide solution. There are four main stages:

- Generator—Heat is supplied to the generator, which is under a vacuum, and a dilute solution of lithium bromide and water is sprayed into the generator. The heat and low pressure cause the solution to boil and separate. Refrigerant (water) vapor enters the condenser, and concentrated lithium bromide solution passes to the absorber.
- Condenser—Cooling water is provided so the refrigerant vapor condenses. The latent heat is removed by a cooling tower. The liquid refrigerant then enters the evaporator.
- Evaporator—A strong vacuum is maintained, so the liquid refrigerant boils and removes heat from a water loop to produce chilled water for air-conditioning. The refrigerant vapor then enters the absorber.
- Absorber—The concentrated lithium bromide solution is sprayed into the absorber, which is under a strong vacuum due to the affinity of the refrigerant and absorbent, where the water vapor is absorbed to create the dilute solution, which returns to the generator. The heat of condensation is removed by a cooling water loop to a cooling tower.
- Absorption chillers generally have a lower coefficient of performance than vapor-compression chillers, but they can utilize waste heat, which improves their overall efficiency. They also avoid the need for chlorofluorocarbon (CFC) refrigerants. Ammonia may also be used instead of lithium bromide.

Chilled Beam Systems

Chilled beam systems are commonly used where space-sensible loads are high relative to ventilation and latent cooling needs. Typical applications include science laboratories and hospital patient rooms. Chilled beam systems also feature low acoustic signatures that make them ideal for sound-sensitive environments like libraries. Chilled beam systems can be used for both heating and cooling.

Passive chilled beams (PCBs) consist of a fin-and-tube heat exchanger suspended from the ceiling. Chilled water flows through the tubes, and the warm air in the space rises and is cooled from the beam. PCBs do not require fans.

Active chilled beams (ACBs) also have a heat exchanger that is suspended from the ceiling. ACBs include an integral air supply where primary air passes through nozzles, inducing air from the space through the cooling coil. ACBs have more cooling capacity than PCBs. ACBs have a two-pipe and a four-pipe design. In the four-pipe design, some zones can receive cool water for colling while other zones receive hot water for heating.

Chilled beam systems do not have a condensate draining system and therefore must rely on the primary air system to maintain the indoor dew point that is below the chilled beam's surface temperature.

Energy Efficiency Ratio (EER)

The Energy Efficiency Ratio (EER) is a measure of cooling output for each unit of electrical energy input:

$$EER = \frac{Cooling\ Energy\ Output\ (Btu)}{Electrical\ Energy\ Input\ (Wh)}$$

It has the units of Btu/Wh, and is often calculated as the ratio of cooling power output to electrical power input:

$$EER = \frac{Cooling\ Power\ Output\ (\frac{Btu}{h})}{Electrical\ Energy\ Input\ (W)}$$

The EER for an air-conditioning unit is determined at a specific set of temperature conditions, so at other temperatures, the performance will be different. A Seasonal Energy Efficiency Ratio (SEER) is also calculated for systems to account for the range of temperatures a unit will operate at on average during the year. The EER can also be calculated from the coefficient of performance (COP) this way:

$$EER = COP \times 3.412 \frac{Btu}{Wh}$$

Coefficient of Performance (COP)

The coefficient of performance (COP) is a measure of the efficiency of a chiller or heat pump and is calculated by the power output divided by the power input:

$$COP = \frac{Power\ Output}{Power\ Input}$$

The COP of a simple electrical resistance heater is 1.0 because all the electrical energy is converted to heat. For a heat pump or chiller, the COP is often 3.0 or more because the refrigeration cycle is able to move a greater amount of heat from the environment than the electrical power it uses. The COP can be found from the Energy Efficiency Ratio (EER) this way:

$$COP = \frac{EER}{3.412 \frac{Btu}{Wh}}$$

Evaluating Chiller Efficiency and Performance

Chiller efficiency is generally evaluated by the power consumed in kilowatts divided by the tons of cooling output. One ton of air-conditioning is equal to 12,000 Btu per hour. Chiller efficiency can be calculated from the Energy Efficiency Ratio (EER) and coefficient of performance (COP) as follows:

$$\frac{kW}{ton} = \frac{12}{EER} = \frac{3.517}{COP}$$

The EER is cooling energy output divided by the electrical energy input and has units of Btu/Wh. The COP is dimensionless and is the power output (kW) divided by the power input (kW). The EER and COP are calculated under specific conditions at full load, so these performance measures are of limited value. The Integrated Part Load Value (IPLV) provides a measure of performance at 100%, 75%, 50%, and 25% of rated capacity. ASHRAE 90.1 states minimum equipment performance for various technologies. Some of these values include the following:

Technology	EER		kW/ton	
	Full Load	IPLV	Full Load	IPLV
Air cooled chiller < 150 tons	> 10.1	> 13.7		
Air cooled chiller > 150 tons	> 10.1	> 14.0		
Water cooled, positive displacement < 75 tons			< 0.75	< 0.60
Water cooled, positive displacement < 150 tons			< 0.72	< 0.56
Water cooled, centrifugal < 300 tons			< 0.61	< 0.55
Water cooled, centrifugal > 300 tons			< 0.56	< 0.52

HVAC Terminology

Enthalpy—the enthalpy of a substance is the sum of its internal energy and the product of its volume and pressure:

$$H = U + PV$$

The enthalpy is the total energy content and is an extensive property, so it is proportional to the size of the system. The total enthalpy of a system is not directly measured; the change in enthalpy from a reference point is what is measured. The specific enthalpy is the total enthalpy divided by the mass of the system and is measured in Btu/lb.

Sensible heat—sensible heat is the energy that increases the temperature of a substance but does not cause it to change phase.

Latent heat—latent heat is the energy associated with a change in phase of a substance. For example, when liquid water is boiling, the temperature remains constant, but it is absorbing latent heat as it changes from a liquid to a vapor, and similarly when water vapor condenses, it is releasing its latent heat as it changes phase from a vapor to a liquid.

Dry bulb temperature—The temperature as measured by a thermometer

Wet bulb temperature—The temperature of air when it has been cooled to saturation by evaporating water into the air with all the latent heat provided by the air

Dew point temperature—The temperature at which water vapor in the air will begin to condense

Relative humidity—The ratio of the actual amount of water in the air to the maximum amount of water that the air could hold at that temperature and pressure (the saturation point)

Moisture content—This is also called the humidity ratio and is the pounds of moisture per pound of dry air

Specific volume—The space occupied by 1 pound of a material; for example, air at 75°F and 30% relative humidity has a specific volume of 13.6ft³/lb.

If two of these properties of air are known, then the remaining properties may be found on a psychrometric chart.

Psychrometric Charts

The information presented on a psychrometric chart is described here with reference numbers indicated in the figure:

1. Dry bulb temperature—The dry bulb temperature is usually known because it is easily measured with a thermometer. It is the vertical lines on the chart with the temperature stated on the horizontal axis at the bottom of the chart.
2. Wet bulb temperature—The wet bulb temperature is also easily measured with a sling psychrometer, so this is often known as well. It is found along diagonal lines that run parallel to lines of enthalpy.
3. Relative humidity—The relative humidity is found on the curving lines that run through the chart. The relative humidity is the value of the line that intersects the dry bulb and wet bulb temperatures.
4. Dew point temperature—The dew point temperature is found by following a horizontal line to the left from the intersection of the dry bulb and wet bulb temperature.
5. Enthalpy—The enthalpy is found along diagonal lines parallel to the wet bulb temperature.
6. Moisture content—Moisture content is found by following a horizontal line to the right from the intersection of the dry bulb and wet bulb temperature.
7. Specific volume—The specific volume is also along diagonal lines, and the value is found from the intersection of the dry bulb and wet bulb temperatures.

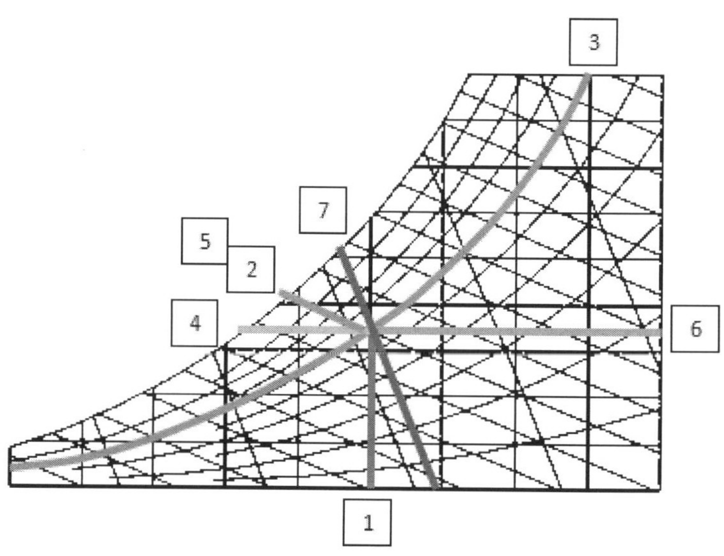

Demand Control Ventilation

Ventilation requirements are stipulated in ASHRAE Standard 62.1. The prescriptive procedure to calculate outdoor airflow in each breathing zone is:

$$V_{bz} = R_p \times P_z + R_a \times A_z$$

Where V_{bz} is the outdoor airflow required in the breathing zone, R_p is the outdoor air flow rate per person, P_z is the number of people in the zone, R_a is the outdoor air flow rate required per unit of area, and A_z is the occupied area of the zone. R_p and R_a are found in tables and depend upon the type of facility. An heating ventilation and air-conditioning (HVAC) system is designed to supply the maximum amount of fresh air to satisfy these conditions, but when occupancy is less than the maximum, then more fresh air is supplied than necessary. This wastes energy to heat and cool the air, if it is much cooler or hotter than the internal conditions, and to move the air through the distribution ducts. A demand control ventilation strategy is allowed whereby carbon dioxide levels are sensed and outside air flow is reduced to maintain a set level of carbon dioxide above ambient conditions, which is usually 700 ppm.

Calculating the Percentage of Outside Air

Mechanical ventilation is required for buildings without any means of natural ventilation. Most air-conditioned buildings rely on supply air fans that mix fresh outside air with conditioned return air to achieve the desired indoor air quality in terms of temperature, humidity, and allowable levels of carbon dioxide or other contaminants. To calculate the percentage of outside air that is present within a supply air stream based on temperature, the following equation is used:

$$Percent\ Outside\ Air = \frac{(RAT - MAT)}{(RAT - OAT)}$$

In this equation *RAT* is the return air temperature, *MAT* is the mixed air temperature, and *OAT* is the outside air temperature. To determine the percent of outside air based on carbon dioxide, a similar equation is used:

$$Percent\ Outside\ Air = \frac{(RCO_2 - MCO_2)}{(RCO_2 - OCO_2)}$$

In this equation RCO_2 is the return carbon dioxide concentration, MCO_2 is the mixed or supply carbon dioxide concentration, and OCO_2 is the outside carbon dioxide concentration. A demand control ventilation strategy based on carbon dioxide levels can be implemented. The general requirement is that the indoor concentration is no more than about 700 ppm above the outdoor concentration, which is generally constant for a particular area. The Percent Outside Air can then be calculated from measurements of return air and M CO_2 levels.

Heat Transfer Through a Building's Fabric

Heat conduction from a building is calculated this way:

$$q = U \times A \times \Delta T$$

In this equation *U* is the overall conductance of the building fabric (measured in Btu/h·ft^2·°F), *A* is the area of the building fabric, and *ΔT* is the temperature difference between the inside of the building and the outside. Describing the thermal weight of a building as being "light" or "heavy" is a means of describing how the building responds to weather conditions. A thermally light building is one that has its heating and cooling demands greatly affected by the weather because the building does not store a lot of heat. A thermally heavy building will have more constant demands for heating and cooling over time because it is able to store and release heat gradually. The thermal weight is influenced by its construction materials and the combination of internal and external heating gains it experiences.

Degree Days and Annual Heating Demand

Degree days are a useful measure of outdoor air temperature when it is not possible or impractical to use hourly temperature data. A temperature of 65°F is usually assumed to be the outside temperature at which no heating or cooling is required. If the average outside temperature for one day was 50°F, then there were 15 heating degree days. An average outdoor temperature of 90°F for one day would mean 25 cooling degree days. Degree days can be used to estimate the heating or cooling demand in a building over a reasonably long period, for example, a seasonal or annual basis. The heat flow can be calculated this way:

$$q_{heating} = U \times A \times 24 \times HDD$$

$$q_{cooling} = U \times A \times 24 \times CDD$$

In this equation *U* is the is the overall conductance of the building fabric (measured in Btu/h·ft^2·°F), *A* is the area of the building fabric, 24 converts degree days to degree hours, *HDD* is the number of heating degree days in the period, and *CDD* is the number of cooling degree days in the period.

Thermal Conductivity and Conductance

The rate of heat transfer through a material is proportional to the temperature difference across the material *ΔT* and its thermal conductivity, *k*:

$$Q \propto k \times \Delta T$$

Thermal conductivity is measured in Btu·in/h·ft^2·°F. The higher a material's thermal conductivity, the more energy that can pass through it in one hour. The thermal conductivity values for some common building materials are as follows:

Brick = 5.0

Wood fiber = 1.4

Plywood = 0.80

Glass fiber = 0.25

The conductance of a material is measured in Btu/h·ft^2·°F. It is the conductivity for a 1-inch thickness of material.

The thermal resistance of a material is its ability to withstand the flow of heat. Thermal resistance is determined by the material thickness, *t*, and its thermal conductivity, *k*:

$$R = \frac{t}{k}$$

Thermal resistance is also the inverse of conductance because conductance vales are given for a material thickness of 1 inch:

$$R = \frac{1}{U}$$

Total Thermal Resistance of Composite Walls

The thermal resistance of a wall made from several layers is equal to the sum of the individual thermal resistances:

$$R_{total} = R_1 + R_2 + \cdots + R_n$$

The thermal resistance of a material is calculated by dividing its thickness by its thermal conductivity:

$$R = \frac{t}{k}$$

For example, a wall made from 4-inch brick (k = 5), 6-inch block (k = 1.7), and ½-inch plasterboard (k = 0.88) has a total thermal resistance calculated this way:

$$R = \frac{4}{5} + \frac{6}{1.7} + \frac{0.5}{0.88} = 4.9\ \frac{h.ft^2.°\text{F}}{Btu}$$

The air film at the outside and inside surfaces also provides some thermal resistance. In still air the thermal resistance through a vertical wall is 0.68 h·ft^2·°F/Btu, and in 15 mph winter air, it is 0.17 h·ft^2·°F/Btu. If these air film resistances were included in the example above, then the total resistance would be 4.9 + 0.17 + 0.68 = 5.75. The total heat flow through this wall if it has an area of 100ft^2, the outside temperature is 40°F, and the inside temperature is 60°F is:

$$q\ = \frac{100 \times (60 - 40)}{5.75} = 348\frac{Btu}{h}$$

Sensible Heat Transfer for Air

Sensible heat causes a change in the dry bulb temperature of air. Sensible heat transfer for air is calculated by this equation:

$$q = \dot{m}\ \times C_p \times \Delta T\ =\ cfm\ \times\ 1.08\ \times\ \Delta T$$

In this equation $\dot{m}$ is the mass flow rate (lb./h), C_p is the specific heat (Btu/lb°F), ΔT is the temperature difference (°F) of the air before and after the heat transfer, *cfm* is the flow rate (ft^3/min), and 1.08 is a multiplication factor that combines the conversion of mass flow rate to cubic feet per minute and the specific heat. For example, if 10,000 cfm of air enters an air handling unit at 40°F and is heated to 70°F without adding or removing any moisture, then the total heat transfer is 10,000 x 1.08 x 30 = 324,000 Btu/h.

General (Sensible and Latent) Heat Transfer for Air

The general heat transfer equation for air includes both the sensible and latent heat transfer and is calculated this way:

$$q = \dot{m} \times \Delta h = cfm \times 4.5 \times \Delta h$$

In this equation $\dot{m}$ is the mass flow rate (lb./h), Δh is the specific enthalpy (Btu/lb.), *cfm* is the flow rate (ft^3/min), and 4.5 is the conversion of mass flow rate to cubic feet per minute (0.075lb/ft^3 x 60min/h). The enthalpy is of an air and water vapor mix:

$$h_{mix} = h_{dry\ air} + h_{water\ vapor} = C_p \times T_{db} + HR \times h_g$$

In this equation $h_{dry\ air}$ is the sensible heat of the air, which is the enthalpy of air without any water vapor and is calculated by multiplying the specific heat, C_p (Btu/lb°F), by the dry bulb temperature, T_{db} (°F); $h_{water\ vapor}$ is the latent heat of the air, or the enthalpy of the water vapor in the air, and is calculated by multiplying the humidity ratio, *HR* (grains of moisture per pound of dry air), and the enthalpy of saturated vapor at the dew point temperature, h_g. These values can be found on a psychrometric chart.

Sensible Heat Transfer for Water

Sensible heat transfer for water is calculated by the equation:

$$q = gpm \times 500 \times \Delta T$$

In this equation *gpm* is the flow rate in gallons per minute, ΔT is the temperature difference of the water before and after the heat transfer, and 500 is a multiplication factor that combines the conversion factor of mass flow rate (lb/h) to gpm and the specific heat (8.34lb/gallon x 60min/h x 1Btu/lb°F). For example, if the flow rate of water through a boiler is 10 gpm and the temperature of the water increases from 50°F to 140°F, then the total heat transfer is 10 x 500 x 90 = 450,000 Btu/h.

Effect of Solar Heat Gains on Building Energy Consumption

Building heat loads are generated by people and equipment inside the building as well as from solar radiation. Solar heat gain is an important design consideration because in winter the solar heat gains will reduce the amount of energy required for heating, but in summer it can be a significant burden on the cooling system. Solar heat gain is primarily through windows and the roof, but there is also solar gain through walls. The size, orientation, and type of windows should be carefully planned to maximize daylight but minimize unwanted heat gain. Automatic shades can be installed that control solar gain through windows depending on the time of day and year. The color of walls and roofs will have an impact on how much solar radiation is absorbed into the building. Lighter colors reflect more light (high albedo) so will reduce solar heat gain compared to darker-colored materials. The thermal mass of the building will also affect the retention of solar heat gain. A building with a higher thermal mass will heat slower and retain heat longer, so this property can be utilized beneficially.

Solar Shading

Solar shading refers to the use of features to control and optimize the amount of solar heat and light that enters a building. Solar shading devices mainly serve three purposes:

- Heat gain reduction: blocking solar heat gain during hot months
- Glare reduction: diffusing sunlight to reduce glare
- Enhancing energy efficiency: lowering energy costs by helping keep the building cooler

There are several types of solar shading options that can be considered:

- Fixed shading devices: These include shutters, external blinds, and overhangs or awnings.
- Glazing design: This considers the size, orientation, and solar heat gain of windows.
- Building design: This includes balconies, eaves, and other architectural features that provide shading. Solar shading devices can be designed to contribute to the building's overall architectural aesthetics.

Passive Design

Passive design is a sustainable architectural approach that optimizes available natural resources. Passive systems, unlike active systems, seek to take advantage of local climate to reduce the reliance on mechanical systems like heating, cooling, and lighting, thus providing cost savings and promoting energy efficiency and environmental sustainability.

There are some common strategies associated with passive design:

- Passive heating strategies: A building's layout can be properly aligned to maximize solar exposure during colder months. Incorporating materials (like concrete and stone) that absorb and release heat slowly is a proven passive strategy.
- Passive cooling strategies: These include designing shading (via overhangs, awnings, or vegetation), natural ventilation, and the use of cool roofs.
- Daylighting: This refers to designing windows and skylights to maximize natural light.

Building Automation, Controls, and Artificial Intelligence Systems

Analog and Digital Inputs and Outputs in Controls Systems

Analog inputs and outputs—Analog signals are sent and received through a continuously variable range. For example, a pressure sensor that operates from 0 to 100 psi might output a 0 to 10V or 4 to 20mA signal proportional to the actual pressure within the sensor's range. Sensors that are most likely to send analog signals to a controller are temperature, humidity, flow, and air quality. Equipment that would receive an analog signal would include valves, dampers, and variable frequency drives.

Digital inputs and outputs—Digital signals are discrete signals that are used for simple on-off or position control. For example, a binary digital signal has just two states: A signal is provided at high level to turn a system on, and then when the signal is at the lower level, the system turns off. Digital signals can also have multiple, discrete levels to replicate an analog signal such as in pulse width modulation signals. Digital signals are often used for switching pumps and fans.

Manual, Open-Loop Automatic, and Closed-Loop Automatic Control Systems

- Manual control—A system that is switched on and off by a person, for example, a light switch, is a manual control system. This is the most basic form of control and has a lot of potential for the system to remain on when it is not needed.
- Open-loop control—Open-loop automatic control systems use an automatic signal to switch a system on and off, but there is no feedback providing information about the system's operation. A timer is one example of an open-loop control system.
- Closed-loop control—Closed-loop automatic control systems receive a signal to determine if the system is operating at the correct settings or if it should be operating at all. For example, a thermostat enables closed-loop control of an heating ventilation and air-conditioning (HVAC) system by sensing the space temperature and sending a signal to a controller, which adjusts the operation of the system to match a desired set point.

On-Off and Floating Control

The simplest control technique is on-off control. If a heating or air-conditioning system is controlled with this technique, then the temperature will vary throughout a range and will not be at the set point for much of the time. In the case of a heating system, when the temperature drops below the set point, the controller switches the equipment on at 100% capacity. The heating system will remain on until the temperature reaches an upper temperature limit, called the differential, and then the controller switches the heating system off. The temperature will then start to decrease again toward the set point as heat is lost. This method of control is simple and low cost but can have problems with overshoot of the set point and differential, and if the response time of the system is too fast, then the equipment will cycle very quickly.

Floating control also uses a set point and differential, but instead of turning equipment on at 100% of capacity when the temperature drops below the set point, it is turned on gradually. When the set point is reached, the equipment then maintains the control position. If the temperature rises above the differential, then the equipment gradually turns off until it goes below the differential, where it again holds the new operating position.

Proportional Control Systems

Proportional control enables modulating control about a set point. The controller detects the size of the error from the set point and will output a control signal that is proportional to the difference between the set point and the actual value. The controller has a fixed gain, which is the response time or sensitivity of the controller; a quicker response time to a small system change will be achieved with a larger gain. If the gain is too high, then the response will be extreme and cause large oscillations about the set point. The difference between the highest value above the set point and lowest value below the set point that the system operates between is called the throttling range. This type of control system has a residual error so that it never reaches the set point exactly, and this is called the offset. A typical proportional controller response pattern is illustrated in the following figure:

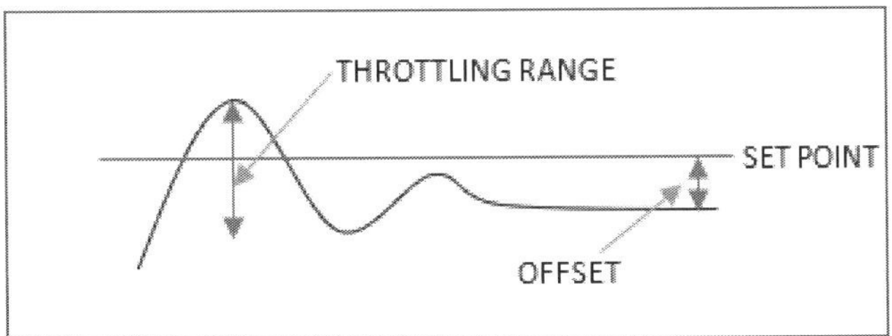

Proportional-Integral (PI) Control Systems

Proportional-integral (PI) control enables better response than proportional control on its own. The integral control eliminates the residual error (offset) from the set point that is present in a proportional-only control system. A proportional control system detects the size of the error from the set point and has a fixed gain that adjusts the control signal output in proportion to the difference between the set point and the actual controlled value. There is always some offset with a proportional control system, but adding integral control will eliminate this residual error. Integral control reacts to the duration of the error by averaging the error over time and adjusts the amount of gain to move the controlled value to the set point. The integral control acts slowly over time, so if a system changes rapidly, it can cause issues with this type of controller. The typical response of a proportional-integral controller is illustrated in the following figure:

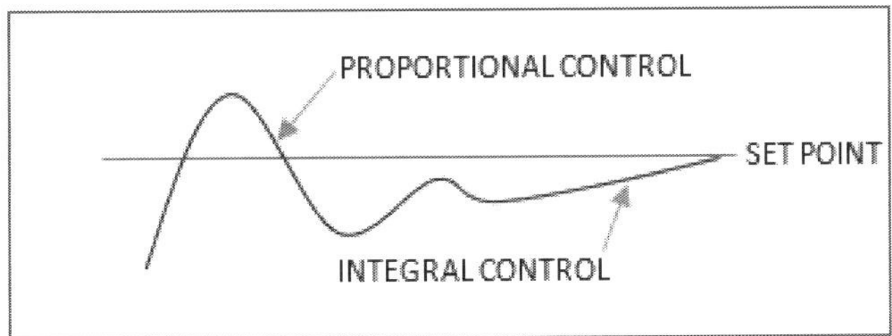

Proportional-Integral-Derivative (PID) Control Systems

Proportional-integral-derivative (PID) control systems offer the most accurate level of system control. PID controllers are able to handle rapid system changes. Proportional control reacts to the magnitude of the error, and integral control reacts to the duration of the error, but adding derivative control enables the rate of change of the error to be measured so that overshoot is minimized and the set point is reached faster than with only proportional or proportional-integral control. One problem with PID control is the initial setup of the derivative control response, which can cause control instability. PID control is mostly used for industrial processes requiring very close control and is rarely used for heating ventilation and air-conditioning (HVAC) system control. The typical response of a PID controller is illustrated in the following figure:

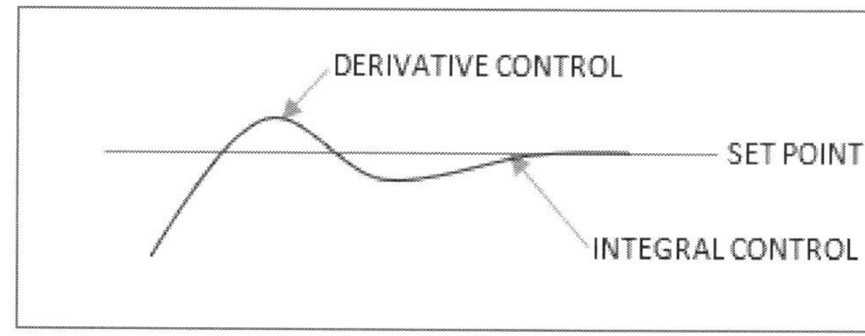

A self-tuning control loop is a PID controller that has a tuning function as well. The tuning function will optimize the system control by continuously updating the proportional, integral, and derivative gains.

Pneumatic Control, Electric Control, and Direct Digital Control (DDC) Technologies

- Pneumatic controls—Pneumatic controls use compressed air to operate system control elements such as valves and dampers. Control signals can be analog or discrete. Analog signals are between a range of 3 and15 psi, which are programmed to represent the change in an external variable, for example, a temperature between 0°F to 200°F. Discrete signals can also be received; if, for example, the control pressure is 0 psi, the system is off, and at 20 psi, the system is on.
- Electric controls—Electric controls can be analog electronic or conventional electric circuits. Analog electronic controls use a continuously variable electrical voltage or current to transmit signals. They are accurate and stable, but they can be difficult to maintain and integrate with computer systems. Conventional electric control is simple and cheap, but they have limited capabilities, especially for optimization of system performance.
- Direct Digital Controls (DDC)—DDC system signals are electrical pulses. They are precise and interface directly with computers or via the Internet. System changes can often be made within the software instead of requiring hardware changes. They are very flexible and provide the most opportunity for system optimization. However, they are expensive to install, and proprietary control systems can make it difficult to integrate different systems.

HVAC Reset Control Optimization Strategies

- Supply air temperature reset—The supply air temperature (SAT) is often set to a constant temperature of 55°F, for example, so some zones may require significant reheating. SAT reset will increase the temperature until the reheat valve in one zone is closed.
- Static pressure reset—The static pressure within variable air volume system ducts is usually controlled to be constant. If zone dampers are almost fully closed during some periods, then the fan is working more than is necessary. Static pressure reset will lower the pressure set point until one zone damper is fully open.
- Chilled water reset—The chilled water set point is often set at a constant point for the highest anticipated cooling demand. The chilled water temperature should be set depending upon the differential between the supply and return temperature and by assessing the position of cooling coil valves. If valves are nearly fully closed, then the temperature could be allowed to increase until valves are nearly fully open.

Optimal Start and Stop Control Strategy

An optimal stop-start strategy is used to minimize the operating time of heating ventilation and air-conditioning (HVAC) systems during scheduled start and stop periods. Optimal start delays the actual starting of equipment during its scheduled operating period to be the minimum time needed to reach the desired internal conditions when building occupants arrive, instead of just starting at a scheduled time. This is useful when the weather is mild and it will not take a long time to bring the building to the occupancy set points after a night setback schedule. For example, if building occupancy begins at 8 am and the equipment is scheduled to begin at 5 am because on the coldest days it can take three hours to reach the set point, then on warmer days the optimal start control will delay HVAC operation until the time it calculates will be needed to bring the building to the correct temperature, which may be 7 am, thereby saving two hours of HVAC operation. An optimal stop strategy turns off equipment at the earliest possible time before the end of the scheduled occupancy time that will still maintain comfortable conditions. In milder weather, the building may be able to maintain a comfortable temperature for several hours before occupants leave so the operation of HVAC equipment up until the end of the occupancy time can be avoided.

Economizer Controls

An economizer is a control system that adjusts the amount of outside air supplied to a building through the ventilation system based on the outside air temperature, and sometimes humidity, to minimize mechanical cooling. An economizer enables more energy-efficient operation when the outside air temperature is low because it will allow more cold air from the outside to be supplied to take advantage of "free cooling." The control methods generally used to decide when the economizer should operate include the following:

- Dry bulb temperature—When the outside air is cooler than the controller set point
- Enthalpy—When the outside air enthalpy is less than the controller set point
- Differential dry bulb—When the outside air is cooler than the return air
- Differential enthalpy—When the outside enthalpy is less than return air enthalpy
- The type of economizer control method will depend upon where the building is located. Warmer and more humid climates will have less opportunities for free cooling, so economizer controls must be set carefully

Building Automation System (BAS) Communication Protocols

Building services equipment such as chillers, air handling units, cooling towers, pumps, valves, and sensors that need to be controlled for effective and efficient operation will be provided by different manufacturers with different inbuilt control system architecture. It is vital that a building automation system (BAS) is able to communicate with the various building services to optimize building operational performance. Therefore, it is necessary for a common communication protocol to be used to facilitate the transfer of information. Some of the most common communication protocols used to enable these different proprietary systems to work together are these:

- BACnet—Developed by ASHRAE, BACnet is an open standard used internationally. It is described in ASHRAE Standard 135 and ISO 16484-6.
- LONWorks—Developed by the Echelon Corporation. This is a group of products utilizing the LONTalk communications protocol described in ISO 14908-1.
- Modbus—A widely used communication protocol originally for programmable logic controllers. It enables serial line data transfer among devices on the same network.

Open Protocol Systems in Building Automation Systems

Protocols are "open" when they are independent of any hardware or system. The main benefit of an open system is that it allows for easy integration of the control devices from multiple manufacturers. The communication rules will be publicly available and can be used in a wide variety of building automation systems (BAS). Additional benefits include no licensing fees, freedom of choice in selecting hardware and software integrations, and support by multiple service organizations, vendors, and manufacturers.

A limitation of open protocols is that they only perform optimally in the exact conditions for which they were designed. For example, if hours of operation or building occupancy change, these protocols will not function optimally. Open protocol systems also normally do not cover all the desired functions of a BAS.

Energy Information Systems

Energy information systems (EIS) are part of the overall energy management information system (EMIS). The EIS shows the energy usage information of a facility. The EIS is different from a traditional energy management system in that it does not rely heavily on manual processes. The EIS works in partnership with the building automation system (BAS) and forms the basis of the EMIS. The BAS is responsible for the controls that run the HVAC and lighting.

Energy information systems have four main functions:

- Reporting that supports energy conservation and sustainability goals and contributes to costs savings
- Early fault detection that helps avoid costly downtime and breakdowns
- Monitoring of energy usage in real time
- Tracking of demand and peak loads, which the facility staff can use to optimize operations

Expert Systems and Artificial Intelligence

An expert system is a type of artificial intelligence system that mimics the decision-making process of a human operator. It does not require a model of the system to operate. An expert system comprises a knowledge base and a set of rules, an inference engine, and a user interface. The knowledge base is a set of data provided by human experts with associated rules for the data, for example if-then rules. A user interface is provided for a user to input queries and receive results. The inference engine searches the knowledge base and applies logical analysis rules to determine the optimal solution to the user's query. Expert systems can be used in building automation systems to determine the optimal control of a heating ventilation and air-conditioning (HVAC) system to minimize energy consumption while ensuring the required internal environmental conditions are met. The quality of the information contained in the knowledge base will determine the effectiveness of the expert systems.

Web-Based Energy Information Systems

A Web-based energy information system (EIS) is used to collect energy consumption data, store the data on a server, and provide software tools to analyze and present the data. An EIS is used to understand the energy performance of the building and facilitate energy conservation actions. Data can be collected from utility meters, building automation systems, or dedicated data acquisition systems. Typical data that is collected will include power demand, inside and outside temperatures, equipment operating times, and other equipment operational data. The data is sent over local or wireless networks to a server that can be accessed via the Internet with TCP/IP protocols. The data is then accessed by a Web-based software tool with suitable analysis and reporting functions appropriate for the facility or portfolio of facilities. The EIS can be used to identify opportunities for energy savings and then track the results using measurement and verification techniques after projects are implemented.

Central Control and Distributed Control

Building automation systems (BASs) require controllers that send control signals to actuators and motors and process signals received from sensors. In a centralized control system, the control processor controls all the points. The controller will either send signals to points along dedicated wires if there are only a small number of control points, or if there are many points, then a shared common data bus network is used. The central controller will need to use a common communication protocol to be able to interface with each different control point. A distributed control system has multiple remote controllers that will communicate with one or more control points independently. A central controller may still be used for overall coordination, monitoring, and reporting, but the remote controllers can often operate independently. Distributed control can offer more overall reliability because problems with a controller will be limited to just one part of the system instead of possibly affecting the entire system. Control signal carriers may be sent via power lines, or in newer systems, over wireless networks.

Internet of Things (IoT)

Existing building automation systems (HVAC, boilers, lighting, etc.) can be modernized by the use of the Internet of Things (IoT). This can help avoid costly renovation and construction. The IoT is transforming traditional building automation systems by allowing them to be proactive as opposed to reacting when problems occur. The IoT is composed of user interfaces, network connectivity, data processing, and sensors.

The IoT is revolutionizing BASs by:

- Providing data-driven insights in real time, which allows for the optimization of occupant comfort and energy consumption
- Early detection of equipment issues, which allows for planned and predictive maintenance
- The use of sensors that continuously gather data on temperature, humidity, air quality, and occupancy and feed that back to the BAS

Cloud-Based Systems in Building Automation Systems

An ideal building automation system will have cloud-based control. This functionality allows for remote access and control of the BAS. Cloud-based control offers flexibility and scalability; however, there are situations in which strictly on-site control is required or preferred. Examples of this are systems in high security or government buildings.

Cloud-based systems offer the following benefits:

- They make it easier for building managers and maintenance staff to access data and manage the building from anywhere. Remote access provides convenience and could contribute to higher maintenance employee satisfaction.
- Cloud computing reduces maintenance and hardware expenses, thus reducing overall costs.
- Cloud-based systems offer disaster recovery capabilities and redundancy.

The main challenges associated with cloud-based systems are protecting and securing sensitive data, cost management, monitoring of cloud expenses, and the dependence on a reliable network.

Using Artificial Intelligence in Building Automation Systems

Artificial intelligence (AI) is being integrated into building automation systems on an increasingly frequent basis. There are several types of AI used in BASs.

- Decision trees: Decisions are made based on rules or conditions. This is effective for optimizing energy use, fault detection, and diagnostics.
- Genetic algorithms: Input variables, like environmental conditions, are used to build hybrid algorithms that calculate a building's thermal load.
- Fuzzy logic: This is useful in controlling HVAC, lighting, and other building functions. Fuzzy logic incorporates imprecise and uncertain data to allow gradual transitions between true and false statements.
- Artificial neutral networks (ANN): These networks adapt to changing conditions in the building's systems and use historical trends and nonlinear processes of inputting data to predict output.
- Particle swarm optimization (PSO): Used in load management and energy efficiency scheduling, PSO algorithms find optimal solutions by simulating the behaviors of particles in a swarm.

Benefits Artificial Intelligence (AI) Brings to Building Automation and Controls

- AI allows for personalization and convenience via smartphone apps that control systems, receive alerts, and report problems.
- AI uses machine learning to continuously monitor spaces, automatically adjust to ensure comfort, and ensure optimized use of energy.
- AI gathers data from all the smart technologies and building management systems in a building to standardize and store key information. AI can accomplish this very quickly and with very few errors. Reports for management and building maintenance can be quickly produced to aid in decisions on maintenance and the replacement of equipment.
- AI uses a scalable and flexible cloud-based system. This means the AI models can quickly adapt to changing workloads, process information efficiently, and allocate resources based on demand.

It must be noted that AI systems are not guaranteed to produce intelligent results if the algorithms are run from poorly derived data.

Issues with Cybersecurity and Information Technology in BASs

Building automation systems have been historically developed as closed environments and, therefore, had little or no cybersecurity issues. With the immense rise in popularity of AI and the Internet of Things (IoT) in building automation systems, however, cyber threats and IT issues are coming to the forefront.

Building automation systems are now vulnerable to cyberattacks that could cause adverse consequences, such as disabling of key equipment, occupant discomfort, or unexpected system downtime. This issue has become a concern for many industries, notably the nuclear power plant industry.

Information technology issues in BASs are also becoming increasingly common. The main issues are related to:

- Privacy concerns: protection of sensitive data
- Labor force concerns: training and retention issues or labor reductions due to automation
- Dependency on reliable networks: unreliable networks causing equipment malfunction, down time, gaps in data, or occupant discomfort

Energy Storage Systems

Design Strategies in Energy Storage Systems

Several strategies need to be taken into account when designing energy storage systems (ESS) to maximize effectiveness and efficiency:

- Proper sizing: Design to meet desired capacity and power output.
- Technology selection: Select the energy storage technology (e.g., TES, flywheels, batteries, or hydro).
- Emissions goals: Identify whether the system will produce net zero emissions or zero emissions. Net zero is typically easier and more cost effective to pursue.
- Co-optimization: Consider how the system will interact with the grid, demand flexibility, and sustainable sources (solar, wind, etc.).
- Storage strategy: Identify a long-term storage solution, such as a lithium-ion battery.

Location, grid specifics, and environmental conditions are a few other factors that also need to be taken into account when designing energy storage systems.

Types of Thermal Energy Storage Systems

There are two types of thermal energy storage systems (TES): sensible heat storage systems and latent heat storage systems.

Sensible heat systems: A storage medium that does not change phase while it absorbs and releases heat (commonly water or another fluid) is used. Sensible heat systems are frequently used in commercial buildings, and they are best for short-term storage. Some examples of these systems are thermal batteries, heat exchange systems, and chilled water stratification. Sensible heat storage systems are the most commercially available and straightforward heat storage systems.

Latent heat systems: A storage medium that changes phase is used (e.g., from liquid to gas or from a liquid to solid). Examples of these systems are thermal energy storage tanks, ice storage systems (usually water), and the phase-change material (PCM) strategy. Latent heat storage systems can be used in both long-term and short-term storage applications.

Partial Energy Storage Systems

Partial energy storage systems (ESS) are those in which only a part of the loads or circuits are backed up by an alternate energy source.

There are four main components of partial energy storage systems:

- Backup loads: Critical equipment and/or essential loads (emergency lighting, sensitive medical equipment, etc.) are connected to the backup power source. If the primary power source or grid goes down, these loads receive power.
- Energy capture: Batteries or solar panels store excess energy that can be used when needed.
- Efficiency: These partial solutions are very efficient; greater than 95% efficiency is generally achieved.
- Greater control for building owners: Building owners can tap into the stored energy as needed, which increases reliability.

Typical partial EES systems are partial load battery backup, ice storage, partial home backup, and cascaded modular photovoltaic (PV).

Full Energy Storage Systems

Full (whole-home) energy storage systems rely entirely on energy from renewable resource technology, such as wind turbines, hydro power, or solar panels. These systems store this energy in high-capacity batteries and detach the user from the traditional utility grid, earning the term "off the grid." Full energy storage systems are self-sufficient in energy consumption and production. Full storage systems can result in positive environmental effects, the elimination of a typical energy bill, and greater energy control and security.

Operating Strategies Employed in Energy Storage Systems

An operating strategy must be designed to minimize cost and maximize performance of the system. There are three key strategies:

- Avoid overcharging/discharging: The system must not allow itself to overcharge or to discharge too much. Tools are available for optimizing storage lifetime and operating ability.
- Peak-demand pricing strategy: The system must produce/charge during off-peak price times and discharge during peak price times. This avoids buying power at the highest price times, thus reducing overall energy costs.
- Self-use optimization: This strategy also chooses to charge/discharge based on peak and non-peak rates. The strategy considers expected future loads, tariff structures, and photovoltaic (PV) generation. This strategy aims to reduce electricity bills for owners of small-scale PV systems.

Benefits of Thermal Energy Storage

The primary benefit of thermal energy storage (TES) systems is reduced operating costs for cooling energy. TES systems store energy during off-peak times so that peak demand charges are reduced and some or all the energy demand for cooling is used outside peak periods when prices are lower. Other benefits of TES are reduced size and cost for new or retrofit chiller projects, chiller operating efficiency can be improved if loaded at optimal efficiency, improved reliability is offered by stored energy, and rebates or rate incentives may be offered for demand side management participation. TES are not cost-effective in all buildings. They are most suitable in these situations:

1. A building has high peak demand charges.
2. The cost of energy at night is much lower than the day.
3. Cooling loads create a large peak demand, and cooling loads are small overnight.
4. Increased cooling capacity is needed, and there is sufficient capacity from an existing chiller that can be utilized with a TES system.

Thermal Energy Storage Operating Strategies

Thermal energy storage (TES) systems are used to reduce peak demand charges and use less energy during periods that have higher costs per unit of energy. Two general strategies can be employed to optimize the cost-saving benefits:

- Load levelling—A thermal energy storage system can be sized and operated so that the chiller energy consumption is constant throughout the day. When the building cooling demand is less than the chiller output, the excess energy is stored by the TES system. When the cooling load is greater than the chiller output, then energy is released from the TES system. The principle is illustrated in the following figure:

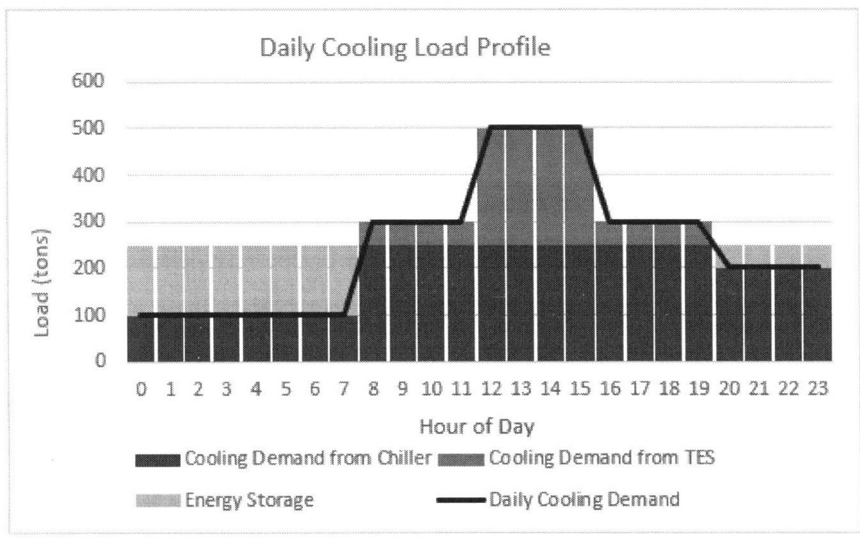

- Load shifting—A thermal energy storage system can be sized and operated so that the chiller will not operate during peak periods when the costs per unit of energy are higher. The total cooling energy demand for the day is produced during off-peak times. The principle is illustrated in the following figure, assuming the peak energy cost is from 12 pm to 8 pm:

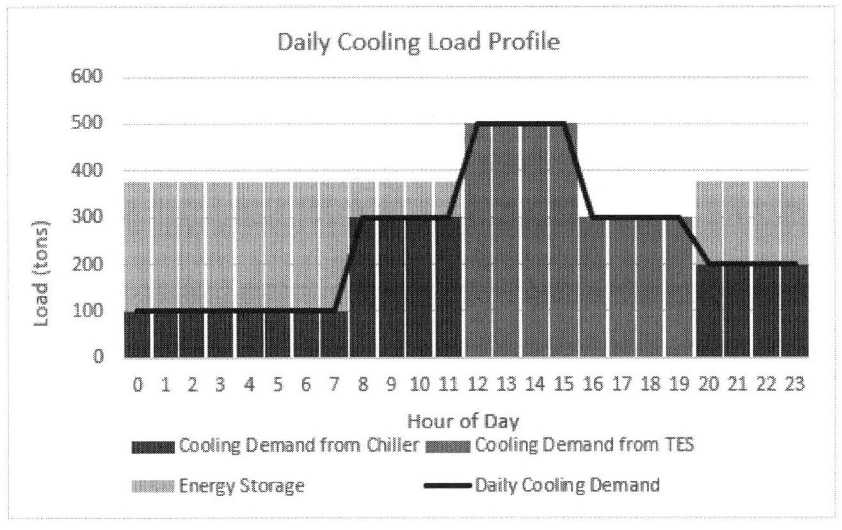

A load-levelling TES system requires less storage capacity and can utilize a smaller chiller than a load-shifting TES system. Load levelling is most cost-effective for new construction, and load shifting may be more suitable for retrofit projects when a large chiller is already installed.

Calculating the Chiller Output and Ton-Hour Storage Capacity for a Partial Thermal Energy Storage System

Partial energy storage is a load-levelling strategy to offset some of the cooling load in peak periods to off-peak periods and reduce demand charges. In a load-levelling strategy, the chiller output throughout the day is constant, and peak cooling demand is met simultaneously by the chiller and a thermal energy storage (TES) system. The total cooling load for the day is measured in ton-hours and is calculated by multiplying the load in tons by the number of hours required during the day. For example, in the figure below the hourly cooling demand profile is shown and the total cooling load is:

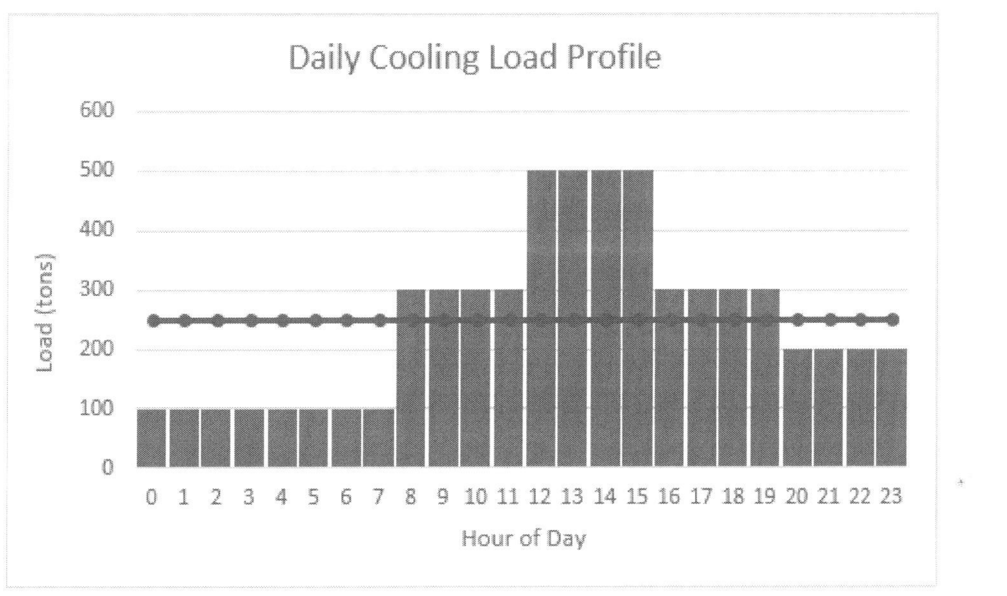

$$Load\ (ton-hours) = 100 \times 8 + 300 \times 4 + 500 \times 4 + 300 \times 4 + 200 \times 4 = 6{,}000$$

The chiller will operate for 24 hours at constant output, so the chiller output indicated by the line in the figure above will be:

$$Chiller\ Output\ (tons) = \frac{6{,}000}{24} = 250$$

The required capacity of a partial TES system is determined by the ton-hour cooling load that must be provided above the output of the chiller. In the example above this would be:

$$TES\ Capacity\ (ton-hours) = 50 \times 4 + 250 \times 4 + 50 \times 4 = 1{,}400$$

Calculating the Chiller Output and Ton-Hour Storage Capacity for a Full Thermal Energy Storage System

Full energy storage is a load shifting strategy to move the cooling load in peak periods to off-peak periods. In a load shifting strategy, the chiller output throughout off-peak periods is assumed to be constant, and it does not operate during peak periods. Peak cooling demand is met only by the thermal energy storage (TES) system. The total cooling load for the day is measured in ton-hours and is calculated by multiplying the load in tons by the number of hours required during the day. For example, in the figure below, the hourly cooling demand profile is shown and the total cooling load is:

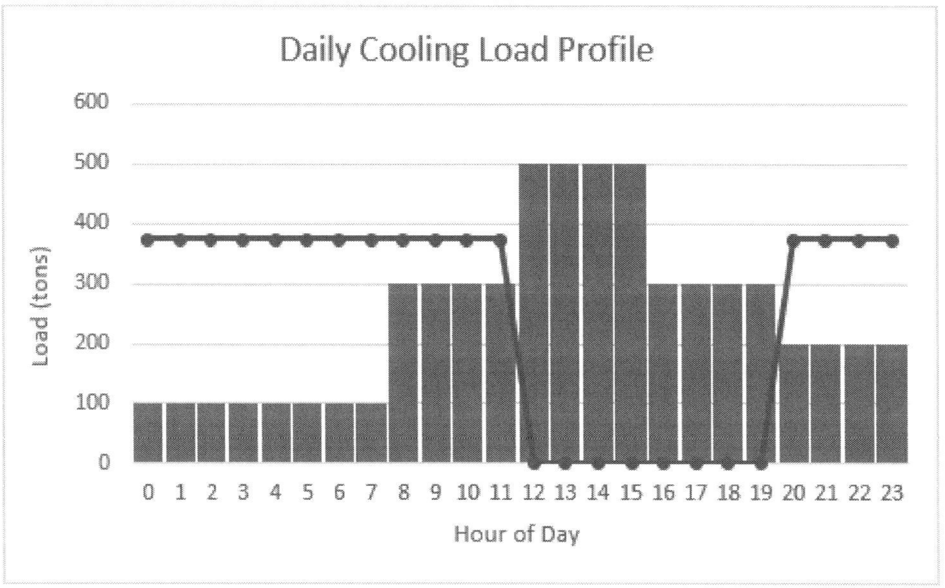

$$Load\ (ton - hours) = 100 \times 8 + 300 \times 4 + 500 \times 4 + 300 \times 4 + 200 \times 4 = 6{,}000$$

The chiller will operate only in off-peak periods. Assuming the peak period is from 12 pm to 8 pm, then the chiller will operate only for 16 hours each day, from 8 pm to noon. Therefore, the chiller output indicated by the line in the figure above will be:

$$Chiller\ Output\ (tons) = \frac{6{,}000}{16} = 375$$

The required capacity of a full TES system is determined by the ton-hour cooling load that must be provided during peak periods when the chiller is not operating. In the example above this would be:

$$TES\ Capacity\ (ton - hours) = 500 \times 4 + 300 \times 4 = 3{,}200$$

Calculating the Minimum Volume of a Chilled Water Storage Tank Based on a Required Ton-Hour Storage Capacity

The ton-hour storage capacity needed for a thermal energy storage (TES) system depends upon the chiller operational settings. Once the energy storage requirements are known, the volume of water needed to store the energy must be calculated. The standard assumptions required are as follows:

1 ton-hour = 12,000 Btu

1 lb. of water can store 1 Btu/°F

1 gallon = 8.34 lb. of water

First, the difference between the chilled water storage temperature and the return temperature needs to be known. A larger temperature differential will result in less water being needed to store the energy. As an example, assuming a storage temperature of 40°F and a return temperature of

58°F, the temperature differential is 18°F, and therefore each pound of water will store 18 Btu. The amount of water required in gallons per ton-hour is:

$$Volume\ of\ Water\ \left(\frac{gallons}{ton-hour}\right)=\frac{1}{18}\frac{lb}{Btu}\times 12{,}000\frac{Btu}{ton-hour}\times\frac{1}{8.34}\frac{gallons}{lb}=80$$

Therefore, if 3,200 ton-hours of storage capacity is required, then a storage volume of about 256,000 gallons is needed (when the temperature differential is 18°F).

Types of Thermal Energy Storage Media Systems

Thermal energy storage (TES) systems can utilize chilled water, ice, or a eutectic salt. Each storage medium has advantages and disadvantages in terms of cost, space required, and complexity.

- Chilled water—Chilled water systems use sensible heat storage, so each pound of water will store about 1 Btu. Storage temperatures are typically 39°F to 42°F. The return temperature should preferably be 58°F to 60°F to minimize the storage volume required. Chilled water systems are the simplest but require the most space. One practical issue is to minimize the mixing of the cold water and warm return water.
- Ice—Ice TES systems use latent heat storage so 1 lb. of water will store 144 Btu. Storage temperature is at 32°F, so the cooling equipment must be able to cool a fluid to between 15°F and 26°F. Ice systems require about one-quarter to one-third less space than chilled water systems but are more complex and usually more expensive.
- Eutectic salt—A eutectic TES system uses a salt that changes phase at a temperature of about 47°F. It stores about 41 Btu per pound and requires about one-third to one-half the space of chilled water. It is a very expensive and rarely used storage medium.

Phase-Change Materials (PCM) Used in Energy Storage Systems

Phase-change materials (PCM) are capable of making and storing significant amounts of thermal energy, which makes them ideal for use in energy storage systems. Advantages of PCMs include high energy-density storage, the ability to operate effectively across a wide range of temperature conditions, and superior isothermal behavior. Use of PCMs is growing, and research on new PCMs continues.

The three main types of phase-change materials are:

- Polymeric materials, such as polyethylene glycol (PEG)
- Organic compounds, such as paraffins (hydrocarbons) and fatty acids
- Inorganic systems, such as metal alloys and salt hydrates

PCM thermal energy storage is widely used in refrigeration and commonly uses paraffin and salt hydrates as the PCM. The materials absorb and release heat while transitioning between solid and liquid phases.

Thermal Storage for Heating

Typically, thermal storage heating systems will store heat during off-peak hours (normally, this is at night), when electricity is at a lower rate. The system will then release the heat gradually (normally, during the day) to warm the space. Water or ceramic is often used to store the heat due to their ability to efficiently retain high heat. Thermal storage systems for heating deliver many of the same benefits as thermal systems for cooling. Namely, they operate during off-peak, lower-rate times to save money, and they help to remove load from the grid during peak periods.

Electric Energy Storage (EES) Systems

Electric energy storage systems are a necessary component of the transition to using more renewable and cleaner energy sources. The benefits to energy storage systems are that they contribute to peak shaving of the grid, they provide a backup power source, and they allow for better integration of renewable energy sources into the grid.

There are many types of electric energy storage systems. The most common types are:

- Batteries: used primarily in electric vehicles and residential applications
- Hydrogen energy storage: converts electricity to hydrogen
- Thermal energy storage: stores cold or heat for later use
- Pumped hydro storage: water reservoirs that store water for later use
- Flywheels: rotating devices that store kinetic energy

Currently, there is a tremendous amount of research going into battery design to increase storage capability and to reduce battery size.

Boiler and Steam Systems

Higher Heating Value (HHV) and Lower Heating Value (LHV)

The heating value of a fuel is the heat energy available when it is combusted. One of the products of combustion is water vapor at high temperature, and this water stores energy as latent heat. The amount of energy stored in the water depends upon the hydrogen content of the fuel; fuels with more hydrogen will produce more water vapor. The higher heating value (HHV) of a fuel, also called the gross calorific value, is calculated assuming that all latent heat of vaporization of the water vapor is recovered. The lower heating value (LHV), or net calorific value, is the heat energy available assuming the latent heat is lost. The latent heat can be recovered if the water vapor is condensed, for example, in a condensing boiler, and used to provide useful heat. Condensing boilers need to operate with a return temperature of less than 131°F for the water vapor in the flue gases to condense so the latent heat can be recovered. The difference between HHV and LHV typically ranges from about 10% for natural gas to about 5% for some oil products.

Boiler Heat Balance

A boiler heat balance is an analysis of the heat content of all inputs and outputs during the combustion process. Analyzing the boiler combustion process enables the efficiency to be determined and opportunities for energy efficiency improvements to be identified. The inputs to a boiler are fuel, air, and feedwater, and the outputs are exhaust gas, hot water or steam, surface heat losses, and boiler blowdown losses. The enthalpy rates (heat content) of all inputs will equal the enthalpy rates of the outputs plus the losses. The heat content of the fluid streams is calculated this way:

$$\dot{H} = \dot{m} \times (h - h_o)$$

In this equation $\dot{H}$ is the enthalpy rate of the fluid, $\dot{m}$ is the mass flow rate of the fluid, h is the specific enthalpy at the fluid's temperature, and h_o is the specific enthalpy at a reference temperature (for example, 70°F). The heat content for a gaseous stream is:

$$\dot{H} = \dot{V} C_p \times (T - T_o)$$

In this equation $\dot{V}$ is the volume flow rate of the gas, C_p is the specific heat, T is the temperature of the gaseous stream, and T_o is the reference temperature.

Condensing Boiler Systems

A condensing boiler system works by using two heat exchangers instead of one. The first heat exchanger is for combustion. The additional heat exchanger captures the heat from the flue gasses that are exhausted. The name is derived from the fact that the boiler removes the latent heat (moisture) from the hot flue gas, causing water to condense out of the flue.

The condensing boiler achieves very high efficiency (>90%) by condensing water in the exhaust gases and recovering its latent heat of evaporation. In older boilers, the flue gas is not captured and may leave the system at over 200 °C. As of 2005, it became a requirement that all boilers be condensing boilers. Condensing boilers have specific venting considerations that must be made and require proper and careful installation to make sure condensation occurs efficiently.

Process of Deriving Enthalpy from Saturated and Superheated Steam Tables

Saturated steam exists at the boiling point of water for a given pressure. It contains both vapor and liquid water. The enthalpy of saturated steam can be found using saturated steam tables. These tables provide values of enthalpy, internal energy, and other properties for different temperatures and pressures. To use a saturated steam table, look up the temperature and pressure of the system and find the corresponding enthalpy of the saturated steam.

Superheated steam is steam that has been heated beyond its boiling point temperature for a given pressure. Superheated steam is a vapor, containing no liquid. The enthalpy of superheated steam can be derived from superheated steam tables. To use a superheated steam table, look up the temperature and pressure of the system. The enthalpy value at that point is the enthalpy value of the superheated steam.

Steam System Configuration

A steam system will comprise a boiler that produces steam from an input fuel, such as natural gas or oil, and the steam distribution system. The components of the steam distribution system include steam lines, steam traps, and possibly waste heat recovery equipment. The steam lines carry steam to where it is needed, and these should be insulated to minimize heat losses. Leaks in the steam lines are a significant source of heat loss and so should be identified quickly through regular maintenance. As the steam gives off heat, some of it condenses. The condensate must be removed, which is the purpose of steam traps. Steam traps also remove air and dissolved gases, which also improves steam quality and efficiency. Condensate should be returned to the boiler to reduce the energy required for the process. Any condensate lost must be made up with lower temperature water, which requires more energy. The energy lost in condensate not returned to the boiler can be calculated this way:

$$\dot{Q} = \frac{\dot{m} \times \left(h_{condensate} - h_{make-up\ water}\right)}{\eta}$$

In this equation $\dot{Q}$ is the energy loss in Btu/h, $\dot{m}$ is the mass of condensate lost (lb/h), $h_{condensate}$ is the specific enthalpy of the condensate at the specified pressure and saturated liquid temperature, $h_{make\text{-}up\ water}$ is the specific enthalpy of a saturated liquid at the temperature of the make-up water, and η is the efficiency of the boiler.

Industrial Boiler Interior Configuration

Boilers may be used to produce either hot water or steam. The usual configuration of industrial boilers is a firetube boiler or watertube boiler; their names describe how the hot gases and water pass through the boiler.

- Firetube boilers—These boilers have many tubes passing through the inside of the boiler that convey the hot combustion gases while being surrounded by boiling water. The gases pass back through the boiler two to four times to maximize heat transfer to the water. The efficiency of firetube boilers can be improved by installing turbulators inside the tubes. Turbulators create turbulent flow that improves heat transfer.
- Watertube boilers—In these boilers the water passes through tubes that are surrounded by the hot combustion gases. Water moves through the tubes due to the difference in density between the colder feedwater and the hotter water and steam at the top of the tubes.

Enthalpy of Water

As the temperature of water increases from 32°F up to its boiling point, the enthalpy increases linearly. Once it boils water becomes a saturated liquid; its temperature stops increasing, but the enthalpy continues to increase as the water begins to turn to a vapor. Once all the liquid has evaporated and becomes steam, the temperature begins to increase again, and the water becomes superheated steam. There are two versions of steam tables: one is based on temperature, and one is based on pressure. The data is the same; it is just presented differently. The information found in the temperature-based steam table is generally ordered as follows:

Temperature (°F)	Absolute Pressure (psi)	Specific Volume (ft^3/lb)		Enthalpy (Btu/lb)		
		v_f	v_g	h_f	h_{fg}	h_g
32	0.08859	0.016022	3304.7	-0.0179	1075.5	1075.5
212	14.696	0.16719	28.878	176.14	972.8	1149.0
300	67.005	0.01745	6.4658	269.7	910.0	1179.7

The absolute pressure given in the table above at each temperature is the pressure at which water will boil. The other values in the table are these:

v_f = specific volume of saturated water (liquid)

v_g = specific volume of saturated steam (gas)

h_f = specific enthalpy of saturated water (liquid); this is the energy needed to heat water from 32°F to the boiling point

h_{fg} = latent heat of vaporization; this is the energy needed to turn all the water to steam

h_g = specific enthalpy of saturated steam (gas); this is the energy needed to generate steam from water at 32°F

Boiler Blowdown

Make-up water is needed to replace water lost from the system, and the boiler make-up water introduces impurities into the system. Mineral deposits form over time because the impurities are not evaporated with the water and end up becoming concentrated in the bottom of the boiler. Boiler blowdown is the term describing the process of periodically removing water from inside a boiler to remove mineral deposits. If the mineral deposits are not removed, then heat transfer is not as effective, and boiler efficiency will decrease. Energy savings can be achieved by ensuring the boiler blowdown schedule matches the boiler load. If the boiler is only partially loaded for a lot of the time, then the blowdown schedule should be reduced to match the boiler operation. This will avoid unnecessary boiler blowdown and associated energy losses. Heat recovery from the hot blowdown water and ensuring any condensate is returned from steam distribution lines and used as make-up water can also be investigated to minimize energy losses.

Condensate and Flash Steam

Steam systems usually produce saturated steam, and as the steam gives up its latent heat, condensate is produced. When high-temperature, high-pressure condensate experiences a reduction in pressure that puts it above the saturation temperature (boiling point) at the lower pressure, the condensate will immediately evaporate and turn to steam. This is called flash steam. This often happens when condensate passes through a steam trap or valve. The percentage of condensate that will become flash steam when a pressure drop is experienced can be calculated this way:

$$Flash\ Steam\ (\%) = \frac{\left(H_{f\ (steam\ pressure)} - H_{f\ (condensate\ pressure)}\right)}{H_{fg\ (condensate\ pressure)}}$$

For example, if steam at 30 psi is vented to the atmosphere the amount of water lost is:

$$Flash\ Steam\ (\%) = \frac{\left(H_{f\ (30psi)} - H_{f\ (14.7psi)}\right)}{H_{fg\ (14.7psi)}} = \frac{(218.9 - 180.17)}{970.3} = 4\%$$

It is best to return the condensate to the boiler at as high of a temperature and pressure as possible to minimize energy losses.

Steam Traps

Steam traps are automatic valves used in steam distribution systems. Steam traps allow condensate and air to be removed from the system while preventing steam from escaping. There are three main types of steam trap, and the best choice of trap will depend upon the application:

- Mechanical steam traps—Inverted bucket and float steam traps are the two types of mechanical steam traps that are widely used. They operate on the principle of different specific gravities of water and steam to regulate the amount of condensate. When condensate is present, the negative buoyancy of the bucket or float prevents a valve from closing the drain. Steam entering the trap pushes the bucket or float upward, thereby closing the valve to the drain. Inverted bucket traps release condensate intermittently once enough condensate has built up inside the trap, but float traps release condensate continuously.
- Thermostatic steam traps—Thermostatic traps have a bellows surrounded by a temperature-sensitive fluid that expands when steam enters to block the drain and contracts when lower temperature condensate is present so the drain opens. A thermostatic steam trap removes condensate continuously.
- Thermodynamic steam traps—Disc traps are a type of thermodynamic trap that operates in response to the balance of forces acting upon a disc that sits on top of a valve. When steam flows below the valve, it is moving at high velocity, so the pressure decreases, which forces the disk onto the valve and prevents any flow. Condensate will push the disk up and drain when no steam is present in the trap. Disc traps operate intermittently.

Air-to-Fuel Ratio and Combustion Process Efficiency

Stoichiometric combustion is the theoretical ideal combustion process that uses only the exact amount of oxygen required to burn all the fuel completely. In practice this cannot realistically be achieved, and if less than the stoichiometric amount of air is supplied, then carbon monoxide and smoke are produced, and unburned fuel may be present in the exhaust gases. Excess air is always needed to ensure complete fuel combustion and to prevent dangerous conditions arising. However, too much air in the combustion process decreases the combustion efficiency because more of the energy in the fuel is used to heat up the excess air. For these reasons it is important to carefully control the amount of excess air. The amount of oxygen and carbon dioxide in the flue gases can be analyzed to determine the optimum amount of excess air. For a natural gas fired boiler, 2% of oxygen in the flue gases is equivalent to about 10% excess air.

Economizers and Recuperators

Economizers and recuperators improve combustion efficiency by reducing the amount of fuel needed to heat combustion air or feedwater.

- Boiler economizer—Exhaust gases from a boiler may be 300°F to 500°F. Boiler economizers recover waste heat from the exhaust gas to preheat boiler feedwater. An economizer is a heat exchanger located in the exhaust stack with boiler feedwater running through tubes within the exhaust gases. The temperature drop in the stack is controlled so that the water in the economizer doesn't boil and the gas temperature does not drop below the dew point, which is around 130°F.
- Recuperator—Exhaust gases in medium- to high-temperature process heating applications such as furnaces and incinerators may be around 1100°F to 2400°F. Recuperators recover waste heat in exhaust gases to preheat the incoming air for the combustion process. Recuperators are either radiation recuperators or convective recuperators, and they may be used in combination. A radiation recuperator comprises a tube around the exhaust stack that the combustion air passes through. A convective recuperator comprises a set of tubes that the exhaust gases pass through, and the combustion circulates past the tubes in a perpendicular direction.

Distributed Generation and Renewable Energy Systems

Combined Heat and Power (CHP)

CHP is the simultaneous production of electrical power and heat. A fuel such as natural gas, oil, biogas, or biomass is combusted to turn a prime mover and generate electricity. The heat from the combustion process is captured in one or more heat exchangers and utilized. The prime mover in a CHP unit is typically a reciprocating engine or turbine. CHP is a distributed generation technology that is generally cheaper and produces less greenhouse gases than separately purchasing grid electricity and burning a fuel for heat. A CHP engine typically needs to operate for at least 4,000 hours each year to be financially beneficial, and the greater the difference in cost between electricity and the fuel used in the CHP engine, the better the financial benefits. CHP is also beneficial in terms of security of electricity supply because on-site generation can provide power when the grid is unavailable.

Regulations That Govern Combined Heat and Power (CHP) Projects

Below is a list of regulations associated with CHP projects:

- Environmental regulations: These are primarily based on output (both thermal and mechanical). Examples of these regulations are the EPA's New Source Performance Standards for CHP prime movers and the National Emission Standards for Hazardous Air Pollutants.
- Interconnection standards regulations: These are Federal Energy Regulatory Commission or state regulations that govern utility policies for interconnection of distributed generation to the utility grid. Interconnection agreements ensure the safety and reliability of the grid.
- Net metering policy regulations: These regulate how CHP customers are compensated for selling excess electricity to the grid. These regulations or policies address eligible systems, treatment of excess generation, and system capacity limits.
- Renewable Portfolio Standards regulations: These regulations require utilities to derive a certain amount of their electricity from specified sources. In the states where this is required, it creates a demand for CHP systems because utilities can capture the CHP systems' environmental and efficiency benefits.

Enablers and Barriers to Entry of CHP Projects

The Renewable Portfolio Standards regulations enable utilities to capture the environmental and efficiency benefits of CHP projects. These are not available in all states. Public benefit funds, which are typically created by putting a charge on customers' electricity bills, are used to support renewable and energy efficiency projects, like CHP projects. Another enabler is state climate plans that local or state governments use to address the reduction of GHG (greenhouse gas) emissions. These plans can provide streamlined regulation and financial incentives to support CHP projects. There are numerous financial incentives that may be available for CHP projects. Examples are feed-in tariffs, C-PACE programs, federal and state bonds, and federal tax incentives.

There are still numerous barriers to entry when it comes to CHP, although there are fewer than there were a decade ago. The main barriers to entry are interconnection issues and complications, spark spread, grid safety issues, high project first cost, and gaps in industry understanding of the numerous regulations and policies.

Delivered Energy from a CHP System vs. Conventional Energy Generation

Electrical energy production from a large natural gas-fired power station is about 40% efficient. Transmission and distribution losses are about 5%, so for every 100 units of energy consumed by a power station, we receive about 35 units of electricity. CHP systems provide a more efficient energy conversion process because the waste heat that is generated may be utilized as well. If a CHP were to provide the same 35 units of electricity, it would also use about 100 units of natural gas but also generate approximately 50 units of thermal energy for an overall efficiency of 85%. To provide the 50 units of thermal energy we are using from the CHP with a gas-fired boiler with 85% efficiency would require a further 59 units of energy. Therefore, using grid electricity and a gas-fired boiler would use a total of about 159 units of energy compared to 100 units for a CHP engine. That is an overall efficiency of 53% for conventional supply compared to 85% with CHP.

Types of CHP Operating Cycles

CHP engines can be operated to prioritize the production of electricity or the production of heat:

- Topping cycle—This is an electrically led system that is designed to produce a constant electrical output, and the thermal energy is used when there is sufficient demand and rejected if demand is insufficient.
- Bottoming cycle—This is a thermally led system that is sized to meet the heat demand with the amount of electricity output not as critical. Unmet electricity demand is supplied by the grid, and any excess electricity is exported to the grid.
- CHP systems can also be a combined cycle. These usually have a gas turbine that generates a large amount of electricity and waste heat. The waste heat is hot enough to drive a steam turbine that generates more electricity and lower-grade process steam.

District Energy Systems

District energy systems are made up of multiple components and are a highly efficient way to heat and cool multiple buildings from a central plant. These are commonly used on college campuses, city centers, and hospital complexes. District energy systems combine loads from multiple buildings to reduce energy costs, create economies of scale, and realize environmental benefits.

The key components of a district energy system are:

- Central plants: This is where steam, hot water, or chilled water is produced.
- Pipes: A network of insulated pipes is necessary to move hot or cold water through the campus or complex.
- Buildings: The water flows to the buildings to provide air conditioning, heating, and hot water.

Prime Movers in a Distributed Generation Energy System

Prime movers are the mechanical machines that convert the primary energy from fluids or fuel into mechanical energy. Prime movers play an important role in distributed energy systems because they drive the electric generators.

Key prime movers are:

- Hydraulic turbines convert potential energy from water into kinetic energy. The water may be held in an upper-level reservoir. The kinetic energy hits the runner of the hydraulic turbine and changes direction and momentum. The motion produces mechanical work that rotates against the electric generator's torque.

- Fossil fuel (gas, coal, oil) produces thermal energy when it's burned in a combustor.
- Gas turbines and internal combustion engines use gas or oil combined with air.
- Wind turbines convert kinetic energy from wind into mechanical energy. They harness wind power to generate electricity.
- Steam turbines use steam as the working fluid for nuclear fuel or coal.

Considerations in Selecting Fuel for Distributed Generation

There are several factors that should be considered when selecting fuel for a distributed generation system:

- Cost and availability of the fuel
- Efficiency of the chosen fuel cell technology
- Energy density and heat recovery
- Environmental impact

Two types of fuels to choose from are fossil fuels and biofuels. Fossil fuels are non-renewable energy sources, such as coal, oil, or natural gas. Burning fossil fuel releases CO_2 into the atmosphere and contributes to climate change.

Biofuels are a renewable, biological source that may come from algae, plants, or organic waste materials. Burning biofuel also releases CO_2 into the air but has fewer negative environmental effects than fossil fuels.

Operating Strategies for Distributed Energy Systems

Distributed energy systems must adopt operating strategies that maximize energy efficiency. Common strategies are:

- Electric load following: This is also known as FEL. FEL is the most common strategy, and it is used when electricity demand is a big concern. FEL adjusts CCHP (combined cooling, heating, and power) operation to meet the building's electrical load requirements.
- Thermal load following: This is also known as FTL and is used frequently in CCHP systems. This strategy adjusts operation based on thermal load demand. The goal is to match the heat output to the building's heating requirements.
- Hybrid approach: In this strategy, the system switches dynamically between FTL and FEL to minimize excess electrical or thermal energy production.

Thermal Efficiency in Distributed Energy Systems (DES)

The thermal efficiency in a DES is the fraction of the heat that becomes useful work. It can be calculated by the following equation:

$$n = W/Qh$$

In this equation, n represents the thermal energy, W is the useful work, and Qh is the total heat energy from the heat source.

There are two main types of thermal efficiency in devices such as turbines and engines.

- Indicated thermal efficiency measures the efficiency of an engine based on the indicated work output during the power stroke. This does not account for losses in heat transfer or losses due to friction.

- Brake thermal efficiency accounts for inefficiencies and losses in the engine. This includes losses in heat transfer and those due to friction. It is calculated based on the actual work of the engine's crankshaft. This is considered to provide a more accurate or "real world" assessment of performance.

Heat Recovery Steam Generators

Heat recovery steam generators (HRSG) are essentially heat exchangers. The HRSG recovers the heat from a hot gas stream, usually from a combustion turbine. The HRSG then produces steam that can be used to drive a steam turbine (this is known as combined cycle) or that can be used in a process (cogeneration). Examples of HRSG system applications are generating steam for district heating or factory processes and driving a steam turbine to generate more electricity in a utility power plant.

Heat recovery steam generators offer numerous benefits. Key benefits are:

- They lead to very high or increased efficiency of the system. They often increase plant efficiency up to 90%.
- They are a cost-effective investment due to the efficiency gains.
- The systems provide environmental benefits and produce minimal CO_2 emissions.

Solar Photovoltaic Systems & Batteries

Solar power systems, or solar photovoltaic (PV) systems, are commonly known as PV systems.

PV systems consist of:

- Solar panels (PV modules): These absorb sunlight and use PV cells to convert the sunlight to electricity.
- Inverter: The inverter converts the DC (direct current) output from the solar panels to AC (alternating current).
- Balance of system: This includes the wiring, circuit breakers, fuses, switches, etc. that go into the mounting of the panels and into collecting and distributing the current.
- Batteries: Batteries play a critical role in the PV system by storing the solar energy produced. In general, the batteries collect excess electricity during the day (sunny days) and release it for use at nights or on cloudy days. Common types of batteries used in PV systems are lead-acid, flow, and lithium-ion batteries.

PV systems may also employ a solar tracking mechanism that follows the sun's path (looking for maximum sunlight potential) and/or a charge controller for regulating battery charging.

Using Micro-Grids in Distributed Generation Systems

Micro-grids are small-scale power grids that generate electricity for a localized area and operate independently from the grid. These units are self-contained and can improve reliability and energy resilience. Micro-grids can interconnect or integrate with the main utility grid or operate independently (island mode). Micro-grids can employ a mix of energy sources, including solar, wind, and backup generators.

Micro-grids are becoming more popular due to their efficiency and resiliency. They are no longer located just in rural or unpopulated areas but are now popping up in cities and urban areas. Micro-grids have the flexibility to serve a single building or an entire city center or neighborhood.

Building-to-Grid Integration

Building-to-grid integration is a relatively new approach that enables buildings to seamlessly connect, coordinate, and communicate with the power grid and other energy sources. When done correctly, it will match energy supply with demand.

Some key points to consider in building-to-grid integration design are:

- Visions and approach: Define how the buildings will communicate with the grid and other energy sources. Buildings will act as "shock absorbers" for the grid in a transactive approach. Sensors, smart meters, loads, distributed generation, and smart appliances should communicate seamlessly.
- Grid balancing: The buildings will essentially become storage options for the grid, balancing supply and demand and grid peaks and valleys.
- New markets and empowered owners: Building-to-grid integration will contribute to sustainability and energy efficiency goals. Owners can create cash flow from energy savings to be reinvested into their businesses.

Waste-to-Energy Systems

Waste-to-energy systems (WtE) do exactly as their name implies: they convert waste to energy. These systems generate fuel, heat, or electricity from materials like municipal solid waste (MSW), plastic, paper, wood, and even yard debris.

Below is a list of typical WtE systems:

- Incineration: This is the most common WtE method. This involves burning (incinerating) waste to produce heat, which then generates steam and, in turn, drives turbines that produce electricity.
- Landfill gas recovery: Methane gas is emitted from landfills as the waste decomposes. The methane gas is collected and used for energy by turbines or engines. Anaerobic digestion also produces methane gas but derives it from the decomposition of organic waste (like food scraps or agricultural residues).
- Gasification: This method converts solid waste into synthetic gas (also known as syngas) by heating it in a low oxygen environment. The gas can be used for electricity production via engines and turbines or as feedstock for chemical production. Pyrolysis produces bio-oil, which can be used for heat.

Public Utility Regulatory Policy Act (PURPA)

PURPA was established in 1978 as part of the National Energy Act. It facilitated the development of combined heat and power (CHP) plants by requiring utilities to purchase power at a competitive rate if the cost was less than the utility's avoided cost for power generation. It also guaranteed small generators the right to connect to the electrical grid and provided exemption from federal and state utility regulations. As the cost of wind and solar have fallen, these generators are now also benefiting from PURPA. PURPA requires a small generator or CHP plant to become a qualifying facility. Small generators qualify if they are less than 80MW and have a renewable primary energy source. A CHP plant must meet minimum efficiency standards but are not limited in size. The Energy Policy Act of 2005 amended the regulations to prevent plants being built just to sell energy to the utility. They must now be built primarily to meet the demands of an industrial or commercial site or process.

Renewable Technologies for Electricity Generation

Renewable electricity generation is used both as a form of distributed generation and as large-scale generation on the main grid network. The most widely deployed technologies included the following:

- Wind generation—Wind turbines may be installed individually or in groups to create a wind farm. Horizontal axis turbines range in size from a few kilowatts to up to 9MW. Wind farms may be built on land or at sea and often have a capacity of several hundred megawatts.
- Solar photovoltaics (PV)—Solar PV systems are being widely installed on the roofs of homes and buildings with capacities of about 2kW up to several megawatts. Large, ground-mounted solar farms are now being built up to several hundred megawatts.
- Hydroelectric—Hydroelectric power generation is also possible on a small scale with microturbines having just a few kilowatts output. However, larger generators using dams are widespread and can have total output of several gigawatts.

Renewable Technologies for Heating Systems

Renewable energy may be used for providing heating to individual buildings or large facilities as well as in district heating schemes within cities. The technologies most commonly employed include the following:

- Solar thermal—Solar radiation is collected to produce heat for space heating and hot water. Glazed or flat plate solar thermal collectors are installed on the roofs of homes or commercial buildings to provide hot water up to about 200°F. Large-scale solar thermal concentrators built using parabolic mirrors can produce high-temperature heat for electricity production and process heat.
- Biomass—Biomass can be used in boilers or combined heat and power plants. The biomass material is sometimes grown specifically for combustion (coppice), or it may be a waste material such as wood chips.
- Geothermal—Reservoirs or hot water underground are often found along tectonic plates. This can be used for power generation. Ground-source heat pumps utilize the heat energy in the ground for space heating and/or cooling.
- Waste-to-energy—Reducing the amount of waste sent to landfills is a high priority in many regions. Waste that cannot be recycled can be incinerated to produce electricity and useful heat for processes or district heating.
- Landfill gas—Methane gas is produced in large quantities at landfills. The gas can be captured and injected into main natural gas distribution networks or burned on site in combined heat and power plants for electricity generation and process or district heating.

Net Metering

Utilities offer a range of incentives for distributed, and most often renewable, generation. Some utilities have net metering regulations that value the generation of electricity at the retail rate and enable customers to receive this financial benefit regardless of when the generation occurs. Wind and solar generation are intermittent and, particularly for solar, have seasonal variability. In some months the generation from a customer's wind or solar installation may exceed their demand for grid electricity. In this case the utility gives the customer credits for the excess generation so that when the customer requires more grid electricity than they are producing from their on-site source of distributed generation, they only have to pay for the electricity that exceeds the total of their credits for previously exported electricity.

Power Purchase Agreement (PPA) Arrangements

A power purchase agreement (PPA) is a contractual arrangement between a distributed generation electricity provider and a buyer. The electricity provider may or may not be the owner of the generation plant, and the buyer may use the electricity generated at the site of generation, or they may export it to the grid. For example, an organization may want to install a source of generation at their facility, but they do not want to own and operate the equipment. A third-party could be contracted to build, own, operate, and maintain the installation and sell the generated electricity to the organization under a PPA at a set rate that is lower than what the organization would buy electricity from the grid. Alternatively, an organization may have excess electricity from an on-site source of generation that they need to sell. A PPA can be established with a utility or another third-party that may stipulate the amount and price for the purchase of the excess electricity that is exported to the grid.

Industrial Systems

Industrial Energy Management

Industrial energy management is best defined as the processes, systems, and strategies put into place to reduce energy consumption in an industrial process and ensure it is as energy efficient as possible. The benefits of a solid industrial energy management system are that it reduces energy waste, helps lower operating costs, and addresses sustainability goals. These benefits contribute to the overall cost competitiveness of the firm. Industrial energy management is critical as industry accounts for over 25% of the United States' greenhouse gas (GHG) emissions and energy usage.

Best practices in industrial energy management include conducting annual energy audits, setting energy management goals and targets, identifying an energy management champion or even a small department dedicated to energy management, installing the most efficient technologies in lighting and HVAC, and using systems to track and manage energy usage. Investing in a renewable energy source, such as wind or solar, is recommended. Energy Star has an information center on their site dedicated to industrial energy management.

Compressed Air Systems

Compressed air is useful for pneumatic control within, for example, heating ventilation and air-conditioning (HVAC) systems; it is useful for cleaning away dry dirt and materials; and it can provide power to machines and tools. The parts of a compressed air system include the following:

- Compressor—There are many types of air compressors, and they are generally categorized according to their method of compressing air, cooling method, number of stages, and method of lubrication. There are two methods of compressing air: increasing the pressure by decreasing the volume using a positive displacement motor or increasing the velocity of the air using a rotodynamic compressor. Positive displacement compressors have either reciprocating motors or rotary motors. Rotodynamic compressors have either a centrifugal or axial flow.
- Aftercooler—Air leaving the compressor is very hot, so it must be cooled by either air or water in a heat exchanger. Moisture in the compressed air is also removed as it condenses.
- Receiver—The receiver is a tank for storing the compressed air until it is needed. Once the receiver reaches its maximum pressure, the compressor turns off. When the tank is at its minimum pressure, the compressor switches back on.
- Dryer—Any remaining condensation is removed in the dryer as the air leaves the receiver.
- Distribution lines—Compressed air is distributed to its end use within pipes.

Compressed Air System Management Options

The demand side of a compressed air system should be the priority for energy management. The first question to ask is whether compressed air is necessary to perform tasks or whether there is a more energy efficient alternative. Air leaks can be a very large cost if they are not found and repaired quickly, so preventive maintenance and leak detection are worthwhile. On the supply side, it is important that the pressure in the system is not higher than necessary. Approximately 1% of energy can be saved for every 2 psi reduction in pressure. The pressure drop through the distribution pipe work should be no more than about 10%. The system pipe layout should be efficient, and receivers could be installed to ensure the pressure at the ends of the distribution pipes is sufficient. Other operational issues to consider include having intake air as cool and dry as possible; sequencing multiple compressors as needed to meet pressure requirements; installing after coolers to remove moisture from air; and recovering waste heat for preheating combustion air or heating process water—usually around 250,000 Btu per 100HP is available.

Leakage Rate for Compressed Air Systems

The information required to calculate the average leakage rate in a compressed air system is the system volume (V), initial pressure (P_i), final pressure (P_f), and the time interval for measurement (Δt). The equation is:

$$Leakage\ Rate\ (cfm) = \frac{V \times (P_i - P_f)}{\Delta t \times 14.7}$$

The system volume includes the receivers and main air headers, but small air lines less than 1 inch in diameter can be ignored. Once the leakage rate is calculated, the annual cost of energy leaks can be determined using the following equation:

$$Cost\ of\ Leaks\left(\frac{\$}{Year}\right) = \frac{Leakage\ Rate \times specific\ efficiency \times 0.746 \times operating\ hours \times energy\ cost}{\eta}$$

The specific efficiency is the horsepower of the compressor divided by the flow rate in cfm, and this value can be found from charts.

Identifying the Locations of Compressed Air Leaks

Air leaks can waste 20% to 30% of an air compressor's output. Compressed air systems are relatively inefficient and expensive, often requiring about 7hp to generate 1hp of compressed air power, so leak detection is very important and cost-effective. Air leaks are not visible, so the best method of detecting them is using an ultrasonic leak detector. Air leaks generate sound at a range of frequencies. Focusing on the sound at ultrasonic frequencies is an accurate method of locating the source of the noise and is not affected by background noises in the range audible to people. The leakage rate in cfm can be estimated from the size of the leak and the system pressure, and these values are given in tables. Some examples include the following:

Leakage Rate (cfm) Based on Hole Size and Pressure				
	Approximate Diameter of Hole (Inches)			
Pressure (psi)	1/64	1/32	1/16	1/8
90	0.37	1.5	5.9	23.8
100	0.41	1.6	6.5	26.0
110	0.44	1.8	7.1	28.2

The annual cost of leaks using this method may be calculated as follows:

$$Cost\ of\ Leaks\left(\frac{\$}{Year}\right) = Leakage\ Rate \times number\ of\ leaks \times \frac{kW}{cfm} \times operating\ hours \times energy\ cost\left(\frac{\$}{kWh}\right)$$

Industrial Process Steam Systems

Industrial steam systems are commonly used in a variety of industries and manufacturing areas. These systems can be found frequently in automotive plants, power plants, the hospitality industry, and food processing. The main benefits of using steam are that it has a very high heat transfer property, the steam can be injected directly into a product, steam can evenly fill or supply a space to keep it at a consistent temperature, and steam is environmentally friendly. Steam systems do pose some safety risks that are mainly associated with burns from the superheated compound, contact with pipes carrying the heated compound, or ruptured pipes.

There are many kinds of steam available, and the type of industry or manufacturing process will dictate which type is best for a given situation. The most common types of steam are dry steam, saturated steam, superheated steam, utility steam, culinary steam, and clean steam. Saturated steam is used in pharmaceutical production, and culinary steam is used in food processing.

Turbines

Turbines harness rotational or kinetic energy from a gas (commonly steam) or liquid and convert that into energy that can be used to power a wide range of equipment for many applications. The most common types of turbines are wind turbines, water (hydro) turbines, steam turbines, and gas turbines.

Turbines are classified by their type. Gas turbines are open- or closed-cycle and are used widely in aviation, power generation, and marine applications. Steam turbines are a bit more complex and can be classified according to the steam flow direction, number of stages, point of steam entry, exhaust condition, and blade design. There are two main types of wind turbines: horizontal-axis wind turbines (HAWT) and vertical-axis wind turbines (VAWT). The two main types of hydropower turbines are reaction turbines and impulse turbines. Reaction types are the most common type used in the United States.

The advantages of using turbines are scalability, efficiency, low maintenance requirements, and high power output. One of the most considerable benefits is that they can—and usually do—run on a sustainable or renewable energy source, such as wind or water.

Using Industrial Fans

Industrial fans are mechanical ventilation systems used to provide airflow for a variety of purposes. The most common purposes are for HVAC or for cooling machinery and equipment. Industrial fans are designed to move large volumes of air at relatively low pressures. They are commonly found in warehouses, gyms, and manufacturing plants. Safety features may include overcurrent protection, vibration control, and thermal protection. These fans have numerous benefits, including occupant comfort due to better air quality, improved working conditions, and odor/moisture control.

There are three main types or categories of industrial fans: axial fans, centrifugal fans, and mixed flow fans.

In centrifugal (also called radial) fans, air blows perpendicular to the fan's axis, generating airflow. These are often used in air conditioning and industrial processing.

In axial fans, airflow is generated by air blowing parallel to the shaft on which the blades rotate. Axial fans are often used in welding shops or paint booths, where air filtration and ventilation are necessary to meet regulatory compliance and for the workers' safety and comfort.

Mixed flow fans are a hybrid between centrifugal and axial fans. They are used in both residential and commercial ventilation systems. These are used to provide fresh air and improve indoor air quality.

Industrial Refrigeration

Industrial refrigeration systems undertake the cooling and freezing of large-scale industrial processes and equipment. Industrial refrigeration is different from standard refrigeration that is commonly found in the hospitality or grocery/convenience store segments. Industrial refrigeration involves much larger cooling equipment and is necessary for industries where maintaining a certain temperature is absolutely critical. Example industries are in the chemical, pharmaceutical, and food and beverage manufacturing fields.

Large industrial refrigeration systems are complex. They have compressors, condensers, evaporators, and elaborate control systems. These systems rely on ammonia or R134A as refrigerants. Ammonia is quite efficient at all load levels but poses a safety risk if there is a leak. It also has a higher first cost. R134A is environmentally friendly and efficient at full load or mostly full load.

Calculating the Amount of Waste Heat Available from a Process

The amount of waste heat that is available from a system can be calculated this way:

$$q = m \times C_p \times (T_i - T_f)$$

In this equation m is the mass flow rate, C_p is the specific heat capacity, T_i is the initial temperature of the waste heat source, and T_f is the final temperature of the waste heat. The suitability and potential application of a waste heat source will depend upon a range of factors including these:

- Temperature—Waste heat may be low temperature (80°F up to about 450°F), medium temperature (up to about 1,200°F), or high temperature (greater than 1,200°F). The temperature of the waste heat source will dictate the potential applications for the heat.
- Amount of heat—The quantity of heat available and the demand need to be assessed. Too little heat to meet the demand may make recovery unfeasible.
- Location and timing—The source of waste heat will usually need to be reasonably close to the location it can be utilized and be available at the appropriate time; otherwise the difficulty or cost of transporting or storing the heat may make heat recovery impractical.

Heat Exchanger Flow Arrangements

Heat exchangers bring two fluids into contact to transfer heat from the higher-temperature fluid to the lower-temperature fluid. The flow arrangement of a heat exchanger is one of three types:

- Parallel flow—The hot stream and cold stream flow in the same direction.
- Counter flow—The hot stream and cold stream flow in opposite directions.
- Cross flow—The hot stream and cold stream flow perpendicular to each other.

The typical temperature differences that can be achieved with each flow arrangement is presented in the following figures:

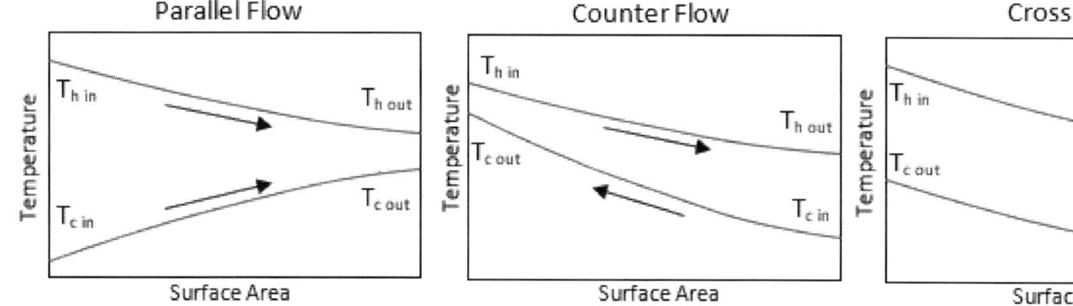

If the leaving temperature of the hot waste stream is to be cooled below the leaving temperature of the cold stream, a counter flow heat exchanger must be used. The effectiveness of a heat exchanger is defined this way:

$$\varepsilon = \frac{actual\ heat\ transferred}{maximum\ possible\ heat\ transfer}$$

The effectiveness increases as the area of a heat exchanger increases, but the increase is nonlinear, so there is a point at which increased area does not significantly improve the effectiveness. Effectiveness is usually between 50% and 90%.

Waste Heat Recovery from Liquid or Gas to a Liquid

- Economizer—An economizer is a finned tube heat exchanger. Waste heat is transferred to a liquid that is carried in pipes through the exhaust gas flue from a combustion process. Economizers are used for low to medium temperature heat recovery, so they may heat domestic hot water, preheat boiler feedwater, or produce water for process heating.
- Shell and tube heat exchanger—Low and medium temperature heat recovery can also be carried out in shell and tube heat exchangers when the fluids are at different pressures. Tubes for the higher-pressure fluid pass through a cylinder (the shell). The lower-pressure fluid or vapor that will condense flows through the shell. There may be baffles within the shell so that the fluid can make multiple passes over the tubes.
- Waste heat boiler—A waste heat water tube boiler recovers heat at medium to high temperature to produce steam. The waste heat is usually from a turbine or incinerator.

Equipment Used for Waste Heat Recovery from Gases

Waste heat recovery from a gas to another gas can be achieved with a variety of heat exchanger technologies:

- Recuperator—Waste heat from medium- to high-temperature exhaust gases from incinerators, furnaces, or ovens are suitable for recovery in a recuperator. The recovered heat is generally used to preheat the air intake for the combustion process. A recuperator recovers heat either through radiation, convection, or both. A radiation recuperator is simply an annulus around the exhaust gas flue with air passing through it that absorbs heat through radiation. In a convective recuperator the exhaust gases are carried in tubes that pass through a shell carrying the air to be heated.
- Heat wheel—A heat wheel is used for low- to high-temperature heat recovery. Heat wheels are made of a porous disk having a high specific heat. Their axis of rotation is parallel to the gas flow and between the ducts carrying the gases. They rotate through both ducts absorbing sensible heat from the hotter gas and releasing the heat into the colder gas. If a hygroscopic material is coated onto the wheel, it can also transfer latent heat.
- Passive air preheaters—Passive air preheaters are used for low- and medium-temperature applications when cross contamination of gas streams cannot occur. Plate reheaters have alternating channels of conducting metal plates. Heat pipes comprise an annular wick carrying a fluid that moves by capillary action toward the hotter end of the heat pipe. As hot gases pass over the heat pipe, the heat transfer fluid evaporates into the center of the heat pipe and flows toward the cooler end of the tube. The fluid then condenses, releasing its latent heat of vaporization into the cooler gas stream.

Determining Values for Resistances to Heat Flow in Industrial Processes

Resistance to heat flow in industrial processes is provided by insulation and the air film at the surface of the insulation.

The steady-state heat flow from a higher temperature to a cooler temperature having a temperature difference ΔT through a section of insulation having area *A* is calculated this way:

$$Q = \frac{A \times \Delta T}{\sum R}$$

The thermal resistance of the insulation is calculated this way:

$$R = \frac{t}{k}$$

In this equation *t* is the thickness of the insulation in inches, and *k* is the thermal conductivity of the insulation in Btu-in/h·ft^2·°F. Industrial insulation has a high thermal resistance, so heat loss is minimized. The surface of the insulation also has some thermal resistance due to an air film that is present close to the surface. The thermal resistance of the air film is governed by the temperature difference between the surface and the ambient air, the ambient air velocity, as well as the emissivity of the surface. The emissivity is the ability of a material to emit thermal radiation. A lower emissivity indicates less heat loss. Glass has an emissivity of about 0.9, and aluminum foil is about 0.03. Air film resistances and thermal conductivity for materials are given in tables.

Calculating the Required Thickness of Industrial Insulation

The temperature at the outside of pipe insulation should be less than 150°F for it to be safe to touch. The steady-state heat flow through a section of insulation having area *A* is calculated this way:

$$\frac{Q}{A} = \frac{temperature\ difference}{resistance\ to\ heat\ flow} = \frac{\Delta T}{\sum R} = \frac{T_{fluid} - T_{ambient}}{R_{insulation} + R_{surface}}$$

In this equation T_{fluid} is the temperature of the contained fluid at the container surface, $T_{ambient}$ is the temperature of the surrounding air, $R_{insulation}$ is the thermal resistance of the insulation, and $R_{surface}$ is the thermal resistance of the insulation surface. Because the heat flow is at steady state, the heat flow through each section is equal. Therefore, the heat flow through the insulation is the same as the heat flow from the surface (at temperature $T_{surface}$) to the environment:

$$Q = \frac{T_{fluid} - T_{surface}}{R_{insulation}} = \frac{T_{surface} - T_{ambient}}{R_{surface}}$$

The thermal resistance of the insulation is calculated this way:

$$R_{insulation} = R_{surface}\left(\frac{T_{fluid} - T_{surface}}{T_{surface} - T_{ambient}}\right) = \frac{t}{k}$$

In this equation *t* is the thickness of the insulation, and *k* is the thermal conductivity of the insulation. For example, if a tank has hot water at 180°F, the ambient air is at 70°F, the surface resistance is 0.8 h·ft^2·°F/Btu, and the thermal conductivity of the insulation is 0.28 Btu-in/h·ft^2·°F, then for a safe touch temperature of 140°F the insulation thickness should be:

$$t = 0.28 \times 0.8 \times \left(\frac{180 - 140}{140 - 70}\right) = 0.3\ inches$$

Calculating Power Required to Operate a Pump

Pumps move a liquid through a pipe distribution system by increasing the pressure within the liquid. The horsepower required for pumping is calculated this way:

$$hp = \frac{\Delta P \times Capacity}{1715 \times \eta}$$

In this equation ΔP is the differential pressure across the pump in psi, *Capacity* is the flow rate in gallons per minute, and η is the pump efficiency. The required horsepower can also be calculated based on the elevation (in feet) the water must be pumped to:

$$hp = \frac{Head \times Capacity}{3960 \times \eta}$$

The pressure the pump must produce needs to be greater than the total static head. The greater the flow rate, the less pressure the pump can produce. Pump power requirements can be reduced by installing a smaller impellor on oversized pumps; reducing motor speed whenever flow rates can be reduced; using a smaller auxiliary pump for part load situations; reducing pipe friction losses by increasing pipe diameter; and ensuring there are no leaks.

Relationship Between Head and Flow Rate for a Typical Pump

A system curve is a representation of the relationship between head and flow rate for a pipe system. The system head is a function of the pipe diameter, length, number of fittings, elevation, and flow rate. Pumps have a head and flow rate performance range with maximum head at zero flow and decreasing head as flow increases. An example system curve and pump curve is shown in the following figure:

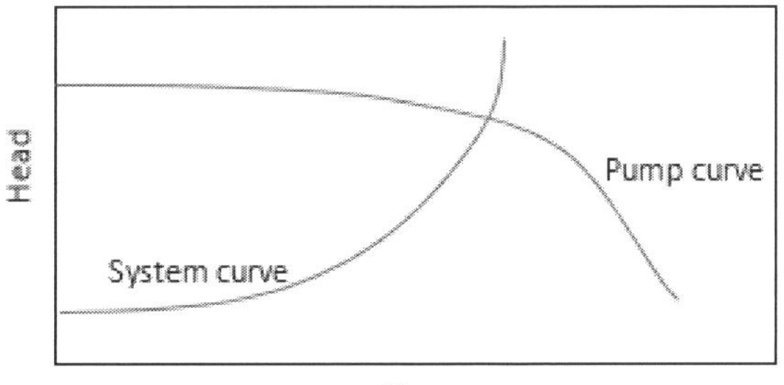

A pump that operates in the system will be operating at the point the pump curve intersects the system curve. Therefore, the pressure a pump can produce at the desired flow rate must match the system head. The pump performance curve can be changed to move the system operating point by changing the size of the pump impellor or changing the pump motor speed. Reducing the pump impeller diameter will shift the pump curve down so less head and flow rate are produced. Reducing the pump motor speed with a variable frequency drive (VFD) also shifts the pump curve downward so it operates at a point on the systems curve with less head and flow rate.

Operations, Maintenance and Commissioning

Computerized Maintenance Management Systems

A computerized maintenance management system (CMMS) optimizes the performance of maintenance operations and centralizes maintenance information and data. A CMMS consists of multiple components that perform and track maintenance and manage asset performance and life cycle. The system can be scaled and designed to meet the organization's unique requirements.

The main benefits of a computerized maintenance management system are:

- It can lead to a reduction in downtime and unplanned failures, achieved via regularly-scheduled inspections, timely repairs, and proactive maintenance.
- Compliance and documentation adherence can be improved because the system maintains a comprehensive record of safety inspections and maintenance activities.
- It leads to improved efficiency in maintenance procedures, achieved by the automation of tasks and optimization of maintenance procedures. Technicians can also make use of real-time maintenance data and efficient scheduling of tasks to reduce downtime. The life cycle of equipment is also enhanced, as the CMMS will track and manage maintenance history and supply replacement schedules.
- It integrates with other software systems, allowing for seamless and efficient data exchange.

Steam Leaks

Steam leaks can often be detected by listening for a hissing sound. When the environment is too noisy to be able to detect leaks audibly, then an ultrasonic leak detector can be used. If the amount of steam leaking from a system (in pounds per hour) cannot be measured directly, it can be estimated using Grashof's formula:

$$Steam\ Loss\left(\frac{lb}{h}\right) = 0.70 \times 0.0165 \times 3600 \times A \times P^{0.97}$$

In this equation 0.70 is a coefficient for hole shape, 0.0165 is a constant, 3600 is the number of seconds in an hour, A is the area of the hole in square inches, and P is the steam pressure in pounds per square inch. Once the steam loss has been calculated, the annual cost of the leak can be calculated using the following equation:

$$Cost\ of\ Steam\ Leak\left(\frac{\$}{yr}\right) = Cost\ of\ Steam\left(\frac{\$}{Btu}\right) \times Steam\ Loss\left(\frac{lb}{h}\right) \times Enthalpy\left(\frac{Btu}{lb}\right) \times Operating\ Hours\left(\frac{h}{yr}\right)$$

Steam Trap Loss

The most common causes of a steam trap malfunction are dirt that causes leaking or plugging of the trap, pressure surges, improper piping, and oversizing that causes the trap to work too hard.

There are three ways to calculate losses from a steam trap malfunction:

- Calculate the cost of the steam lost: $/yr = ($A$ x B x C)/1000.

A is the steam leakage in kg/h, B is operations hours/year (h/yr), and C is the steam unit cost ($/1000).

- Approximate annual steam loss (XSL): Estimate the XSL as 4% of the maximum condensate load, multiply by the number of traps, and divide by the expected life of the traps. This is widely considered the "rule of thumb method" to calculate steam trap losses.
- Estimate through an orifice using this formula: steam flow (lb/h) = 24.24 x *Pa* x *D*^2

  Pa is system pressure, and *D* is the diameter of the orifice.

Calculating the Annual Savings from Adding Insulation to the Wall of a Tank

The heat lost through an uninsulated tank wall per square foot is calculated using the basic heat loss equation:

$$\frac{q}{A}\left(\frac{Btu}{h.ft^2}\right) = U \times \Delta T$$

If the conductance, U, is not given and instead the thermal resistance, R, is given then the equation becomes the following:

$$\frac{q}{A}\left(\frac{Btu}{h.ft^2}\right) = \frac{\Delta T}{R}$$

An uninsulated metal wall will have negligible thermal resistance, but there is an air film resistance at the surface that can be found in tables. The ΔT is the temperature of the tank contents less the temperature of the ambient air. If the ambient air is moving, then the surface air film resistance will be lower, and this value can also be found in tables. The thermal resistance, R, of insulation is calculated this way:

$$R = \frac{t}{k}$$

In this equation t is the insulation thickness and k is its thermal conductivity. The total thermal resistance of an insulated metal tank wall includes the thermal resistance of the air film at the surface:

$$R_{total} = R_{insulation} + R_{surface}$$

The heat loss through the insulated wall is then calculated using the heat loss equation. The energy savings are:

$$energy\ savings\left(\frac{Btu}{h.ft^2}\right) = q_{uninsulated} - q_{insulated}$$

To determine the annual energy savings in Btu/ft^2, the result above must be multiplied by the hours of use each year and divided by the efficiency of the system:

$$annual\ energy\ savings\left(\frac{Btu}{ft^2}\right) = \frac{(q_{uninsulated} - q_{insulated}) \times h}{\eta}$$

The annual cost savings in $/ft^2 are then found by multiplying the annual energy savings by the cost of energy in $/Btu.

Boiler Scale

Boiler scale is caused by impurities in the boiler water precipitating onto the internal heat transfer surfaces of the boiler. Typical impurities that cause boiler scale are calcium and magnesium salts as well as phosphate, iron, and silica. Scale has a low thermal conductivity, so the heat transfer efficiency of the boiler decreases as the thickness of the scale increases. The approximate percentage of energy lost due to boiler scale is illustrated in the following figure:

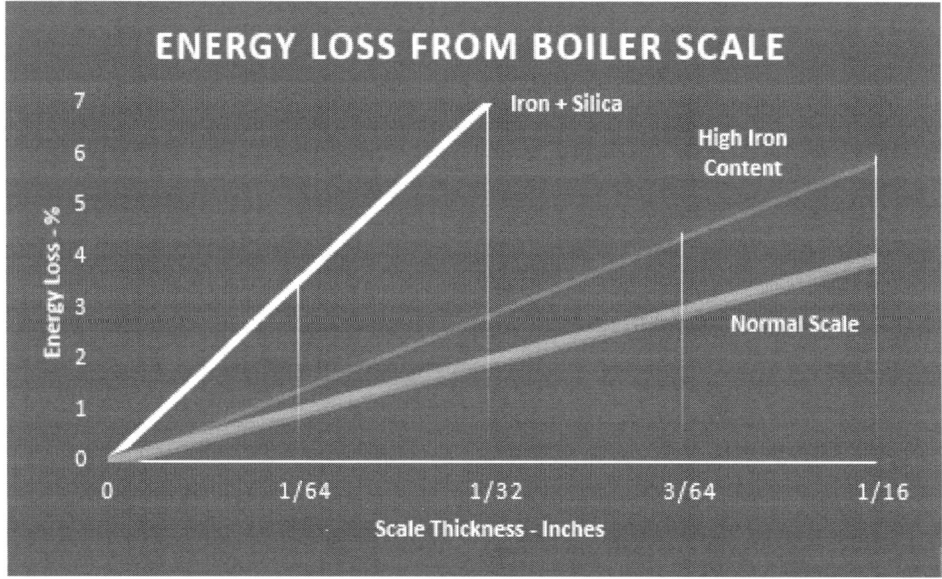

If boiler scale is not removed, it can cause blockages in tubes, corrosion of tubes can occur, and eventually the boiler may overheat, and tubes can rupture. Boilers have a water treatment system that demineralizes boiler feedwater and adds chemicals that prevents scale buildup. The water treatment system must also be regularly checked as part of a scheduled boiler maintenance program.

Group Re-Lamping Benefits

Group re-lamping is the practice of replacing lamps at scheduled intervals based on lamp life and operating hours instead of replacing lamps as they fail. Group re-lamping provides the following benefits:

- Reduced labor costs—The average time to replace an individual lamp can be significantly longer than when replacing groups of lamps in one area.
- More consistent light output—Lamps in each area have a similar output over their life; the same types of lamps are more likely to be used, and there are fewer failed lamps.
- Improved maintenance scheduling—Re-lamping can be scheduled in advance with consideration to other maintenance tasks and to minimize disruption to facility occupants.

The group re-lamping interval (GRI) is calculated this way:

$$GRI = \frac{Average\ Rated\ Lamp\ Life \times Percent\ of\ Life}{Annual\ Hours\ of\ Operation}$$

For example, the GRI for replacing lamps with a rated life of 20,000 hours at 70% of their life when they operate for 5,000 hours each year is:

$$GRI = \frac{20{,}000 \times 70\%}{5000} = 2.8\ years$$

The group re-lamping interval should be calculated based upon the site-specific costs for lamps and labor, the time it takes to change lamps individually and as a group, as well as the rated life of the lamps and the average daily hours of use. For example, a facility has 1,000 lamps having a rated life of 20,000 hours and 5,000 hours of annual operation. It takes 15 minutes to replace an individual lamp and 5 minutes to replace each lamp when part of a group re-lamping operation. Labor costs are $20 per hour, and lamp costs are $2 per lamp. The total re-lamping costs for spot re-lamping and group re-lamping at 70% of rated life are in the following table:

	Spot Re-lamping	**Group Re-lamping (70%)**
Number of lamps	1,000	1,000
Rated life (hours)	20,000	20,000
Annual hours of operation	5,000	5,000
Group re-lamping interval (years)	*n/a*	$= \frac{20{,}000 \times 70\%}{5{,}000} = 2.8$
Average annual lamp replacements	$= \frac{5{,}000}{20{,}000} \times 1{,}000 = 250$	$= \frac{1{,}000}{2.8} = 357$
Lamp replacement cost	$= \$2 \times 250 = \$500$	$= \$2 \times 357 = \$714$
Maintenance cost	$= \$20 \times \frac{15}{60} \times 250 = \$1{,}250$	$= \$20 \times \frac{5}{60} \times 357 = \$595$
Total cost	$= \$500 + \$1{,}250 = \$1{,}750$	$= \$714 + \$595 = \$1{,}309$

In the example above the cost savings from group re-lamping are about 25%. With these conditions, it would be cost-effective to carry out group re-lamping down to 52% of the lamps' rated life.

Using Infrared (IR) to Identify Maintenance Issues

Infrared (IR) imaging is a useful diagnostic tool that may be used for identifying problems requiring maintenance. IR can be used to show where areas of the building fabric have higher heat losses due to missing or inadequate insulation or gaps where air is able to pass through. Electrical connections that are faulty will be hotter than other connections, and these are easier to find with an infrared image. IR may also be used to identify steam traps that have failed; find heating ventilation and air-conditioning (HVAC) equipment with poor air flows, duct leakages, compressor problems, or poor fluid flows in coils; and assess heat generated in mechanical systems such as motor bearings. IR imaging requires some expertise to use the systems and interpret the results. The equipment is relatively expensive, but it is likely to pay for itself if one major malfunction is identified.

Problems Leading to Excessive Vibrations

Vibrations are a common indication of problems in rotating machinery such as motors for pumps and fans. Excessive vibrations may be caused by machines being out of balance or alignment, bent shafts, bearing failures, loose mountings, motor faults, or resonance. A condition based monitoring program including vibration analysis can identify issues before equipment fails. Failure of equipment or critical components will likely cost far more than the vibration analysis if an expensive repair or replacement is needed and there is significant down time while repairs are made. There are also potential safety and environmental issues if equipment fails because vibrations were not detected early. There are two main diagnostic techniques using vibration analysis: taking instantaneous snapshots to produce vibration signatures, which are then compared with baseline vibration signature values to provide an indication of a machine's condition, and taking regular measurements over the long term to identify trends so that an ongoing evaluation of condition can be gained.

Preventive, Predictive, and Proactive Maintenance Programs

Maintenance can be performed using a variety of procedures that will be influenced by the type of equipment within a facility and the budget and staff available. The most basic maintenance program is reactive maintenance, whereby equipment operates until it fails and is then repaired or replaced. This is an expensive method and would only suit a facility that could handle equipment shutdowns. Better maintenance methods include the following:

- Preventive maintenance—This is scheduled maintenance that repairs or replaces equipment at predetermined times to prevent problems occurring. This is suitable for equipment that does not operate continuously and staff who have sufficient time and skills.
- Predictive maintenance—Condition-based monitoring of equipment on an ongoing basis allows staff to identify problems before they become critical. When issues are detected, the equipment is repaired or replaced to prevent a more serious problem from occurring.
- Proactive maintenance—This method utilizes both preventive and predictive maintenance techniques, and it also identifies precise problems that cause equipment wear. This ensures that maintenance is only performed when needed and ways to improve reliability are investigated, including considering modifications or redesign.

Human Behavior in Energy Management

It is critical to understand the human component of energy management in order to have a successful and profitable energy management system. This involves understanding human-related effects on the success of energy management systems through behavior-related data and analytics.

Some examples of human behavior in energy management are allowing the controls to operate the lighting and air-conditioning systems rather than overriding to suit the occupants' needs, choosing to recycle, and observing water-conservation practices.

Many energy management systems are installed with the best of intentions, but as time goes on, training may become outdated, employees may try to circumvent maintenance procedures, employees or occupants may fall back on old habits, and new employees may not be advised of the culture or rules related to energy conservation and efficiency. Combating these behavior-related issues can help maintain proper energy management. Examples of interventions that target behavior-related issues are home energy reports (HERs) and default energy saving features for appliances.

Behavior-Based Energy Efficiency Programs

Behavior-based energy efficiency programs are divided into two main categories.

1. Education and outreach programs: These programs provide the consumer with tips on energy efficiency and ways to save money. The information can come in many forms, such as booklets, educational webinars, and mailers. Popular programs include utility-sponsored seminars and contests held in schools and universities.

2. Feedback programs: These are characterized by the consumer receiving direct or indirect feedback from a device, such as a home energy report (HER), smart meter, and/or a community or peer comparison report. Utilities often offer a home energy report program. The DOE offers a Home Energy Score program.

Benefits of behavior-based energy efficiency programs are that they are easy to implement, they often allow for direct engagement with the consumer, and they contribute to a utility's energy reduction goals while lowering the consumer's bill.

The main challenge with these programs is that the savings attributed directly to the programs are difficult to measure.

Types of Commissioning in New and Existing Buildings

- Commissioning—The process of ensuring the systems in a new building operate as intended is called commissioning. It is a systematic process to verify equipment is installed, tested, and operating as intended in the planning and design phase. Systems are documented and building operators are trained to ensure optimal operation.
- Recommissioning—The performance of buildings that were commissioned during the construction and handover phase will gradually decline as changes are made to meet new operational needs and equipment gets older. Recommissioning existing buildings will bring systems back to the original design intent or ensure that they are operating efficiently to meet current conditions.
- Retro-commissioning—A commissioning process for existing buildings that were not commissioned when they were built and handed over to the occupants is called retro-commissioning. The process is similar to commissioning a new building, but the design intent may no longer be valid under actual operating conditions, so the retro-commissioning process will aim to optimize equipment to meet current operational needs.
- Continuous commissioning—Also called real-time commissioning, continuous commissioning is an ongoing process throughout the life of a building to make sure that all systems are operating optimally to meet current conditions rather than just the original design intent.

Building Commissioning

Building commissioning is a systematic process that ensures building systems are documented, are properly installed and tested, and their operational performance is validated as meeting the intended original building design in accordance with the operational needs of the building occupants. Systems that typically require commissioning include mechanical, electrical, building automation, fire, and security systems as well as the building fabric. The purpose of commissioning is to prevent or eliminate problems with building operational performance, lower first-cost and life-cycle costs of building ownership, and improve operations and maintenance with better documentation and records. Commissioning should be considered as early as possible in the planning and design phases and implemented throughout the life of the building using a continuous commissioning process. Cost savings are the primary benefit of building commissioning. Other benefits of proper building commissioning include the following:

1. Lower energy consumption
2. Improved environmental conditions
3. Better building operation and maintenance
4. Longer equipment life

5. Increased occupant satisfaction
6. Better system documentation

PHASES, PARTICIPANTS, AND DOCUMENTATION REQUIREMENTS

Commissioning should be considered throughout every phase of a building's life. The general commissioning activities that take place during each phase include the following:

- Planning phase—Commissioning should begin in the pre-design phase. The project manager should schedule commissioning activities, and the commissioning team should be decided. A preliminary commissioning plan and budget are prepared at this stage.
- Design phase—A commissioning agent, who should ideally be an independent third-party contracted by the building owner, should lead the commissioning process. The design and owner requirements are reviewed, the commissioning plan is updated, and commissioning specifications decided.
- Construction phase—The commissioning team's goals during construction are to ensure the system requirements are met and the quality of the installation meets the necessary standards. Installation, start-up, functional tests, documentation, and operator training are carried out. The documentation required includes the owner's requirements, design intent, commissioning plan, results of facility system checks and functional tests, systems manuals and training guides, and a final commissioning report.
- Occupancy phase—The performance of systems gradually alters over time, and the needs of occupants can change, so the commissioning team will resolve any issues that arise, carry out seasonal testing and a post-occupancy review, and prepare a final commissioning report. A plan for ongoing commissioning throughout the building's life should be prepared.

ROLE OF THE COMMISSIONING AGENT/AUTHORITY

Commissioning agents (CxA) play a critical role in the construction process. They are highly specialized professionals who oversee and manage the commissioning process. The commissioning authority, also commonly known as CxA, has responsibilities broader than commissioning agents. Agents have specific, project-focused tasks, while the authority has a responsibility to develop commissioning standards, guidelines, and strategies. The CxA is an independent third party who acts as a liaison between the contractor, building owner, and all other key stakeholders.

Primary responsibilities of the CxA are:

- Ensuring that the building systems and components operate optimally and in accordance with the owner's project requirements (OPR)
- Quality assurance: ensuring that the building meets requirements, industry standards, and design specifications
- Energy efficiency optimization: achieving the maximum benefits of HVAC, lighting, and control systems
- Issue resolution and maintenance of an issue log
- Long-term/ongoing system monitoring and recommissioning plan

FACILITY DESIGN INTENT

Facility design intent is the purpose and overall vision behind creating a space or building. Properly setting the design intent helps maximize overall efficiency of time, materials, and human resources. The primary components of facility design intent include efficiency, clear documentation, training and integration, and sustainability:

Efficiency: A crucial aspect of facility design intent is carefully and thoughtfully laying out the design and placement of equipment, workstations, fixtures, offices, restrooms, etc.

Clear documentation: Clear communication and documentation of construction, operations, and maintenance procedures are essential to ensuring they are adhered to.

Training and integration: Facilities and building operations staff must be trained to ensure the facility is operated and maintained as outlined in the design intent. Strict attention to training new personnel who come on board as others retire or leave the company is critical.

Sustainability: This should be built into the facility design intent by incorporating guidelines to ensure water conservation efforts are in place, energy efficiency equipment (lighting, HVAC, controls) is selected, and recycled or reclaimed materials are used when possible.

Documentation Requirements for Building Commissioning

There are four main documentation phases in building commissioning. Each phase includes multiple documentation needs as well as a matrix for the overall commissioning process that indicates owners, approvers, and the status of the documents in each phase.

3. Pre-design/project initiation phase: Key documents are the owner's project requirements (OPR), training requirements outline, and issues log.
4. Design phase: Key documents are the updated OPR, design review comments, construction specifications, and system manual outline.
5. Construction phase: Key documents include basis of design updates, evaluation, test procedures, test data submittals, and meeting agendas and minutes. This phase has the greatest number of required documents.
6. Occupancy and operations phase: Key documents include maintenance programs, test procedures, final commissioning reports, and recommissioning plans.

The owner's project requirements (OPR) are prepared jointly by the owner and the commissioning agent. These requirements are commonly labeled as being the most critical document in the building commissioning process.

Components and Systems That Should Undergo Functional Testing

There are three main components and systems that should undergo functional testing:

Mechanical and electrical: The main areas to test include all heating, ventilation, and air-conditioning (HVAC) systems (including test and balance (TAB) procedures and duct work), fume hoods, air supply, lighting systems and controls, emergency power, grounding, and fault systems.

Building envelope: This includes testing for infiltration air leaks, interior and exterior shading control, and window tinting/glazing.

Laboratory: This includes testing process and specialty gas distribution systems, process cooling water systems, life safety systems, and toxic gas monitoring (CO, fire, etc.) systems.

Energy Savings Performance Contracting and Measurement & Verification

Measurement & Verification (M&V)

Energy savings cannot be measured directly because they are the absence of energy use. Savings are determined by measuring energy use before an energy conservation project is implemented and comparing this to the energy use after the project. Measurement & Verification (M&V) is the process for carrying out this comparison. The purpose and fundamental principles of M&V are described in the International Performance Measurement and Verification Protocol (IPMVP). M&V will, among other things, provide valuable feedback of energy conservation measures to improve design or operations and ensure the persistence of savings over time; increase project credibility and reduce risk so financing is more easily obtained; describe financial transactions in energy performance contracts; and help manage energy budgets. M&V activities should meet the following criteria:

- Accurate—Savings will be calculated as accurately as the M&V budget will allow.
- Complete—All aspects of a project should be considered, even indirect savings.
- Conservative—Savings should be underestimated where uncertainty exists.
- Consistent—Project effectiveness should be consistent for different project types.
- Relevant—Measurements of important, known parameters should be made, whereas estimates can be made of less critical parameters.
- Transparent—All M&V activities should be clearly specified.

M&V Protocols

Measurement & Verification (M&V) protocols provide a framework and options for determining energy savings. The most widely used protocol internationally is the International Performance Measurement and Verification Protocol (IPMVP). It provides four options for determining energy savings: retrofit isolation, key parameter measurement; retrofit isolation, all parameter measurement; whole facility; and calibrated simulation. The IPMVP is published by the Efficiency Valuation Organization (EVO) in three volumes. The Federal Energy Management Program (FEMP) M&V Guidelines was devised by the Department of Energy (DoE), and it must be used for all federal projects. FEMP M&V Guidelines have the same four options as IPMVP but are more specific and focused on federal energy savings performance contracts. The other M&V protocol used in the United States is the ASHRAE Guideline 14 Measurement of Energy and Demand Savings. These guidelines have three M&V options, which are the same as the IPMPVP, less the key parameter measurement option. ASHRAE Guideline 14 is more technical than the other protocols, but the fundamental principles of M&V are the same for all three protocols.

Calculating Energy Savings

Energy savings cannot be directly measured because they represent avoided energy consumption. A savings calculation is used to compare energy demand before and after an energy conservation measure is implemented:

$$Savings = \left(Energy\ Use_{Baseline\ Period} - Energy\ Use_{Reporting\ Period}\right) \pm Adjustments$$

The baseline energy use must have sufficient data to accurately represent the energy performance before the project. The baseline performance is used to predict how much energy would have been used if the project had not been implemented. The reporting period energy use is subtracted from the baseline to determine the savings. The reporting period should be at least one operating cycle to fully capture the new energy performance. The Adjustments term represents routine and non-routine adjustments to the energy performance. A routine adjustment would be energy consumption drivers that are expected to change, such as the weather. Non-routine adjustments are changes that do not usually occur, such as a change in facility size.

Energy Performance Contract Advantages and Disadvantages

Energy performance contracts enable an organization to improve its energy performance by implementing energy conservation measures without making a significant initial investment. The ability for an organization to carry out a large-scale retrofit project without using their own capital or obtaining a loan is one of the major benefits of a performance contract. Other benefits include lower risk of failure because the contractor takes on performance risk, and the ongoing maintenance of the equipment will be included in the contract. The disadvantages of a performance contract include entering a long-term contract that will mean some control is relinquished to the contractor in terms of facility operations and further upgrades to building energy services. The cost savings achieved by the project will be shared with the contractor for a significant period of time, so the overall value of savings will be reduced compared to other means of in-house financing. The performance contract will also be a more complex process that will require time and expertise to manage throughout the contract.

Financing Energy Projects

- Equity—Using in-house capital is the simplest form of financing and is usually the most cost-effective because there is no interest to pay. The cost of financing projects using in-house capital is the rate of return that could be achieved by using that capital for other alternatives. Insufficient capital and taking on all the project risks are two drawbacks to using in-house capital.
- Loans—Borrowing funds for projects can be financially beneficial if the cost of borrowing is low enough for the life of the project. All the project risk is with the organization because the loan will still need to be repaid even if the project does not achieve the expected savings.
- Leases—Leasing options include capital leases and operating leases. These arrangements allow an organization to pay for equipment in installments with various conditions.
- Performance contract—A performance contract is an agreement between an organization and an energy services company (ESCO) whereby the ESCO finances the project and the organization pays the ESCO a fee that is less than the value of the energy savings. Performance contracts enable an organization to reduce or almost eliminate project risk.

Loans, Stocks, and Bonds as Financing Instruments

Loans offer a straightforward method for financing Energy Savings Performance Contracts (ESPC). Loans can be initiated through a bank or other financial institution, much like a mortgage. The energy savings derived from the project can be used to pay the loan. This is a common approach. Stocks are not often used, due to their volatility, but a corporation could issue shares to raise capital for the ESPC project. Bonds are issued by governments or organizations and can also be used as financing instruments. Tax-exempt lease-purchase agreements (TELP) allow for tax-exempt financing of energy efficiency projects. These can be utilized by state and local governments. Not-for-profits may also qualify.

Tax-Exempt Lease-Purchase Agreements (TELP)

Tax-exempt lease-purchase agreements (TELPs) allow a public entity, such as a city, county, school district, or public university, to enter into a purchase agreement that is paid for by its annual revenues. This is the most common type of lease arrangement used by public entities. With a TELP, a public entity can acquire equipment and assets without incurring long-term debt and own the assets at the end of the lease term. Tax-exempt lease-purchase agreements can, in some cases, be extended to 501(c)(3) not-for-profit entities, special purpose districts, and hospitals. The list of eligible items is extensive and includes both personal property and real property. Examples of eligible items include energy management systems, vehicles, software, HVAC systems, and modular buildings. The main benefits of TELPs are preservation of capital, low rates, improved cash flow, and the fact that no voter approval is required. This allows for a much quicker and simpler approval process.

Utility Financing

Also known as utility on-bill financing, this uses the utility bill as the vehicle for payment of the project. This is particularly attractive if a client wants to embed the payment into the utility bill. The project may be financed by the utility itself or by a third-party entity or lender. Advantages include the possibility of the utility offering lower loan rates, the ease of there being no additional bill for the project, and the ability to pay any incentives or rebates directly to the client or apply them to the project. Utility on-bill programs will differ by utility and state due to regulatory structure. They can be run as tariffs, loans, or service agreements, though loans are the most common.

Capital and Operating Leases for Financing Energy Projects

- Capital lease—A capital lease is an arrangement whereby the equipment is an asset on the balance sheet of the lessee. They are suitable for long-term leases of equipment that will not become obsolete. To be considered a capital lease, at least one of the following must be true:
- Ownership of the property transfers to the lessee at the end of the contract term.
- There is a bargain purchase option at the end of the lease for less than the fair market value, sometimes for just $1.
- The lease term is more than 75% of the useful life of the equipment.
- The present value of the lease payments is more than 90% of the fair market value of the equipment.
- Operating lease—An operating lease is a type of rental agreement whereby the lessor owns the equipment, so the equipment does not show on the lessee's balance sheet. These leases are suitable for short-term use of equipment and do not meet any of the criteria for capital leases. The lessee may have the option to buy the equipment at the end of the contract or have the equipment removed.

Utility Energy Services Contracts (UESCs)

A utility energy services contract (UESC) is an agreement between a federal agency and its serving utility for energy management services. These services can include energy and water efficiency improvements and energy-demand reduction efforts. The utility energy services contract is a limited-source acquisition between the federal agency and the utility. This is often called *sole source procurement*, and it allows a government entity to enter into a contract with a supplier without going through the typical lengthy, competitive bid process. There is no limit on the size of the project, and a UESC greatly simplifies energy efficiency projects and strengthens the relationship with the serving utility. UESC is part of the FEMP (Federal Energy Management Plan) Utility Program, and billions of dollars have been awarded to fund UESC projects. Energy conservation measures can include simple lighting retrofits and controls, HVAC improvements, complex thermal energy storage, and renewable energy projects.

Energy Performance Contracts

Principles and Stakeholders

An energy performance contract is an agreement between an organization seeking to reduce its energy costs and an energy services company (ESCO) that designs, builds, operates, and maintains equipment to achieve reduced energy costs. The ESCO will generally arrange finance for the capital investment, and the organization will pay for the project from the energy savings achieved. At the end of the contract, the full benefits of the energy savings are retained by the organization. A lender that provides the necessary capital is often a party to the energy performance contract and will carefully evaluate the project's risks, such as the ability of the ESCO to achieve the savings and the organization to make payments. Utility companies may also be stakeholders if they offer a rebate to the ESCO for certain equipment or demand response participation.

Energy Performance Contract Structures

There are a variety of contractual arrangements that an energy services company (ESCO) will use to reduce a customer's energy costs:

- Guaranteed savings—The ESCO designs and implements a project and guarantees the amount of energy savings that will be achieved. The ESCO accepts the performance risk for the project, so any savings shortfall will be met by the ESCO. The ESCO may facilitate financing arrangements, but the customer will contract directly with a lender.
- Shared savings—The ESCO designs, finances, and implements a project, and the energy savings are shared between the customer and the ESCO for a specified period. The amount of savings is not guaranteed, and contracts may be longer than needed for guaranteed savings, so the ESCO can recover the investment costs.
- Chauffage—An ESCO will take over the operation and maintenance of equipment and charge fees to provide specified services, such as cooling and heating. Any investment in equipment upgrades will be made by the ESCO, but ownership remains with the customer.

Savings and/or Avoided Cost Calculations Associated with an Energy Savings Performance Contract

In addition to savings that come from a reduction in energy and resource usage, savings can come from the elimination of maintenance contracts or from the reduction of maintenance staff. The savings are calculated from a simple equation:

O&M Cost Savings = (Adjusted Baseline O&M Costs) – (Actual O&M Costs)

Savings can also come from a decreased need for equipment replacement. More efficient, longer-lasting lighting is a prime example of this. A reduction of contract labor associated with installing new equipment should also be factored into savings calculations.

Projects should include adequate documentation and verification of performance savings. Items to include:

- Dates and times of on-site verification activities (note: witnessing is required for federal ESPCs). The main verification activities include determining a baseline, developing the M&V plan, a post-installation M&V report, and continuing to perform M&V annually.

- Review of key variables that impact the realization of savings. These include weather, occupancy, change in building usage, disruption or malfunction of building automation systems (BAS), and fuel and utility rates.
- Verification that standards of performance have been met.

Key Parameter Measurement Option for M&V

Option A of the International Performance Measurement and Verification Protocol (IPMVP) and Federal Energy Management Program (FEMP) M&V Guidelines describe a retrofit isolation method for determining energy savings whereby only one important parameter is measured and other parameters may be estimated. Estimation of non-critical parameters is allowed if the uncertainty in the estimation does not significantly affect the calculated savings. The choice of parameter to measure should be the parameter of interest that is affected by the energy conservation project. For example, if a lighting retrofit project is being carried out that will reduce the power, but the hours of operation are not expected to change, then the power before and after the project should be measured, and the hours can be estimated. This option enables M&V cost to be minimized by avoiding measurements of some parameters. This method is also called the spot measurement method because measurements are often taken only once for a short period of time.

All Parameter Measurement Option for M&V

Option B of the International Performance Measurement and Verification Protocol (IPMVP) and Federal Energy Management Program (FEMP) M&V Guidelines describe a retrofit isolation method for determining energy savings whereby all parameters that determine the energy consumption are measured and no estimates are allowed. This option is used when parameters affecting energy are highly variable, the energy conservation measure can be isolated and metered appropriately, and overall savings are relatively small compared to the entire facility. Option B is generally the most accurate M&V method, but costs can be greater depending upon the number of meters required and length of measurement period. A typical application for Option B may be the addition of a variable frequency drive to a pump, which would require continuous measurement because the power and operating time would be variable. The measurement period may be short or long term depending upon the operating cycle of the equipment because the full range of operating conditions should be measured to capture all potential savings.

Whole Facility Option for M&V

Option C of the International Performance Measurement and Verification Protocol (IPMVP) and Federal Energy Management Program (FEMP) M&V Guidelines describe a whole facility method for determining energy savings whereby the energy consumption of the entire facility is measured and energy savings are determined by comparing total energy consumption before and after one or more energy conservation measures are implemented. This option is used when the expected savings are large, usually greater than 10% of the total facility energy consumption, so the impact of the energy conservation measures can be detected in utility meter bills; therefore, this method is also called the utility bill comparison method. This option is best suited for when there are many retrofit projects within one facility, when retrofit projects are difficult to measure independently, and the relationship between energy consumption and independent driving factors is well established. A retrofit project that may be best suited to Option C is one including building fabric upgrades, occupant behavior change, and building recommissioning because these are difficult to measure independently and there are many interactive effects that are not easy to isolate. The cost of M&V using this option may be low because the use of existing meters is often sufficient.

CALIBRATED SIMULATION OPTION FOR M&V

Option D of the International Performance Measurement and Verification Protocol (IPMVP) and Federal Energy Management Program (FEMP) M&V Guidelines describe a computer simulation method for determining energy savings whereby the energy consumption of the entire facility or individual systems is estimated using a calibrated model that accurately predicts energy use. Energy savings are determined by comparing predicted energy consumption with actual energy consumption. The simulation model may be used to predict either baseline energy consumption or reporting period energy consumption but not both. This method is usually used only when no other option is feasible. It is a good option for new buildings that do not have baseline data, so the performance of energy-efficiency measures beyond standard building specifications can be evaluated. In this case the simulation model would be calibrated so that it closely matches actual energy consumption, and then the energy-efficiency measures are removed from the model to determine what energy consumption would have been without the efficiency measures.

Practice Test

Want to take this practice test in an online interactive format?
Check out the online resources page, which includes interactive practice questions and much more: **mometrix.com/resources719/energymanager**

1. The Coefficient of Performance of a chiller is 3.2. What is its efficiency in kW/ton?

a. 1.10
b. 1.25
c. 1.33
d. 1.56

2. Consider a 30 horsepower three-phase motor with name plate rated performance of 93.6% efficiency drawing 35 A at 460 V. What is the power factor of this motor at 100% load?

a. 0.80
b. 0.86
c. 0.90
d. 0.92

3. Which of the following statements regarding net zero energy buildings is true?

a. Net zero energy buildings do not need to purchase electricity from the grid
b. There are no net greenhouse gas emissions from net zero energy buildings
c. All the energy used in a net zero energy building is produced using renewable sources
d. Net zero energy buildings generate at least as much energy as they use each year

4. A company plans to invest the savings generated by a boiler retrofit project to pay for a lighting upgrade five years from now. The lighting project is expected to cost $80,000 and the company has fixed price contracts for the next five years of $0.085/kWh and $7/Mcf. How many Btu's of energy must the new boiler save each year if the company can invest the savings at 10%? (Assume 1 Mcf = 1,037,000 Btu).

a. 526 MMBtu
b. 1217 MMBtu
c. 1941 MMBtu
d. 3126 MMBtu

5. Which of the following conditions is not typically a primary indication that thermal energy storage is suitable for a facility?

a. High peak demand charges
b. Low cooling loads at night
c. Lower energy costs at night
d. Low cooling system efficiency

6. Which of the following conditions will occur if insufficient oxygen is provided to a boiler during combustion of natural gas?

a. The amount of carbon dioxide in the flue gas will increase
b. The efficiency of the boiler will improve because there is less air to heat
c. Less heat is lost in the stack
d. Carbon monoxide will be produced

7. Which of the following actions is the most appropriate at the start of an energy audit?

a. A walk-through of the facility to identify energy efficiency opportunities
b. An analysis of at least 12 months of utility bills to understand the rate structures and monthly energy demands
c. Set-up of metering and monitoring equipment for all energy end-uses
d. Calculation of potential savings from no-cost and low-cost energy conservation measures such as changes to equipment schedules

8. The HVAC system in a building was recommissioned at a cost of $18,000 and produced annual savings of $5,700. What is the minimum amount of time the savings need to persist if the building owner uses a discount rate of 10%?

a. 3 years
b. 4 years
c. 5 years
d. 6 years

9. What is the required minimum floor area to be eligible for LEED Operations + Maintenance certification?

a. 250 ft^2
b. 1,000 ft^2
c. 2,500 ft^2
d. 10,000 ft^2

10. The apparent power in a facility with a real power demand of 600 kW and a power factor of 0.87 is:

a. 522 kVA
b. 612 kVA
c. 690 kVA
d. 705 kVA

11. Which of the following is not typically part of a lender's risk assessment of an Energy Savings Performance Contract?

a. Value of savings
b. Customer creditworthiness
c. Project complexity
d. Contract terms

12. A natural gas fired combined heat and power engine can produce 500 kW of power and 2.2 MMBtu/hour at an overall efficiency of 90%. What is its rate of fuel consumption in Mcf/hour? (Assume 1 Mcf = 1,037,000 Btu)

a. 3.77 Mcf/hour
b. 4.19 Mcf/hour
c. 4.42 Mcf/hour
d. 4.77 Mcf/hour

13. What is the primary benefit of VRF (variable refrigerant flow)?

a. It serves extremely large spaces.
b. It takes advantage of using varying types of refrigerants.
c. It precisely controls the amount of refrigerant flowing to multiple zones.
d. It operates at full capacity at all times.

14. Calculate the annual heat loss through the roof of a building having an area of 5,000 ft2 and a U-value of 0.04 when there are 4,000 heating degree days.

a. 16,800,000 Btu/year
b. 19,200,000 Btu/year
c. 21,300,000 Btu/year
d. 23,900,000 Btu/year

15. Which of the following is a key component of greenhouse gas (GHG) reporting?

a. Compliance with US climate change policy
b. ESG governance
c. Qualification for state funds
d. Carbon footprint calculation

16. A facility has a power factor of 0.83 and would like to increase this to 0.90 by installing a capacitor bank. If the demand in the facility is 1,200 kW, what size capacitor bank should be connected?

a. 207 kVAR
b. 218 kVAR
c. 225 kVAR
d. 236 kVAR

17. Which of the following is not a financial mechanism commonly employed by utilities to encourage the development of distributed energy technologies?

a. Net metering
b. Power-Purchase Agreement
c. Energy performance contract
d. Rebate

18. Why does a supply air reset control strategy save energy?

a. The ventilation system fans are slowed down using VFDs when the pressure in the system is too high
b. The amount of outside air supplied to rooms is adjusted depending upon the outside air temperature
c. When a building is unoccupied the heating setpoint is allowed to decrease or the cooling setpoint can increase
d. The supply air temperature is allowed to increase in order to minimize the amount of reheat required

19. Which of the following statements regarding heat exchanger effectiveness is not true?

a. Effectiveness increases non-linearly with increasing area after a certain size
b. The effectiveness of counter flow heat exchangers is generally better than parallel flow heat exchangers
c. Effectiveness is usually between 50% and 90%
d. The effectiveness is the ratio of potential heat transfer possible depending upon the temperatures of the two streams to the actual heat transfer

20. In January a facility had a peak demand of 525 kW and used 190,000 kWh. What was the facility's load factor?

a. 8%
b. 36%
c. 41%
d. 49%

21. During the past 12 months a 150,000 square foot facility used 1,350,000 kWh of electricity and 7,500 MMBtu of natural gas. The cost of electricity is $0.085/kWh and the cost of natural gas is $7.50/Mcf. What is the Energy Cost Index of the facility? (Assume 1 Mcf = 1.037 MMBtu).

a. $1.11/ft2
b. $1.13/ft2
c. $1.15/ft2
d. $1.17/ft2

22. Which of the following factors is not relevant when considering the feasibility of installing a waste heat recovery system on an air compressor?

a. The pressure of the compressed air system
b. The horsepower of the air compressor
c. When the air compressor operates each day
d. What the waste heat will be used for

23. A chilled water thermal storage system requires a capacity of 4,000 ton-hours. If the chilled water is stored at 39°F and the return temperature is 59°F, then what volume of water is required for this storage system?

a. 287,600 gallons
b. 294,300 gallons
c. 303,100 gallons
d. 310,700 gallons

24. The purpose of ASHRAE Standard 189.1 is to

a. specify minimum requirements for HVAC system energy performance.
b. establish a green building assessment protocol.
c. specify minimum requirements for the design of green buildings.
d. establish methods of testing the seasonal efficiency of air conditioners and heat pumps.

25. Which of the following best describes demand in electrical power systems?

a. It is measured in kilowatt-hours (kWh).
b. It represents the total amount of energy used over a period of time.
c. It represents the maximum amount of power consumed at a given instant.
d. It refers to electricity used during off-peak hours.

26. A natural gas fired boiler operates with a combustion air inlet temperature of 80°F with flue gas at 730°F and 3% flue gas oxygen. It is proposed that an economizer be installed that will reduce the flue gas temperature to 630°F. The annual gas consumption of the boiler is 7,000 Mcf and gas costs $8.00/Mcf. What are the expected fuel cost savings by installing the economizer?

a. $1,904/year
b. $1,650/year
c. $1,825/year
d. $2,030/year

27. Which of the following economic analysis methods does not consider the time value of money?

a. Simple Payback Period
b. Present Worth Analysis
c. Life Cycle Cost
d. Benefit Cost Ratio

28. Which of the following is not a LEED rating system?

a. LEED for Homes
b. LEED for Neighborhood Development
c. LEED for Interior Design + Construction
d. LEED for Schools

29. Which of the following is not one of the four allowable criteria for a capital lease?

a. The ownership of the asset is transferred to the lessee by the end of the lease term
b. There is a bargain purchase option, so the lessee can buy the asset at less than the market value
c. The lease period is at least 75% of the asset's useful life
d. The value of the asset at the end of the lease must be at least 20% of its value at the start of the lease

30. An office building uses 1,200,000 kWh of electricity each year and 4,000 Mcf of natural gas. A lighting retrofit will save 80,000 kWh each year by reducing the power demand when the lights are switched on. Which measurement and verification method would be most appropriate?

a. Spot measurement
b. Continuous measurement
c. Utility bill comparison
d. Calibrated simulation

31. A company is considering a lighting retrofit project that will cost $86,000 to implement and have projected annual savings of $27,000. The company uses a discount rate of 12% and will need to invest $90,000 in a new boiler in three years' time. The lighting project can only proceed if the savings produced by the project over three years are greater than the investment required for the boiler. Should the company invest in the lighting project?

a. Yes
b. No

32. Which of the following is not a combined heat and power system operating cycle?

a. Topping cycle
b. Bottoming cycle
c. Combustion cycle
d. Combined cycle

33. Natural gas is currently trading at $8.50/Mcf but the weather during the next winter is expected to be milder than average so the price may fall. A hospital facility manager would like to set a maximum cost for natural gas for the next year but does not want to pay more than necessary if the price drops later in the year. Which would be the best pricing strategy for this facility manager?

a. Index pricing
b. Fixed pricing
c. Index with a cap
d. Interruptible supply

34. A chiller retrofit project is being considered that will reduce energy consumption in a building by 150,000 kWh per year. The cost of electricity is currently $0.09/kWh, and this price is expected to increase by $0.009/kWh each year for the next 5 years. The new chiller will cost $200,000 and will have a useful life of 15 years. If the tax rate is 35% and the organization's discount rate is 15%, what is the present value of the after-tax savings after 5 years? (Use straight-line depreciation.)

a. $13,441
b. $45,056
c. $50,124
d. $66,317

35. Which lamp technology generally has the better Color Rendering Index?

a. Metal halide
b. Fluorescent
c. LED
d. Incandescent

36. The outside air has a dry bulb temperature of 70°F and a wet bulb temperature of 64°F. What is the dew point of the air?

a. 58°F
b. 61°F
c. 64°F
d. 66°F

37. Which of the following is not typically a goal of a facility energy audit?

a. Identify the sources and costs of energy used
b. Understand how energy is used and where any waste occurs
c. Determine which energy end-use services are not required
d. Calculate the potential energy and cost savings from implementing suitable energy conservation measures identified during a facility walk-through

38. The output of a chiller is 100 tons of cooling with a supply water temperature of 45°F. If the return water temperature is 55°F, what is the chilled water flow rate?

a. 200 gpm
b. 215 gpm
c. 233 gpm
d. 240 gpm

39. The electrical bills for a facility are charged according to the following rate structure:

Customer charge = $18.00/month
Electricity cost = $0.028/kWh
Fuel cost adjustment = $0.031/kWh
Demand charge = $4.20/kW/month
Delivery charge = $4.50/kW/month

A lighting retrofit project is undertaken that exchanges 200 T8 lamps that have a power demand of 36 W with LED lamps that each use 18 W. The lamps operate for 4,380 hours each year. What are the annual electricity cost savings from this retrofit?

a. $644
b. $932
c. $961
d. $1,306

40. Which key performance indicator is NOT commonly calculated in an energy audit?

a. Site energy use intensity (EUI)
b. Lumens per square foot
c. Cost savings in energy consumption and ROI
d. Carbon footprint reduction

41. Which of the following methods of control is an example of an automatic, open loop system?

a. Thermostat
b. Manual switch
c. Pressure sensor
d. Timer

42. What is the reduction in heat loss from an uninsulated 4.5" diameter steel pipe carrying 170°F water if 2 inches of fiberglass insulation with an aluminium cover is added? The ambient air temperature is 70°F, the thermal conductivity of fiberglass is 0.33 Btu.in/hr.ft2.°F, the thermal resistance of steel is 0.72 hr.ft2.°F/Btu, and the thermal resistance of aluminium is 0.8 hr.ft2.°F/Btu.

a. $118.1\,\frac{\text{Btu}}{\text{ft}^2\cdot\text{hr}}$
b. $122.3\,\frac{\text{Btu}}{\text{ft}^2\cdot\text{hr}}$
c. $127.8\,\frac{\text{Btu}}{\text{ft}^2\cdot\text{hr}}$
d. $131.6\,\frac{\text{Btu}}{\text{ft}^2\cdot\text{hr}}$

43. A building owner replaced a #2 fuel oil-fired boiler which had an efficiency of 80% with a natural gas condensing boiler which has an efficiency of 92%. The price of oil is $2.30 per gallon and the price of gas is $0.85 per therm. If the facility uses 4,100 MMBtu each year and the new boiler will cost $140,000, what is the simple payback period?

a. 2.8 years
b. 3.0 years
c. 3.7 years
d. 4.9 years

44. The efficiency of an old natural gas fired boiler is 76% and it has a remaining life of 5 years. A boiler economizer was installed that cost $15,000 and improved the overall boiler efficiency to 81%. The value of the economizer after the boiler is taken out of service is $10,000. The annual fuel demand before the economizer was installed was 6,500 MMBtu and gas costs $8.00/Mcf. If the company's discount rate is 12%, what is the Net Present Value of the economizer? (Assume 1 Mcf = 1,037,000 Btu).

a. -$3,849
b. -$288
c. $1,825
d. $6,151

45. A 25,000 ft^2 building used 900,000 kWh of electricity and 1,200 Mcf of natural gas over the past 12 months. What is the Energy Use Index of the building? (Assume 1 Mcf = 1,037,000 Btu)

a. 97.3 kBtu/ft^2
b. 112.4 kBtu/ft^2
c. 122.8 kBtu/ft^2
d. 172.6 kBtu/ft^2

46. Which of the following systems would be most suitable to have measurements taken with a bourdon gauge?

a. Lighting
b. Electrical supply
c. Building envelope
d. Boiler

47. The cooling load profile for a building is shown in the figure below. Determine the load the chiller should operate at under a load levelling strategy.

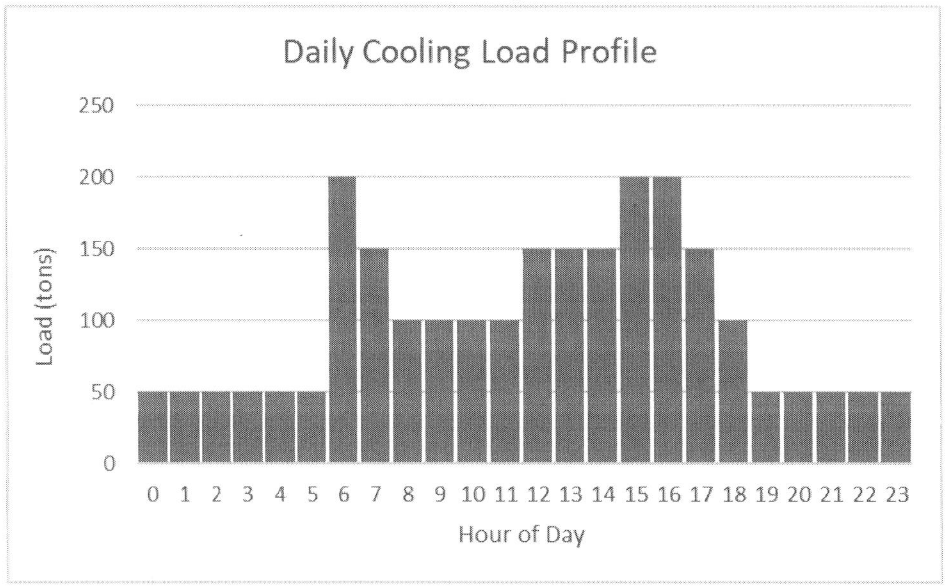

a. 100 tons
b. 125 tons
c. 133 tons
d. 150 tons

48. A 100 psi steam distribution line has a 3/16th inch diameter leak. The steam boiler has an efficiency of 85% and operates for 6,570 hours each year. What is the energy loss from this leak each year? (Hint: first use Grashof's formula to estimate the amount of steam leaking in lb/hour, and assume a 0.70 coefficient of discharge.)

a. 780 MMBtu
b. 918 MMBtu
c. 1,176 MMBtu
d. 1,312 MMBtu

49. What is the state of a refrigerant in a vapor compression cycle chiller as it leaves the condenser?

a. A high temperature, high pressure vapor
b. A low temperature, low pressure vapor
c. A high temperature, high pressure liquid
d. A low temperature, low pressure liquid

50. What is the purpose of building commissioning?

a. To ensure that building services systems operate as they were intended
b. To provide documentation of the building design and construction to improve operation and maintenance over the life of a building
c. To reduce operating costs and optimize energy use
d. All of the above

51. To recover waste heat from a liquid, which of the following technologies should be used?

a. Recuperator
b. Shell and tube heat exchanger
c. Heat pipe
d. Heat wheel

52. What is the measure of how well a lamp produces light and has units of lumens per watt?

a. Luminous flux
b. Efficacy
c. Coefficient of Utilization
d. Efficiency

53. How much flash steam can be recovered from 4000 lb/hour of boiler blowdown in a 100 psia steam system if the flash steam is recovered in a vessel at 30 psia?

a. 227 lb/hour
b. 296 lb/hour
c. 304 lb/hour
d. 336 lb/hour

54. Which of the following factors affecting natural gas prices is not a demand side impact?

a. Seasonal weather variations
b. Natural disasters
c. The economy
d. The price of alternative fuels

55. What is the annual after-tax cash flow of a new boiler economizer if it costs $50,000 to install, will save $8,000 per year, and has a useful life of 10 years after which it is worth nothing? Assume a tax rate of 30% and use straight-line depreciation.

a. $2,600
b. $5,600
c. $6,500
d. $7,100

56. ASHRAE Standard 90.1 specifies energy standards for which type of building?

a. Existing buildings
b. High-performance green buildings
c. Low-rise residential buildings
d. Buildings except low-rise residential buildings

57. What type of measurements are taken by a pyrometer?

a. Temperature
b. Carbon dioxide level
c. Relative humidity
d. Light intensity

58. How does the efficiency and power factor of an AC induction motor vary as the percentage of rated load applied to the motor changes?

a. Efficiency and power factor increase linearly as the load factor increases and reach a maximum at 100% of rated load
b. Efficiency and power factor increase linearly up to about 75% of rated load and then remain constant until 100% of rated load
c. Efficiency and power factor increase non-linearly as the load factor increases, but efficiency peaks at about 75% of rated load and then begins to decrease
d. Efficiency increases proportionately to an increase in applied load, but power factor increases non-linearly until about 75% or rated load and then begins to decrease

59. Which of the following solutions for use in a variable volume system has power input performance most closely matched to a variable frequency drive?

a. Outlet damper
b. Variable inlet vane
c. Eddy current drive
d. Valve damper

60. Which of the following is an example of a smart city technology?

a. AI-powered smart parking solutions
b. Laptop computers for the public
c. Online bus schedules
d. Large number of top colleges and universities in the city

61. At 100% load, what is typically the largest type of loss within an AC motor?

a. Friction and windage losses
b. Core losses
c. Stray load losses
d. Resistive losses

62. Which of the following is the best definition of a demand ratchet?

a. The kW demand charge for the peak power demand above a predetermined level of power in a single month
b. The kW demand charge for the difference between the peak kW demand and the average kW demand in a single month
c. The difference in the kW demand charge between the on-peak demand charge and the off-peak demand charge
d. The minimum monthly kW demand charge that is calculated as a percentage of the highest peak demand over the previous year

63. Which of the following statements is true of thermally heavy buildings?

a. The R2 value in a regression analysis of fuel consumption vs. degree days is generally higher than 0.8.
b. They heat up and cool down quickly
c. Less energy savings can be expected when the Building Load Coefficient (UA) is improved through building fabric upgrades
d. They are made of materials with low specific heat capacity

64. If the air to fuel ratio of a natural gas boiler is 10:1, approximately how much excess oxygen is present?

a. 2%
b. 5%
c. 10%
d. 80%

65. What is the load factor of a 10 HP motor with an efficiency of 94.1% when it is producing 6.3 kW of power?

a. 79%
b. 81%
c. 83%
d. 85%

66. How much waste heat is recovered from a process that reduces the temperature of hot water flowing at 20 gallons per minute from 200°F to 140°F?

a. 542,900 Btu/hour
b. 570,100 Btu/hour
c. 586,020 Btu/hour
d. 600,480 Btu/hour

67. Which of the following is not a source of current harmonics in an electrical system?

a. incandescent lighting
b. fluorescent lighting
c. variable frequency drives
d. computers

68. What is the minimum score required for a building to become Energy Star certified?

a. 50
b. 70
c. 75
d. 95

69. Which of the following HVAC systems described below is a multizone system?

a. Return air and outside air are mixed, a portion of the air is heated and the other portion is cooled, before being mixed at the air handling unit to reach the desired supply temperature for each separately ducted zone
b. Return air and outside air are mixed and then a portion of the air is heated and the other portion is cooled. The hot and cold air are distributed through separate ducts and mixed in terminal boxes at each zone
c. Return air and outside air are mixed before entering a conditioning section where the air is heated and/or cooled to a varying supply temperature before being supplied via a constant speed fan to each zone which are equipped with reheat units
d. Return air and outside air are mixed before entering a conditioning section where the air is heated and/or cooled to a predetermined temperature, and then supplied via a variable speed fan to at least one zone, which have dampers to control the amount of air supplied and may also have reheat units

70. Which of the following is not usually considered to be a light loss factor when assessing a lighting system using the lumen method?

a. Lamp lumen depreciation
b. Ballast factor
c. Lamp life
d. Luminaire dirt depreciation

71. Which of the following statements regarding the relationship between pump and systems curves is not correct?

a. As the flow rate increases, the system head increases
b. The head and flow rate of a pump is the point where its performance intersects the system curve
c. Pumps have a maximum head at zero flow rate
d. The pump performance curve cannot be changed

72. Which of the following methods is not a method of depreciation?

a. Declining-balance
b. Sum-of-Years Digits
c. Accelerated Cost Recovery System
d. Life-Cycle Cost

73. Which of the following data communication protocols is described in ASHRAE 135-2016?

a. LonWorks
b. Modbus
c. BACnet
d. Zigbee

74. The power demand in a facility with a three-phase supply is 200 kW. The voltage is 460 V and the current is 270 A. What is the power factor?

a. 0.89
b. 0.91
c. 0.93
d. 0.95

75. The speed of a 60 Hz, 75 HP motor is measured at 1744 RPM. If the Full Load RPM of the motor is 1780, what is the true slip?

a. 20
b. 36
c. 56
d. 66

76. If a lighting system has a Visual Comfort Probability rating of 80% then it means that

a. 80% of people will not complain about the level of illumination.
b. 80% of people will be comfortable with the amount of glare from the light fixtures.
c. 80% of people will be able to distinguish colors correctly.
d. 80% of people will be comfortable with the contrast in the room.

77. The high bay lamps in a factory are mounted 45 feet above the floor. The lighting level at the floor is 10 footcandles. One area of the warehouse needs to increase the lighting level to 50 footcandles, so it is proposed that the lamps in this area be lowered. What is the greatest lamp height that would provide the required lighting level?

a. 20 feet
b. 24 feet
c. 27 feet
d. 31 feet

78. During a compressed air system audit, a pressure drop of 20 psi was observed over 15 minutes. The system operates at 110 psi and has a total volume of 400 cubic feet. Calculate the average leakage rate in the system.

a. 36 cfm
b. 40 cfm
c. 42 cfm
d. 46 cfm

79. The air handling unit for an office has a 20 HP motor that operates at full speed. An energy audit of the office has determined that the air flow of the HVAC system can be reduced by 20%. What is the new HP requirement for the air handling unit motor?

a. 10.2 HP
b. 12.4 HP
c. 15.1 HP
d. 16.0 HP

80. Which standard specifies minimum requirements for ventilation and indoor air quality?

a. ASHRAE 55
b. ASHRAE 62.1
c. ASHRAE 90.2
d. ASHRAE 189.1

81. What is the main goal of demand-side management (DSM)?

a. Infrastructure efficiency
b. To give customers money to change out equipment
c. For utilities to lower a customer's bill
d. Building new efficient power plants

82. Which of the following best describes passive design?

a. Systems that do not include any active mechanical systems
b. Systems that seek to eliminate all active HVAC systems
c. An approach that aims to use local climate and natural resources to reduce reliance on mechanical systems
d. An approach that seeks to use only local climate and resources to provide cooling and lighting to a building

83. What is the maximum contract term a federal agency may have for an Energy Saving Performance Contract?

a. 10 years
b. 15 years
c. 25 years
d. 40 years

84. Which of the following control signals is an analog input?

a. Temperature
b. Valve position
c. Lighting switch
d. Smoke detector

85. Which Act required utilities to purchase power generated by qualifying cogeneration facilities?

a. Public Utilities Regulatory Policy Act (PURPA)
b. Public Utility Holding Company Act (PUHCA)
c. The Energy Independence and Security Act of 2007
d. The Energy Policy Act of 2005

86. Two potential projects to replace a fuel oil fired boiler have been identified. The first option is to install a natural gas fired boiler that will cost $150,000 to install and will provide annual savings of $30,000 for 15 years. The second option is to install a biomass boiler that will cost $200,000 after a rebate of $25,000 is received, and will save $40,000 per year for 12 years. Which project is a better investment if the minimum attractive rate of return on the investment is 15%?

a. Option 1 – natural gas boiler
b. Option 2 – biomass boiler
c. Neither option
d. Both options are equal

87. Calculate the annual heating cost savings per square foot for a facility that adds insulation which drops the overall U-value of the building from 0.25 to 0.18. The heating system is a natural gas boiler with an efficiency of 85%, the cost of gas is $8.50/Mcf, and there are 5,000 heating degree days each year. (Assume 1 Mcf = 1,037,000 Btu)

a. $0.048/ft2
b. $0.053/ft2
c. $0.069/ft2
d. $0.081/ft2

88. A building owner is considering two potential lighting retrofit projects. Project 1 will cost $25,000 and produce savings of $6,000 per year. Project 2 will cost $40,000 and produce savings of $9,000 per year. If both projects have an expected life of 8 years, which project should be chosen if a return on investment of 15% is required?

a. Project 1
b. Project 2
c. Neither Project 1 or Project 2
d. Both projects have the same return

89. A pump is used to move 120 gpm of water from the basement of a building 100 feet vertically to the top floor. If the efficiency of the pump is 93%, what is the horsepower required?

a. 3.0 hp
b. 3.3 hp
c. 3.6 hp
d. 3.9 hp

90. Which of the following is NOT a commonly used phase-change material (PCM) in thermal energy storage systems?

a. Inorganic compounds, such as calcium oxide (CaO)
b. Polymeric materials, such as polyethylene glycol (PEG)
c. Organic compounds, such as paraffins (hydrocarbons)
d. Inorganic materials, such as salt hydrates

91. A building is heated with a boiler that has an efficiency of 85%. Last year there were 4,000 heating degree-days and the total natural gas consumption was 500 Mcf. What is the Building Load Coefficient (UA)? (Assume 1 Mcf = 1,037,000 Btu)

a. 4,037
b. 4,591
c. 5,401
d. 6,354

92. Which of the following facility characteristics indicate that a real-time pricing electricity contract may be beneficial to take advantage of daily and seasonal price variations?

a. The facility has little control over when electricity is used, but the cost of electricity is not important compared to other costs
b. The facility does not generate its own electricity, and it does not use a lot of electricity at night
c. The facility has a production line that uses a lot of electricity, but has excess production capacity so it has flexibility in planning when production lines operate
d. All of the above

93. A hot water heating coil is used to heat 500 cfm of air at 60°F and 60% relative humidity to 85°F. If the ΔT of the water in the heating coil is 10°F, what is the flow rate of the water?

a. 2.7 gpm
b. 4.1 gpm
c. 7.4 gpm
d. 11.25 gpm

94. Proper grounding in a facility will help to maintain

a. power quality.
b. power factor.
c. load factor.
d. reactive power.

95. When a capacitor bank is added to an electrical system with a lagging current, the power factor is increased because

a. total reactive power is increased.
b. total reactive power is decreased.
c. total real power is increased.
d. total real power is decreased.

96. ISO 50001 is

a. an international measurement and verification standard.
b. a green building rating system.
c. a green building standard.
d. an international energy management standard.

97. The results of an efficiency test of a natural gas fired boiler indicate 8% of the flue gas is oxygen and the stack temperature is 620°F with a combustion air inlet temperature of 70°F. If the amount of combustion air to the boiler is adjusted so that only 3% oxygen is present in the flue gas, what is the potential boiler efficiency improvement?

a. 3%
b. 4%
c. 5%
d. 6%

98. What is the heating load required in Btu/hour to heat 5,000 cfm of outside air at 53°F and 80% relative humidity to 73°F?

a. 86,100 Btu/hour
b. 112,500 Btu/hour
c. 167,300 Btu/hour
d. 222,900 Btu/hour

99. To achieve a cold fluid exit temperature higher than a hot fluid exit temperature, what type of heat exchanger flow arrangement needs to be used?

a. Parallel flow heat exchanger
b. Counter flow heat exchanger
c. Cross flow heat exchanger
d. None of the above

100. The U-value for the walls of a building needs to be 0.084 Btu/hour.ft2.°F or better. The wall will have ¾" plywood (U = 1.07) on the outside and ½" plasterboard inside (U = 2.25). The gap between these layers will be filled with insulating material. If mineral wool fiber (k = 0.27 Btu.in/hour.ft2.°F) is used for the insulation, what is the minimum wall gap (insulation thickness) that could be used?

a. 2.75"
b. 3.0"
c. 3.25"
d. 3.5"

101. Which instrument could be used during an energy audit to measure the air velocity from a vent?

a. Psychrometer
b. Manometer
c. Pyrometer
d. Anemometer

102. Which of the following is NOT addressed in the IES (Illuminating Engineering Society) handbook?

a. Lighting measurement and testing standards
b. Lighting science standards
c. Roadway and parking facilities lighting standards
d. Pricing standards and purchasing tips for lighting sets

103. Calculate the cost of an air leak from a compressed air system if the leakage rate is found to be 6 scfm, the compressor specific efficiency is 22 BHP/scfm, overall efficiency is 90%, and the compressor operates for 6,000 hours each year. The cost of electricity is $0.06/kWh.

a. $35,450
b. $39,389
c. $41,232
d. $43,210

104. Which type of steam trap would be most suited to an application that requires excellent ability to handle dirt, operate well against back pressure, and failure in an open position?

a. Inverted bucket
b. Float and thermostatic
c. Disk
d. Bellows thermostatic

105. For a given period of time, what is the ratio of the average energy consumption in a facility divided by the peak demand in the facility called?

a. Energy balance
b. Demand charge
c. Energy Use Index
d. Load factor

106. The input of a boiler is 4,185,000 Btu/hour. If it is 85% efficient, what is its boiler horsepower output?

a. 89 BHP
b. 99 BHP
c. 106 BHP
d. 125 BHP

107. Which of the following are all LEED 2009 (New Construction) credit categories?

a. Thermal comfort, green power, sustainable sites
b. Energy and atmosphere, materials reuse, alternative transportation
c. Water efficiency, measurement and verification, materials and resources
d. Indoor environmental quality, sustainable sites, energy and atmosphere

108. A facility manager is considering the installation of a combined heat and power (CHP) system that will produce 300 kW of electricity and 1.33 MMBtu/hour at an overall efficiency of 87%. The annual demand in the facility for electricity is 2,400,000 kWh and the annual heat demand is 6,200 MMBtu, which is generated by a natural gas fired boiler with an efficiency of 85%. The facility currently buys electricity for $0.08/kWh and natural gas at $7.50/Mcf. What will the annual cost savings be if the CHP unit operates for 6,600 hours each year? (Assume 1 Mcf = 1,037,000 Btu)

a. $80,735
b. $82,021
c. $88,650
d. $114,335

109. Which of the following is NOT a section/component of a primary power supply?

a. Feeders
b. DC conversion
c. Primary loops
d. Lateral taps

110. How many tons of cooling is needed to cool 2,000 cfm of air at 90°F and 70% relative humidity to 55°F and 100% relative humidity?

a. 4.0 tons
b. 8.0 tons
c. 12.5 tons
d. 16.5 tons

111. A 75,000 ft^2 warehouse operates 24 hours per day but has a reduced number of workers from 10pm to 6am. There are 180 high bay fittings each with a single 250W SON lamp. The facility manager is considering retrofitting the lamps with 190W LEDs that are dimmable to 10% of rated power when an area is unoccupied. Calculate the potential annual cost savings assuming that a quarter of the lights will dim to 10% power for 5 hours each day. The electricity rate structure is:

Customer charge = $20.00/month
Electricity cost = $0.033/kWh
Fuel cost adjustment = $0.025/kWh
Demand charge = $6.50/kW/month

a. $4,656
b. $5,431
c. $7,145
d. $9,588

112. What is a district energy system?

a. A system that is designed and paid for by a district authority
b. A system designed to combine loads to heat and cool multiple buildings from a central plant
c. A system characterized by individual heating and cooling units that are designed to service an individual building
d. A design where each building operates independently

113. A chiller retrofit project will cost $100,000 to implement and will have a useful life of fifteen years. If the company pays $0.09/kWh for electricity and uses a discount rate of 10%, how many kilowatt-hours must the project save each year to pay for itself?

a. 350,000
b. 286,000
c. 146,000
d. 35,000

114. An energy audit of a facility found that the dual-fuel boiler was using #2 fuel oil and its efficiency was found by combustion analysis to be 70%. It is proposed that the boiler start using natural gas and be tuned to improve its efficiency to 80%. What are the expected cost savings in $/MMBtu if the price of #2 fuel oil is $2.00/gallon and the price of natural gas is $7.00/Mcf? (1 Mcf = 1,037,000 Btu)

a. $8.05/MMBtu
b. $9.28/MMBtu
c. $10.23/MMBtu
d. $11.97/MMBtu

115. What is the rate of heat loss per square foot through a 4-inch cinderblock wall when the internal temperature is 69°F and the outside temperature is 37°F?

Assume:

Masonry block conductance $= 0.90\,\frac{\text{Btu}}{\text{hr}\cdot\text{ft}^2\cdot{}^\circ\text{F}}$

Inside air film resistance $= 0.68\,\frac{\text{hr}\cdot\text{ft}^2\cdot{}^\circ\text{F}}{\text{Btu}}$

Outside air film resistance $= 0.17\,\frac{\text{hr}\cdot\text{ft}^2\cdot{}^\circ\text{F}}{\text{Btu}}$

a. $16.3\,\frac{\text{Btu}}{\text{hr}\cdot\text{ft}^2}$
b. $18.3\,\frac{\text{Btu}}{\text{hr}\cdot\text{ft}^2}$
c. $56.0\,\frac{\text{Btu}}{\text{hr}\cdot\text{ft}^2}$
d. $264.1\,\frac{\text{Btu}}{\text{hr}\cdot\text{ft}^2}$

116. A 50 foot by 30 foot office requires 50 footcandles of illumination on the work surface. LED lamps, each with an output of 2200 lumens, will be used in fixtures that hold two lamps. The light loss factor has been calculated to be 0.71 and the Coefficient of Utilization is 0.80. How many LED lamps will be required?

a. 30
b. 44
c. 56
d. 60

117. Which type of control system is characterized by a residual error?

a. On-off control
b. Floating control
c. Proportional control
d. Proportional-Integral control

118. A three phase 80 HP motor has an efficiency of 91% and operates at a load factor of 0.7. The voltage is 480V and power factor is 0.75, so a capacitor bank will be installed at the motor to increase the power factor to 0.95. How much reactive power must the capacitor bank provide?

a. 25.4 kVAR
b. 28.4 kVAR
c. 31.7 kVAR
d. 37.2 kVAR

119. What is the main goal of the US's climate change policy?

a. To solidify the Paris Agreement
b. To promote adoption and mitigation
c. To reduce greenhouse gas (GHG) emissions by 50% by 2030
d. To reach net zero by 2040

120. Which of the following does human centric lighting design NOT aim to elevate?

a. Mood
b. Energy efficiency
c. Productivity
d. Social interaction

121. Which organization develops and maintains the LEED green building rating system?

a. EPA
b. ASHRAE
c. USGBC
d. ISO

122. A compressed air system operating at 90 psi uses 500,000 kWh each year. If the system pressure is dropped to 80 psi, what are the approximate energy savings?

a. 5,000 kWh
b. 10,000 kWh
c. 25,000 kWh
d. 50,000 kWh

123. Which of the following is a typical Energy Use Index?

a. MMBtu/kWh
b. $/Mcf
c. kWh/ft2
d. therm

124. A facility manager replaces all the T5 lights in an office when they have reached 80% of their rated life of 20,000 hours. The lights operate for 12 hours each day, 5 days per week, for 52 weeks of the year. What is the group re-lamping interval for these lights?

a. 3.7 years
b. 4.6 years
c. 5.1 years
d. 6.4 years

125. Which of the following is NOT a key element of sustainable design?

a. Environmental impacts
b. Integration of ESG factors
c. Minimizing cybersecurity threats
d. Health and well-being

126. Calculate the percentage of outside air provided to a building when the outside air temperature is 50°F, the return air is 70°F, and the mixed air temperature is 65°F.

a. 20%
b. 25%
c. 33%
d. 40%

127. A chilled water reset control strategy is implemented when:

a. the supply air temperature set point is increased.
b. the chilled water supply temperature is increased.
c. the chilled water return temperature is decreased.
d. the return air temperature set point is increased.

128. Which of the following is not a benefit of thermal energy storage?

a. Decreased cooling demand
b. Lower peak demand
c. Improved reliability
d. Better chiller efficiency

129. An energy audit has found that the HVAC system performance has drifted from its designed operation when it was originally commissioned. What process should the building owner undertake?

a. Recommissioning
b. Retrocommissioning
c. Measurement and Verification
d. Benchmarking

130. A 20 HP motor operates at full load for 7,000 hours each year at an efficiency of 91%. It is replaced by a new 20 HP motor with an efficiency of 93%. What are the annual energy savings achieved by installing the new motor?

a. 2,206 kWh
b. 2,520 kWh
c. 2,840 kWh
d. 3,308 kWh

131. The three phases of an electrical supply have voltages of 235 V, 245 V, and 246 V. Calculate the percentage of voltage imbalance in this system.

a. 1.7%
b. 2.9%
c. 3.1%
d. 4.2%

132. Why should a true RMS meter be used to measure the voltage or current of an AC power supply during an energy audit?

a. Other meters are not safe to use
b. Only a true RMS meter is accurate when there are non-linear loads
c. Only a true RMS meter can measure voltage, current, and instantaneous power
d. A non-RMS meter is not approved for measurement and verification plans

133. Calculate the Room Cavity Ratio of a 40 by 50-foot room with lamps mounted on a nine-foot-high ceiling and a work surface 32 inches high.

a. 1.42
b. 1.46
c. 1.51
d. 1.54

134. Which of the following is a potential application for an infrared camera?

a. Finding faulty electrical connections or overloaded circuits.
b. Determining areas of heat loss from a building.
c. Identifying mechanical faults such as excessive bearing friction
d. All of the above

135. Which of the following descriptions of maintenance programs most closely matches a preventive maintenance system?

a. Maintenance activities are scheduled at predetermined times and carried out regardless of equipment condition
b. Equipment maintenance is carried out according to regular condition-based assessments
c. Maintenance is carried out at a predetermined time or as a result of a condition based assessment and may involve redesign of systems to prevent failures that have occurred from happening in the future
d. Equipment is repaired after it fails

136. A 5,000 square foot office area has 90 fixtures each with two lamps. The lumen output of each lamp is 2,800 lumens and they have a light loss factor of 0.7 and a coefficient of utilization of 0.75. A lighting retrofit is proposed that will reduce the total power required by installing lamps with an output of 2,400 lumens each, a light loss factor of 0.85, and a coefficient of utilization of 0.80. How many fixtures would be required so that the new lights provide the same number of footcandles as the existing lights?

a. 81
b. 85
c. 90
d. 93

137. What is the maximum interest rate an organization should accept if it is to finance an energy saving product that saves $20,000 per year over its useful life of 10 years if the initial cost is $112,000?

a. 2%
b. 12%
c. 17%
d. 20%

138. Which of the following regulatory activities is the responsibility of the Federal Energy Regulatory Commission?

a. Approves the siting of interstate natural gas pipelines
b. Regulates retail sales of electricity and natural gas
c. Approves the construction of new electricity generating facilities
d. Regulates local natural gas distribution pipelines

139. Which of the following is NOT outlined in the ASHRAE standard 211?

a. Steps to conduct an energy audit
b. Measurement and verification approaches
c. Data collection approaches
d. Compliance and certification guidelines

140. If a new building earns 41 points in the LEED rating scale, what level of certification will it receive?

a. LEED Certified
b. LEED Silver
c. LEED Gold
d. No certification

141. A new high efficiency 100hp motor that costs $8,900 is installed instead of a standard efficiency motor that costs $7,600. The high efficiency motor saves 4,000 kWh each year. The expected life of the motor is 20 years and electricity costs $0.09/kWh, but this cost is expected to increase by 3% each year. What is the simple payback of the motor?

a. 2.5 years
b. 3.6 years
c. 4.1 years
d. 7.7 years

142. In which Energy Savings Performance Contract structure will an Energy Services Company (ESCO) pay the customer if the savings are less than expected?

a. Shared savings
b. Guaranteed savings
c. Chauffage
d. Deemed savings

143. Which of the following regulations was not part of the Energy Policy Act of 2005?

a. A requirement for electric metering in all federal buildings by 2012.
b. The requirement that total energy use in federal buildings be reduced by 30% by 2015 compared to the 2005 level
c. New federal buildings must incorporate life-cycle costing
d. Renewable energy consumption in federal buildings must be greater than 7.5% from 2013 onwards.

144. The minimum ventilation rates for offices in ASHRAE Standard 62.1 are:

People Outdoor Air Rate (cfm/person)	Area Outdoor Air Rate (cfm/ft2)	Default Occupant Density (#/1,000 ft2)	Default Combined Outdoor Air Rate (cfm/person)
5	0.06	5	17

If a 5,000 ft2 office has 30 people, what is the outdoor airflow requirement according to the ventilation rate procedure prescribed in ASHRAE 62.1?

a. 375 cfm
b. 425 cfm
c. 450 cfm
d. 510 cfm

145. Regression analysis of electricity consumption against cooling degree days for a building produces a performance line having the equation y = 95.2x + 12,320 with an R2 value of 0.82. Which of the following statements about the electricity consumption in this building is not a reasonable assumption?

a. The electricity demand in the building is not dependent on heating degree days
b. The electricity demand in the building can be predicted based on cooling degree days
c. The building uses 95.2 kWh for each cooling degree day
d. The monthly base load electricity demand is 12,320 kWh

Answer Key and Explanations

1. A: The performance of an HVAC system can be measured by:

$$\frac{kW}{ton} = \frac{12}{EER} = \frac{12}{COP \times 3.412}$$

Where EER is the energy efficiency ratio. Therefore, the kW/ton efficiency is:

$$\frac{\text{kW}}{\text{ton}} = \frac{3.517}{3.2} = 1.1$$

2. B: the power in kilowatts of the motor is calculated by:

$$P_{kW} = \frac{\text{Horsepower } \times 0.746 \times \% \text{ of Full Load}}{\text{Efficiency}} = \frac{30 \times 0.746 \times 1}{0.936} = 23.9 \text{ kW}$$

The power is also calculated by:

$$P_{kW} = \sqrt{3} \times \text{kV} \times I \times Power\ Factor = \sqrt{3} \times 0.46 \times 35 \times PF$$

Therefore:

$$PF = \frac{23.9}{\sqrt{3} \times 0.46 \times 35} = 0.86$$

3. D: Net zero energy buildings are constructed to be very energy efficient so that their annual energy demands are low. The energy needs are met through utility connections and on-site generation from renewable energy sources such as solar (PV panels). Over the course of a year, the on-site renewable generation is at least as much as the energy that is imported.

4. C: The future value (F) of the lighting project in five years (n) is $80,000. The annual savings (A) that will be invested at 10% (i) must be determined. The interest factor (A/F) should be used on the 10% interest table in row n=5. The annual savings must therefore be $\$80{,}000 \times 0.1638 = \$13{,}104$. At a cost of $7/Mcf the amount of gas saved each year needs to be 1,872Mcf, which is equivalent to about 1941×10^6 Btu.

5. D: The efficiency of the cooling system is not a primary consideration for installation of a thermal energy storage system. The efficiency of cooling energy production may be improved if the chiller is loaded more optimally, but this is secondary to reduced peak demand charges, and taking advantage of low off-peak energy rates at night when there is spare cooling capacity.

6. D: If there is insufficient oxygen available for combustion then incomplete combustion will occur. This results in dangerous conditions whereby carbon monoxide is produced and fuel may travel up the exhaust stack.

7. B: An energy audit should begin with an analysis of historical energy consumption so that the total energy use and costs are known, and the building performance can be benchmarked with other similar buildings. The utility rate structures are important to understand since there may be large peak demand charges or power factor penalties that will guide an energy auditor to consider or discount certain energy conservation measures during a walk-through survey of the facility.

8. B: The present worth of the annual savings should be larger than the cost of recommissioning. Therefore, the compound interest factor $\left(\frac{P}{A}\right)_{10,n}$ should be larger than $\frac{\$18,000}{\$5,700} = 3.1579$. The interest factor for year 4 is 3.1699, which is the closest interest factor greater than 3.1579 and the present worth of the savings would be $\$5,700 \times 3.1699 = \$18,068$.

9. B: Both LEED Building Design + Construction and LEED Operations + Maintenance require a minimum floor area of 1,000 square feet.

10. C: The apparent power is calculated by:

$$\text{Apparent Power (kVA)} = \frac{\text{Real Power (kW)}}{\text{Power Factor}} = \frac{600}{0.87} = 690 \text{ kVA}$$

11. A: The value of the energy savings to the customer are not important to the lender since they are only concerned with receiving repayment for the loan. The ability of the customer to repay the loan is dependent upon their creditworthiness, how likely the project is to succeed and produce savings, and the terms of the contract such as how long the contract will last, how savings are calculated, and how savings are shared.

12. B: The total fuel consumption each hour is:

$$\text{Fuel}\left(\frac{\text{MMBtu}}{\text{hour}}\right) = \frac{\text{Electrical Energy} + \text{Thermal Energy}}{\text{Overall Efficiency}}$$

$$\text{Fuel}\left(\frac{\text{MMBtu}}{\text{hour}}\right) = \frac{500 \text{ kW } \times 1 \text{ hour} \times 0.003412 \frac{\text{MMBtu}}{\text{kWh}} + 2.2 \text{ MMBtu}}{90\%} = 4.34 \frac{\text{MMBtu}}{\text{hour}}$$

The amount of gas used each hour is:

$$\text{Natural Gas}\left(\frac{\text{MCf}}{\text{hour}}\right) = \frac{4.34 \frac{\text{MMBtu}}{\text{hour}}}{1.037 \frac{\text{MMBtu}}{\text{Mcf}}} = 4.19 \frac{\text{Mcf}}{\text{hour}}$$

13. C: VRF is an HVAC technology that precisely controls the amount of refrigerant flowing to multiple areas or zones within a building. VRF allows for a single compressor to serve multiple indoor units. The system will adjust the refrigerant flow based on demand. VRF could be used to serve many different sizes of buildings – small, medium, or large. *Variable* refers to the flow, not the type of refrigerant. The ability to operate at full capacity (only or at all times) would be found in a non-inverter system. Non-inverter systems do not have the ability to vary the flow of the refrigerant.

14. B: The heat loss is calculated by:

$$Q = U \times A \times 24 \times HDD = 0.04 \times 5,000 \times 24 \times 4,000 = 19,200,000 \text{ Btu/year}$$

15. D: The carbon footprint calculation is a major component of GHG reporting. The carbon footprint calculation follows the GHG protocol and involves identifying emissions sources, collecting relevant data, applying emissions factors, and calculating the total carbon footprint. This data could be used in a portion of a corporation's ESG plan. GHG accounting is not specified in complying with US climate change policy.

16. C: The power triangle for this facility is:

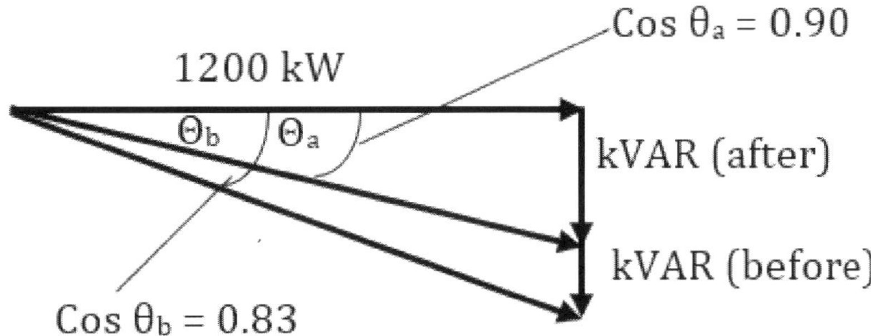

The reactive power needed to improve the power factor from 0.83 to 0.90 is:

$$\text{kVAR (before)} - \text{kVAR (after)} = 1200 \times [\tan\{\cos^{-1}(0.83)\} - \tan\{\cos^{-1}(0.90)\}] = 225\ \text{kVA}$$

The answer may also be found from tables: $1200 \times 0.188 = 225$ kVAR

17. C: Energy performance contracts can be used to finance distributed energy projects, but they are not usually offered by utilities for this purpose. An energy performance contract will generally be focused on energy efficiency improvements with some form of financial and performance risk sharing mechanism.

18. D: A supply air reset strategy is employed when the supply air temperature is significantly different to the room set point temperature and a lot of reheat is required. Static pressure reset is used to reduce fan energy consumption; an economizer optimizes the mixed air temperature by adjusting the amount of outside air supplied; and an unoccupied setback strategy adjusts the setpoint when the building is unoccupied.

19. D: The effectiveness of a heat exchanger is the actual heat transfer from a hotter fluid to a colder fluid divided by the maximum heat transfer possible based on area of the heat exchanger, the overall heat conductance, and the mass flow rate and specific heat of the fluids.

20. D: The load factor is the actual energy used divided by what the energy would have been if the demand during the period was equal to the peak load at all times:

$$\text{Load factor} = \frac{190{,}000\ \text{kWh}}{525\ \text{kW} \times 24\ \dfrac{\text{hours}}{\text{day}} \times 31\ \text{days}} = \frac{190{,}000}{390{,}600} = 0.49$$

21. B: The cost of electricity is $1{,}350{,}000\ \text{kWh} \times \$0.085/\text{kWh} = \$114{,}750$. The cost of natural gas is:

$$\frac{7{,}500\ \text{MMBtu}}{1.037\ \dfrac{\text{MMBtu}}{\text{Mcf}}} \times \frac{\$7.50}{\text{Mcf}} = \$54{,}243$$

So the total cost is $168,993. The Energy Cost Index is:

$$\frac{\$168{,}993}{150{,}000\ \text{ft}^2} = \frac{\$1.13}{\text{ft}^2}$$

22. A: The compressed air system pressure is not relevant since the amount of heat available will be determined by the motor horsepower (about 250,000 Btu/100 HP). The timing of when waste heat is available can be important since it is not likely to be economical to store relatively low grade heat for extended periods of time of the demand for waste heat does not match its availability from the compressor.

23. A: Firstly, the amount of energy that the water can store needs to be calculated. Since 1 lb of water will store 1 Btu/°F:

$$\frac{\text{Btu}}{\text{lb}} = 1\frac{\text{Btu}}{°\text{F}} \times \Delta T$$

Where ΔT is the difference between the supply and return temperatures (59 – 39) = 20°F. Therefore, each pound of water will store 20 Btu.

Next, the volume of water required per ton-hour must be calculated:

$$\frac{\text{gallons}}{\text{ton-hours}} = \frac{1}{20}\frac{\text{lb}}{\text{Btu}} \times 12{,}000\frac{\text{Btu}}{\text{ton-hours}} \times \frac{1}{8.34}\frac{\text{gallons}}{\text{lb}} = 71.9$$

The required storage capacity is 4,000 ton-hours, so the number of gallons needed is:

$$71.9 \times 4{,}000 = 287{,}600 \text{ gallons}$$

24. C: ASHRAE 189.1 is the Standard for the design of high-performance green buildings. Minimum requirements for HVAC system performance is specified in ASHRAE.

25. C: Demand, measured in kilowatts (kW), refers to the maximum amount of electrical power consumed at a given instant. The amount of energy used over a given period of time is measured in kilowatt-hours. Utilities often incentivize customers to move some of their demand to off-peak hours in order to reduce the need for new generation.

26. A: The stack temperature rise is 730°F - 80°F = 650°F. A combustion efficiency chart for natural gas shows that at 3% flue gas oxygen the efficiency is 74.1%. When the flue gas temperature is decreased to 630°F, the stack temperature rise is reduced to 550°F and the efficiency is 76.7%. The percentage of fuel savings is calculated by:

$$\text{Fuel Savings} = \frac{\text{New Efficiency} - \text{Old Efficiency}}{\text{New Efficiency}} = \frac{76.7 - 74.1}{76.7} = 3.4\%$$

Therefore, the savings are $3.4\% \times 7{,}000\frac{\text{Mcf}}{\text{year}} = 238\frac{\text{Mcf}}{\text{year}}$ and $238\frac{\text{Mcf}}{\text{year}} \times \$8.00 = \$1{,}904$ per year in fuel cost savings.

27. A: Simple Payback Period is calculated by dividing the initial costs by the annual savings and does not consider how costs or the value of money changes over time.

28. D: LEED does not have a specific rating system for schools. A school may be rated under LEED for Building Design + Construction or LEED Operations + Maintenance.

29. D: The residual value of the asset is not a condition of a capital lease. A fourth alternative criterion for capital leases is that the present value of the of the minimum lease payment is at least 90% of the fair market value of the asset at the beginning of the lease.

30. A: A spot measurement of the reduction in lighting power would be the best method since the power will not vary over time and the hours of operation are not being changed. The expected savings are only about 7% of the total electricity demand so utility bill comparison is not suitable.

31. A: The future value of the savings after three years are calculated by:

$$\text{Future Worth} = A \times \left({}^{F}\!/_{A}\right)_{12,3} = \$27{,}000 \times 3.374 = \$91{,}098$$

32. C: A combustion cycle is a process for combustion of a fuel, for example in an internal combustion engine, which may be the type of engine used in a CHP unit, but it is not an operating cycle for a CHP system. A topping cycle primarily produces electricity and recovers waste heat. A bottoming cycle primarily produces thermal energy and residual thermal energy produces electricity. A combined cycle produces electricity in two stages and recovers thermal energy at least once.

33. C: An index with a cap pricing strategy sets a maximum price that a customer will pay but if the gas price index drops below this level then the customer will only pay the index price plus a small margin. This enables the customer to benefit from lower gas prices whilst ensuring they have price certainty of the gas price index rises.

34. C: The after-tax savings is calculated using the formula

$$\text{After-Tax Savings} = (1 - I) \times A + ID$$

Where I is the tax rate, A is the annual savings, and D is the annual depreciation. The annual savings are $150{,}000\text{kWh} \times \frac{\$0.09}{\text{kWh}} = \$13{,}500$. The annual depreciation is $\frac{\$200{,}000}{15 \text{ years}} = \$13{,}333$. The first year after-tax savings are calculated as follows:

$$\text{After-Tax Savings} = (1 - 0.35) \times \$13{,}500 + 0.35 \times \$13{,}333 = \$8{,}775 + \$4{,}666$$

The present value of the after-tax savings over 5 years is calculated in three parts: the depreciation savings, the base energy cost savings, and the gradient (increasing) energy cost savings.

$$\text{Depreciation Savings} = \$4{,}666 \times \left(\frac{P}{A}\right)_{15,5} = \$4{,}666 \times 3.3522 = \$15{,}641$$

$$\text{Energy Cost Savings (Base)} = \$8{,}775 \times \left(\frac{P}{A}\right)_{15,5} = \$8{,}775 \times 3.3522 = \$29{,}415$$

$$\text{Energy Cost Savings (Gradient)} = \$8{,}775 \times 10\% \times \left(\frac{P}{G}\right)_{15,5} = \$877.5 \times 5.775 = \$5{,}068$$

$$\text{Present Value} = \$15{,}641 + \$29{,}415 + \$5{,}068 = \$50{,}124$$

35. D: The CRI of incandescent and halogen lamps is 100, which means it is the best approximation of natural daylight possible. LEDs generally have a CRI of around 90, but some can achieve a CRI of up to 98.

36. B: The properties of moist air can be determined using a psychrometric chart. The dry bulb temperature is found on the horizontal axis at the bottom of the chart (Point 1). A vertical line is drawn to the point that it intersects the wet bulb temperature (Point 2) which is found on the left

that and almost aligned with the lines of enthalpy. A horizontal line is drawn to the left from this point and where it crosses the saturation point (Point 3, 100% relative humidity), this is the dew point temperature.

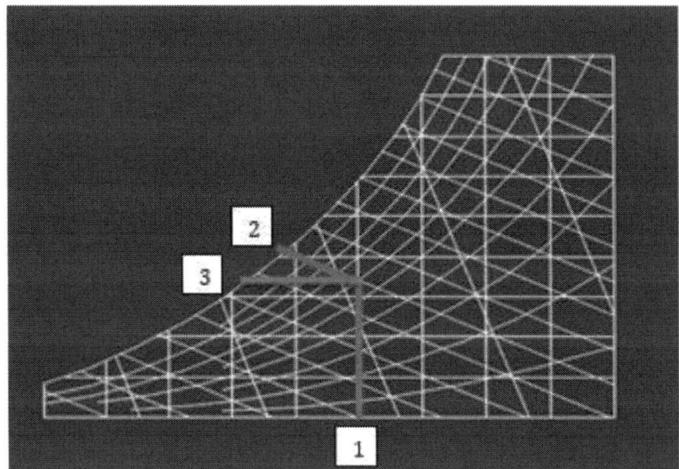

37. C: A goal of an energy audit is to identify wasteful energy use, but not unnecessary end-use services.

38. D: The sensible heat exchange for water is calculated by:

$$q = \text{gpm} \times 500 \times \Delta T$$

The cooling power q is calculated by the relationship that 1 ton of air conditioning is 12,000 Btu/hour. To find the flow rate in gpm, the calculation is:

$$\text{gpm} = \frac{q}{500 \times \Delta T} = \frac{1{,}200{,}000}{500 \ \times 10} = 240 \text{ gpm}$$

39. D: The total electrical energy savings for the year are $200 \times 18\ W \times 4{,}380 \text{ hours} = 15{,}768$ kWh. The power reduction is $200 \times 18\ W = 3.6$ kW. The total cost savings are:

$$15{,}768 \text{ kWh} \times \frac{\$0.028 + \$0.031}{\text{kWh}} + 3.6 \text{ kW} \times \frac{\$4.20 + \$4.50}{\text{kW/month}} \times 12 \text{ months} = \$930.31 + \$375.84 = \$1306.15$$

40. B: Lumens per square foot is not commonly a KPI that is reported in an energy audit. In lighting design, it would be calculated and discussed. In the audit, normally a light count and savings using a more efficient technology are recorded. EUI, ROI, and carbon footprint are routinely calculated as part of the audit. Also routinely included is a 12-to-24-month usage history and a record of all building systems (lighting, HVAC, building envelope).

41. D: An open loop, automatic control system receives no feedback from a system as to the effect of its operation on the system, but it can operate without manual intervention. A manual switch is an open loop system but is not automatic. Both thermostats and pressure sensors are automatic, closed loop systems since they receive feedback about the state of the system.

42. C: The heat loss per square foot of area through the uninsulated pipe is:

$$Q_{uninsulated} = \frac{T_{surface} - T_{ambient}}{R_{surface}} = \frac{170 - 70}{0.72} = 138.9\ \frac{\text{Btu}}{\text{ft}^2 \cdot \text{hr}}$$

The heat loss through the insulated pipe is:

$$Q_{insulated} = \frac{T_{fluid} - T_{ambient}}{R_{insulation} + R_{surface}} = \frac{170 - 70}{\frac{t}{k} + 0.8}$$

The thickness of the pipe is the equivalent thickness of the pipe plus insulation which is calculated by:

$$t = r_{insulation} \ln\left(\frac{r_{insulation}}{r_{pipe}}\right) = (2.25 + 2)\ln\left(\frac{(2.25 + 2)}{2.25}\right) = 2.70$$

Therefore, the heat loss through the insulated pipe is:

$$Q_{insulated} = \frac{170 - 70}{\frac{2.7}{0.33} + 0.8} = 11.1\frac{\text{Btu}}{\text{ft}^2.\text{hr}}$$

The reduction in heat loss is therefore 138.9 – 11.1 = 127.8 $\frac{\text{Btu}}{\text{ft}^2.\text{hr}}$

43. B: The price of fuel oil per Btu is:

$$\frac{\$2.30}{\text{gallon}} \times \frac{1\text{ gallon}}{140{,}000\text{ Btu}} \times \frac{1{,}000{,}000\text{ Btu}}{\text{MMBtu}} \times \frac{1}{0.80} = \$20.54/\text{MMBtu}$$

The price of natural gas per Btu is:

$$\frac{\$0.85}{\text{therm}} \times \frac{1\text{ therm}}{100{,}000\text{ Btu}} \times \frac{1{,}000{,}000\text{ Btu}}{\text{MMBtu}} \times \frac{1}{0.92} = \$9.24/\text{MMBtu}$$

The savings are therefore \$11.30/MMBtu. The annual fuel cost savings are therefore $\frac{\$11.30}{\text{MMBtu}} \times 4{,}100\text{ MMBtu} = \$46{,}330$. The simple payback period will be $\frac{\$140{,}000}{\$46{,}330} = 3.0$ years.

44. C: The Net Present Value (NPV) is the present worth of cash inflows minus the present value of cash outflows. The cash inflows in this case are the annual savings and the salvage value of the economizer. The annual savings are:

$$\text{New Fuel Demand} = \frac{6{,}500\text{ MMBtu} \times 0.76}{0.81} = 6{,}099\text{ MMBtu}$$

$$\text{Fuel Cost Savings} = \frac{(6{,}500 - 6{,}099)\text{ MMBtu}}{1.037\frac{\text{MMBtu}}{\text{Mcf}}} \times \frac{\$8.00}{\text{Mcf}} = 386.7\text{ Mcf} \times \frac{\$8.00}{\text{Mcf}} = \$3{,}094$$

The present worth of the annual savings are:

$$\$3{,}094 \times \left(\frac{P}{A}\right)_{5,12} = \$3{,}094 \times 3.6048 = \$11{,}151$$

The present worth of the economizer after 5 years is:

$$\$10{,}000 \times \left(\frac{P}{F}\right)_{5,12} = \$10{,}000 \times 0.5674 = \$5{,}674.$$

The NPV = -$15,000 + $11,151 + $5,674 = $1,825

45. D: The EUI is in kBtu/ft^2 so kWh and Mcf must be converted to kBtu.

$$900{,}000 \text{ kWh} \times 3.412 \text{ kBtu/kWh} = 3{,}070{,}800 \text{ kBtu}$$

$$1{,}200 \text{ Mcf} \times 1{,}037 \frac{\text{kBtu}}{\text{Mcf}} = 1{,}244{,}400 \text{ kBtu}$$

Therefore, the EUI is $\frac{(3{,}070{,}800 + 1{,}244{,}400) \text{ kBtu}}{25{,}000 \text{ ft}^2} = 172.6 \frac{\text{kBtu}}{\text{ft}^2}$

46. D: A bourdon gauge is a mechanical pressure measurement device. They are often installed in boiler systems to measure the pressure in steam or hot water pipes.

47. A: Under a load levelling strategy the chiller operates at a constant load at all times. The total cooling load can be found by summing up the load at each hour of the day. Therefore, the total daily cooling load is:

$$(11 \text{ hours} \times 50 \text{ tons}) + (5 \text{ hours} \times 100 \text{ tons}) + (5 \text{ hours} \times 150 \text{ tons}) + (3 \text{ hours} \times 200 \text{ tons}) = 2{,}400 \text{ ton-hours}$$

The constant chiller load needed to meet the total cooling load for a 24-hour period is therefore $\frac{2{,}400 \text{ ton-hours}}{24 \text{ hours}} = 100 \text{ tons}.$

48. B: The amount of steam loss from a leak according to the estimated calculation method using Grashof's formula is:

$$\text{leak}\left(\text{lb}/_{\text{hour}}\right) = 0.7 \times 0.0165 \times 3{,}600 \times \left(\pi \times \left(\frac{3}{32}\right)^2\right) \times 100^{0.97} = 100 \frac{\text{lb}}{\text{hour}}$$

The boiler operates for 6,570 hours per year and the enthalpy of the steam is 1187.2 Btu/lb, so the energy lost is $100 \frac{\text{lb}}{\text{hour}} \times 1187.2 \frac{\text{Btu}}{\text{lb}} \times 6{,}570 \text{ hours} = 780 \text{ MMBtu}.$

Because the boiler has an efficiency of 85%, the overall energy loss is therefore $\frac{780 \text{ MMBtu}}{0.85} = 918 \text{ MMBtu}.$

An approximate answer can also be found from a steam leak chart provided in the CEM materials.

49. C: As the refrigerant passes through the condenser it releases heat to the environment. It condenses into a high temperature liquid from a high temperature vapor.

50. D: There are many goals and benefits of building commissioning. These include producing adequate documents that record the design, construction, testing, and intended operation of building energy services. This will help building managers to operate and maintain equipment correctly so that the life of the equipment is as long as possible with reduced maintenance and energy costs.

51. B: A shell and tube heat exchanger can be used to recover heat from a liquid. The other technologies recover heat from gases.

52. B: The efficacy of a lamp is measured in lumens per watt. The useful lumens that can be detected by the eye and the total power used are measured. Efficacy is typically about 20 lumens/Watt for incandescent, 80 lumens/Watt for fluorescent, and can be over 100 lumens/Watt for LEDs.

53. D: The amount of flash steam produced is:

$$\%\text{ Flash Steam} = \frac{h_{f\ steam} - h_{f\ condensate}}{h_{fg\ condensate}} = \frac{h_{f\ 100psia} - h_{f\ 30psia}}{h_{fg\ 30psia}} = \frac{298.5 - 218.9}{945.2} = 8.4\%$$

Therefore, the amount of flash steam that can be recovered is $8.4\% \times 4{,}000\frac{\text{lb}}{\text{hour}} = 336\frac{\text{lb}}{\text{hour}}$.

54. B: The seasonal temperature variations impact the demand for natural gas by customers for heating and also utilities for power production, but natural disasters tend to impact the supply side of the natural gas market. For example, damage to infrastructure or disruption to the local workforce may reduce the amount of natural gas production.

55. D: The after tax cash flow is calculated by:

$$\text{Before-tax income} - (\text{Before-tax income} - \text{deductions}) \times \text{tax rate}$$

Straight-line depreciation is calculated by:

$$\frac{\text{Cost} - \text{Salvage Value}}{\text{Useful Life}} = \frac{\$50{,}000 - 0}{10} = \$5{,}000$$

1	2	3	4	1 - 4
Before-tax income	Deductions (depreciation)	Taxable income	Taxes (30%)	After-Tax Cash Flow
$8,000	$5,000	$3,000	$900	$7,100

56. D: The energy standard for buildings except low-rise residential buildings is ASHRAE 90.1. It sets minimum energy efficiency requirements for the design of new buildings, new portions of buildings, and new systems and equipment in existing buildings.

57. A: Temperature is measured by a pyrometer.

58. C: The efficiency and power factor of a motor increase rapidly up to about 50% of rated load. Efficiency peaks at about 75% of rated load and then decreases slightly as resistive losses begin to increase proportionately to the square of the current. The power factor of a motor continues to gradually increase as the applied load increases.

59. C: Eddy current drives are able to control motor speed most similarly to a variable frequency drive. They do not produce any harmonics but are bulky and heavy on the motor shaft.

60. A: Smart cities are urban environments that use technology and data to drive sustainability and improve infrastructure. It is a relatively new term. AI-powered smart parking solutions would be considered smart city technology. Laptop computers for the public may allow access to smart city technologies, like smart parking management or autonomous vehicles, but are not considered a smart city technology themselves. Online bus schedules and a large number of top universities are great things for a city to have but are not components of smart cities.

61. D: The stator and rotor have resistive losses that are equal to the square of the current flowing through them multiplied by their resistance. This is the largest type of loss in an AC motor as the load and current are at a maximum.

62. D: A demand ratchet is a mechanism used by utilities to ensure that customers with very seasonal demands pay for the cost of providing additional generation capacity needed to meet their peak demand. For example, a resort that is only open for six months of the year may have a high peak demand when it is open, but the remainder of the year it has no demand. The utility will charge the resort a percentage of their annual peak demand every month even if some months they do not use any power.

63. C: Thermally heavy buildings have a high thermal mass, which is achieved by using materials that are dense, have a relatively high specific heat capacity, and moderate thermal conductivity. This enables them to store heat during the day and release it gradually at night. They tend to maintain a relatively constant temperature, so the heating and cooling demands of these buildings is less affected by fluctuations in weather conditions.

64. A: A boiler efficiency chart for a natural gas fired boiler will show that when the percent excess air is 10% (air-to-fuel ratio), the percent of excess oxygen in the flue gas is 2%.

65. A: The load factor of the motor may be calculated by:

$$\text{Load factor} = \frac{\text{Power (kW)} \times \text{Efficiency}}{\text{HP} \times 0.746} = \frac{6.3 \times 0.941}{10 \times 0.746} = 0.79$$

66. D: The amount of waste heat that is available is calculated by:

$$q = \dot{m} \times C_p \times \Delta T$$

Where m is the mass flow rate and Cp is the specific heat. The mass flow rate is:

$$20\text{ gpm} \times 8.34\frac{\text{lb}}{\text{gallon}} \times 60\frac{\text{minute}}{\text{hour}} = 10{,}008\frac{\text{lb}}{\text{hour}}$$

$$q = 10{,}008 \times 1 \times (200 - 140) = 600{,}480\ \frac{\text{Btu}}{\text{hour}}$$

67. A: Non-linear loads such as lighting with magnetic ballasts and equipment that draws current in pulses produce harmonics. Incandescent lights are linear loads and do not produce harmonics.

68. C: A building must perform in the top 25% for energy efficiency among all similar buildings to earn Energy Star certification.

69. A: A multizone system mixes and conditions the air in a central air handling unit, but the unit has separate conditioning and mixing chambers for each zone in the building. A dual duct system heats and cools the air separately, but the air is also distributed to each zone in separate ducts and only mixed at the zone. Constant and variable air volume systems condition a single stream of air in a central unit for distribution to one or more zones.

70. C: Light loss factors are used to account for gradual loss of light output from lamps over time due to maintenance, system components, and the environment. The rated useful life of the lamp is not accounted for in the light loss factor.

71. D: The pump performance curve can be altered by changing the size of the pump impeller, or altering the pump motor speed. For example, reducing the pump impeller size and reducing the pump motor speed both shift the pump performance curve downwards, so the pump produces less head and flow rate.

72. D: Life-cycle cost is a method of determining the total cost of ownership over the life of a product with consideration to the value of money over time.

73. C: BACnet is an open communication protocol maintained by ASHRAE and described in ASHRAE Standard 135.

74. C: The power factor in a three-phase system is calculated by:

$$\text{Power factor} = \frac{\text{kW}}{\sqrt{3} \times \text{kV} \times \text{I}} = \frac{200}{\sqrt{3} \times 0.46 \times 270} = 0.93$$

75. C: The true slip of the motor is:

$$\text{True Slip} = (\text{No Load RPM} - \text{Actual RPM})$$

At 60 Hz, the No Load RPM can only be 3600, 1800, 1200, 900, etc. depending upon the number of pole pairs. Since the Full Load RPM is 1780 the No Load RPM must be 1800. Therefore, the true slip is 1800 - 1744 = 56.

76. B: Visual comfort is affected by many lighting conditions including the level and uniformity of illumination, appearance of colors, contrast, and glare. Visual Comfort Probability is a rating specifically for glare to indicate how comfortable people are with the glare from a light fixture.

77. A: The fundamental law of illumination, or the inverse square law, states the relationship between illuminance (footcandles), luminous intensity (lumens), and distance (feet):

$$E = \frac{I}{d^2}$$

$10 = \frac{I}{45^2}$ and $50 = \frac{I}{d^2}$ Therefore, $d^2 = \frac{10 \times 45^2}{50}$, so $d = \sqrt{\frac{20{,}250}{50}} = 20$ feet

78. A: The leakage rate in a compressed air system is given by:

$$\text{Leakage Rate} = \frac{V \times \Delta P}{T \times 14.7} = \frac{400 \times 20}{15 \times 14.7} = 36 \text{ cfm}$$

79. A: The affinity laws for fan motors can be used to determine the new motor horsepower by reducing the air flow by 20%:

$$\frac{HP_2}{HP_1} = \left(\frac{CFM_2}{CFM_1}\right)^3$$

$$HP_2 = 20 \times \left(\frac{0.8}{1}\right)^3 = 10.2$$

80. B: ASHRAE 62 specifies minimum ventilation rates and acceptable standards for air quality.

81. A: Demand-side management allows utilities to avoid adding new generation and transmission lines and to use current infrastructure as efficiently as possible. Customers sometimes qualify for rebates if they install the proper equipment. Bills are not normally lower due to DSM, although customers may get rebates that can be applied to their bill.

82. C: The goal of passive design is to utilize local climate and natural resources to reduce the reliance on mechanical systems. Passive design does aim to reduce the use of active mechanical systems, but only in the rarest of occasions can active systems be eliminated completely. Passive heating strategies can be employed to maximize solar exposure (to help reduce need for active heating), and passive cooling strategies can be designed into the building to the help reduce air conditioning load; however, these are potential benefits of passive design, not the main goal.

83. C: The Federal Acquisition Regulations (FAR Part 23.205) state that an ESPC cannot exceed 25 years.

84. A: Temperature is read by a thermometer and sent to a control system as an input signal. An analog signal is able to be control or be monitored through a continuously variable range, for example 0 °F to 200 °F, 4 mA to 20 mA, or 0 V to 10 V.

85. A: PURPA was enacted in 1978 and resulted in greater development of cogeneration and renewable energy facilities. PUHCA dates from 1935 and allowed the Securities and Exchange Commission to regulate utility holding companies; it was repealed in 2006 after the Energy Policy Act of 2005 was passed.

86. A: Because the lives of the projects are different, they cannot be compared using the present worth method. An equivalent annual worth must be calculated for each option.

The annual worth of Option 1 is:

$$\text{Annual Worth} = A - P \times \left(\frac{A}{P}\right)_{15,15} = 30{,}000 - 150{,}000 \times (0.1710) = \$4{,}350$$

The annual worth of Option 2 is:

$$\text{Annual Worth} = A - P \times \left(\frac{A}{P}\right)_{12,15} = 40{,}000 - 200{,}000 \times (0.1845) = \$3{,}100$$

Therefore, Option 1 is the better choice since it has a higher annual worth.

87. D: The annual heating system energy is calculated by:

$$q = U \times A \times 24 \times HDD$$

Therefore, the annual energy savings per square foot are:

$$\frac{q}{A} = (0.25 - 0.18) \times 24 \times 5{,}000 = 8{,}400\ \frac{\text{Btu}}{\text{ft}^2}$$

The cost savings are:

$$Savings\left(\frac{\$}{\text{ft}^2}\right) = \frac{8{,}400\text{ Btu}}{0.85\text{ ft}^2} \times \frac{1\text{ Mcf}}{1{,}037{,}000\text{ Btu}} \times \frac{\$8.50}{1\text{ Mcf}} = \$0.081\text{ per ft}^2$$

88. A: The project with the largest equivalent present worth greater than zero should be chosen. The present worth of Project 1 is:

$$-\$25{,}000 + \$6{,}000 \times \left(\frac{P}{A}\right)_{8,15} = -\$25{,}000 + \$6{,}000 \times 4.4873 = \$1{,}923.80$$

The present worth of Project 2 is:

$$-\$40{,}000 + \$9{,}000 \times \left(\frac{P}{A}\right)_{8,15} = -\$40{,}000 + \$9{,}000 \times 4.4873 = \$385.70$$

Both projects are viable since they have a positive present worth, but Project 1 provides a better return.

89. B: The pump horsepower is calculated by:

$$\text{HP} = \frac{\Delta P \times \text{gpm}}{1715 \times \eta}$$

Where ΔP is the differential pressure (in psi) and η is the pump efficiency. The differential pressure can be converted to head (in feet) by:

$$\text{Head} = \frac{P \times 2.31}{\text{Specific Gravity}}$$

Combining the equations, the pump horsepower is:

$$\text{HP} = \frac{\text{Head} \times \text{Specific Gravity} \times \text{gpm}}{2.31 \times 1715 \times \eta} = \frac{100 \times 1 \times 120}{3962 \times 0.93} = 3.3\text{ hp}$$

90. A: Calcium oxide is rarely used in thermal energy storage systems. It is often used as a desiccant and in sugar refinement. PCM thermal energy storage is widely used for refrigeration and commonly uses salt hydrates and paraffins. Polyethylene glycol is widely used as the PCM material in thermal energy storage systems designed to cool buildings.

91. B: The annual fuel demand for a building can be calculated by:

$$\text{Fuel Demand} = \frac{BLC \times 24 \times DD}{\eta \times CF}$$

Where DD is the number of degree-days, η is the efficiency, and CF is the fuel conversion factor, in this case Btu/Mcf. Therefore, the BLC can be calculated by:

$$BLC = \frac{500\text{ Mcf} \times 0.85 \times 1{,}037{,}000\,\frac{\text{Btu}}{\text{Mcf}}}{24 \times 4{,}000} = 4{,}591$$

92. C: The most important factors for real-time pricing to be beneficial are the ability to shift demand to off-peak rate times when necessary or generate electricity on-site, particularly during peak-times. If the cost of electricity at a facility is relatively low, then the added complexity of shifting demand and the potential for higher prices if the strategy is carefully managed may not make real-time pricing worthwhile.

93. A: The air in this case is being heated sensibly with no addition or removal of moisture (latent heat). The sensible heating of air is calculated by either:

$$Q = \text{cfm} \times 1.08 \times \Delta T = 500 \times 1.08 \times (85 - 60) = 13{,}500 \frac{\text{Btu}}{\text{hour}}$$

or

$$Q = \text{cfm} \times 4.5 \times \Delta h = 500 \times 4.5 \times (27.6 - 21.6) = 13{,}500 \frac{\text{Btu}}{\text{hour}}$$

The water heat transfer is calculated by:

$$Q = 500 \times \text{gpm} \times \Delta T$$

Therefore,

$$\text{gpm} = \frac{13{,}500}{500 \times 10} = 2.7$$

94. A: Up to 80% of power quality issues may be caused by poor grounding and wiring systems. Grounding of electrical systems should be inspected for loose connections or configurations that do not meet current standards to help maintain power quality.

95. B: A lagging current is a result of inductive loads, which increase the reactive power to produce the magnetizing field required for their operation. Capacitor banks draw a current that leads the voltage and can therefore decrease the total reactive power that must be supplied.

96. D: ISO 50001 is a framework for implementing an energy management system developed by the International Organization for Standardization.

97. B: The stack temperature rise is 620°F - 70°F = 550°F. A combustion efficiency chart for natural gas shows that at 8% flue gas oxygen the efficiency is 76%. When the flue gas oxygen is reduced to 3%, the efficiency when the stack temperature rise is 550°F is 80%. Therefore, there is a 4% improvement in efficiency.

98. B: The Btu/hour heating load is calculated by:

$$q = \text{cfm} \times 4.5 \times \Delta h$$

The enthalpy of air at 53°F and 80% RH is found on a psychrometric chart to be 20 Btu/lb. The enthalpy of the air increases to 25 Btu/lb at 73°F. Therefore:

$$q = 5{,}000 \times 4.5 \times (25 - 20) = 112{,}500 \text{ Btu/hour}$$

99. B: It is possible in a counter flow heat exchanger for the exit temperature of the cold stream to exceed the exit temperature of the hot stream.

100. B: The overall U-value required is 0.084, so the total R-value is $\frac{1}{0.084} = 11.9$

The R-values of the plywood and plasterboard are $\frac{1}{1.07} = 0.93$ and $\frac{1}{2.25} = 0.44$, respectively. Therefore, the required insulation R-value is 11.9 – 0.93 – 0.44 = 10.53. The minimum thickness of insulation is:

$$t = k \times R = 0.27 \times 10.53 = 2.8 \text{ inches}$$

So the wall gap should be at least 3.0 inches to achieve the minimum U-value.

101. D: An anemometer measures air velocity. They may operate by means of a rotating vane, deflecting vane, hot wires, ultrasonic sound waves, plate, or pitot tube.

102. D: The IES handbook does not address purchasing and pricing of lights. The function of the handbook is to provide comprehensive information on lighting design, applications, measurements, and practices. The IES provides guidelines for lighting levels for numerous applications/spaces, and the most recent version is the 10th edition.

103. B: The equation to determine the cost of an air leak with the information provided is:

$$\text{Leak Cost} = \frac{\text{Leak rate (scfm)} \times \text{Specific Efficiency} \left(\frac{\text{BHP}}{\text{scfm}}\right) \times 0.746 \frac{\text{kW}}{\text{HP}} \times \text{hours} \times \frac{\text{dollars}}{\text{kWh}}}{\eta}$$

$$\text{Leak Cost} = \frac{6 \text{ scfm} \times 22 \left(\frac{\text{HP}}{\text{scfm}}\right) \times 0.746 \frac{\text{kW}}{\text{HP}} \times 6{,}000 \times \frac{\$0.06}{\text{kWh}}}{0.9} = \$39{,}389$$

104. A: An inverted bucket steam trap operates intermittently and fails in an open position. They are robust with excellent resistance to wear, corrosion, and dirt. They operate very well against back pressure and can handle light loads.

105. D: A building's load factor is an indicator of the shape of the daily demand profile. A high load factor indicates a relatively high base load compared to the peak; whereas a low load factor indicates that there is a period with a high peak load relative to other times in the day.

106. C: 1 boiler horsepower is 33,475 Btu/hour. This is because the definition of boiler horsepower is the amount of energy needed to evaporate 34.5 lb of water at 212°F in one hour ($34.5 \frac{\text{lb}}{\text{HP-hour}} \times 970.3 \frac{\text{Btu}}{\text{lb}}$). If the input rating is 4,185,000 Btu/hour then the output at 85% efficiency is 3,557,250 Btu/hour, which is 3,557,250 ÷ 33,475 = 106 boiler horsepower.

107. D: The credit categories for LEED 2009 (New Construction) are: sustainable sites, water efficiency, energy and atmosphere, materials and resources, indoor environmental quality, innovation and design process, and regional priority.

108. B: The current cost of energy at the facility is:

Electricity: $2{,}400{,}000 \text{ kWh} \times \frac{\$0.08}{\text{kWh}} = \$192{,}000$

Natural gas: $\frac{6{,}200 \text{ MMBtu}}{85\% \text{ efficiency}} = 7{,}294 \text{ MMBtu}$

$$\frac{7{,}294 \text{ MMBtu}}{1.037 \frac{\text{MMBtu}}{\text{Mcf}}} = 7{,}034 \text{ Mcf}$$

$$7{,}034 \text{ Mcf} \times \frac{\$7.50}{\text{Mcf}} = \$52{,}755$$

$$\text{Total cost: } \$192{,}000 + \$52{,}755 = \$244{,}755$$

The new cost of energy is calculated by determining the total fuel input to the CHP and any residual energy that the facility must purchase that is not met by the CHP.

Fuel demand (electricity):300 kW × 6,600 hours = 1,980,000 kWh

$$1{,}980{,}000 \text{ kWh} \times 3{,}412 \frac{\text{Btu}}{\text{kWh}} = 6{,}755.8 \text{ MMBtu}$$

Fuel demand (natural gas): $1.33 \frac{\text{MMBtu}}{\text{hour}} \times 6{,}600 \text{ hours} = 8{,}778 \text{ MMBtu}$

Total Fuel: $\frac{6{,}755.8 \text{ MMBtu} + 8{,}778 \text{ MMBtu}}{87\%} = 17{,}855 \text{ MMBtu}$

$$\frac{17{,}855 \text{ MMBtu}}{1.037 \frac{\text{MMBtu}}{\text{Mcf}}} = 17{,}218 \text{ Mcf}$$

$$17{,}218 \text{ Mcf} \times \frac{\$7.50}{\text{Mcf}} = \$129{,}134$$

Electricity not provided by CHP: 2,400,000 kWh − 1,980,000 kWh = 420,000 kWh

$$420{,}000 \text{ kWh} \times \frac{\$0.08}{\text{kWh}} = \$33{,}600$$

More heat energy is provided by the CHP than is required by the facility (8,778 MMBtu compared to demand of 7,294 MMBtu) so there is no additional cost of gas than what is used by the CHP.

Total cost: \$129,134 + \$33,600 = \$162,734

Cost savings = \$244,755 − \$162,734 = \$82,021

109. B: Secondary power supplies convert DC electricity from one voltage to another. Secondary power requires distribution transformers and metering. A primary power supply consists of feeders, primary loops, main trunks, and lateral taps.

110. D: The cooling load is calculated by using a psychrometric chart to determine the change in enthalpy:

$$\text{Cooling}\left(\frac{\text{Btu}}{\text{hour}}\right) = \text{cfm} \times 4.5 \times \Delta h = 2{,}000 \times 4.5 \times (45 - 23) = 198{,}000 \frac{\text{Btu}}{\text{hour}}$$

1 ton of cooling is 12,000 Btu/hour, so 16.5 tons of cooling are required.

111. C: The lighting power (kW) reduction is 180 × 0.25 kW − 180 × 0.19 kW = 10.8 kW.

When a quarter of the LEDs are dimmed to 10% (for $5 \times 365 = 1{,}825$ hours), the power reduction is

$$180 \times 0.25 \text{ kW} - (135 \times 0.19 + 45 \times 0.019) \text{ kW} = 18.50 \text{ kW}$$

The energy saved when the LEDs are at full power is $10.8 \text{ kW} \times (8{,}760 - 1{,}825)$ hours $=$ 74,898 kWh. The energy saved when the LEDs are dimmed to $18.5 \text{ kW} \times 1{,}825$ hours $=$ 33762.5 kWh. Therefore, total energy savings are 108,660.5 kWh.

The peak demand will occur when the lamps are at full power, so the peak is reduced by 10.8 kW.

Therefore, the total annual cost savings are:

$$\frac{\$0.033 + \$0.025}{\text{kWh}} \times 108{,}660.5 \text{ kWh} + \frac{\$6.50}{\text{kW/month}} \times 10.8 \text{ kW} \times 12 \text{ months}$$
$$= \$6{,}302.31 + \$842.40 = \$7{,}144.71$$

112. B: District energy systems are designed to combine loads of multiple buildings and serve and control them from a central energy plant. District energy plants are designed to reduce energy costs and create economies of scale. These are common on hospital campuses, colleges, and city centers.

113. C: The present worth of the investment (P), interest rate (i), and period of time (n) are known. The annual value (A) is what needs to be found, so the interest factor (A/P) should be found in the 10% interest table on row n=15, which is 0.1315. $\$100{,}000 \times 0.1315 = \$13{,}150$ per year. Dividing by the cost of energy gives the number of kilowatt-hours that need to be saved: $\frac{\$13{,}150}{\$0.09 \text{ per kWh}} =$ 146,000 kWh.

114. D: The price of #2 fuel oil per Btu is:

$$\frac{\$2.00}{\text{gallon}} \times \frac{1 \text{ gallon}}{140{,}000 \text{ Btu}} \times \frac{1{,}000{,}000 \text{ Btu}}{\text{MMBtu}} \times \frac{1}{0.70} = \frac{\$20.41}{\text{MMBtu}}$$

The price of natural gas per Btu is:

$$\frac{\$7.00}{\text{Mcf}} \times \frac{1 \text{ Mcf}}{1{,}037{,}000 \text{ Btu}} \times \frac{1{,}000{,}000 \text{ Btu}}{1 \text{ MMBtu}} \times \frac{1}{0.80} = \frac{\$8.44}{\text{MMBtu}}$$

The savings are therefore $20.41 – $8.44 = $11.97/MMBtu.

115. A: The rate of heat loss through a building element is given by:

$$q = U \times A \times \Delta T$$

The conductance, U, is the reciprocal of the sum of the resistances:

$$U = \frac{1}{R_1 + R_2 + R_3 + \cdots} = \frac{1}{0.68 + \frac{1}{0.9} + 0.17} = 0.51$$

Therefore,

$$\frac{q}{A} = 0.51 \times (69 - 37) = 16.3 \frac{\text{Btu}}{\text{hr} \cdot \text{ft}^2}$$

116. D: The number of lamps required can be calculated using the lumen method:

$$\text{No. lamps} = \frac{FC \times \text{Area}}{\text{Lumens} \times LLF \times CU} = \frac{50 \times (50 \times 30)}{2200 \times 0.71 \times 0.80} = 60 \text{ lamps}$$

117. C: Proportional only control senses an error from the set-point and outputs a control signal proportional to the size of the error. It does not reach the exact set-point because the controller gain is fixed. The size of the residual error is larger with higher gains and results in large oscillations.

118. A: The motor power is:

$$\text{kW} = \frac{\text{HP} \times 0.746 \times \text{Load Factor}}{\eta} = \frac{80 \times 0.746 \times 0.7}{0.91} = 45.9 \text{ kW}$$

The Reactive Power (kVAR) that must be provided by the capacitor bank to correct the power factor is:

$$\text{kVAR} = 45.9 \times [\tan\{\cos^{-1}(0.75)\} - \tan\{\cos^{-1}(0.95)\}] = 25.4 \text{ kVAR}$$

This result can also be found from power factor correction tables: $45.9 \times 0.553 = 25.4$ kVAR

119. C: The main goal and commitment made when the US rejoined the Paris Agreement was to reduce GHG by 50% by 2030. The Paris Agreement is a legally binding international treaty on climate change adopted by 196 parties in 2015. The US formally joined the agreement in 2016. There is a target to reach net zero by 2050. The climate policy focuses on adaptation, which is defined by building resilience against climate change impacts.

120. B: Human centric lighting design takes into account the human circadian rhythm and the natural cycles of daylight and darkness. The relatively new design practice aims to elevate mood, productivity, and social interaction to spur creativity, collaboration, and focus. While energy efficiency benefits could potentially be realized through the use of natural lighting or tunable LEDs, energy efficiency is not a goal of human centric lighting design.

121. C: The US Green Building Council develops and maintains the LEED rating system.

122. C: A general rule of thumb for compressed air systems is that for each 2 psi drop in air pressure, 1% of energy savings can be realized.

123. C: kWh/ft¬2. is an Energy Use Index (EUI) that is typically used in energy benchmarking to compare the energy performance of similar building types of different size.

124. C: The group re-lamping interval is calculated by:

$$GRI = \frac{\text{Average Rated Life } \times \text{\% of Rated Life}}{\text{Annual Operation Hours}} = \frac{20{,}000 \times 0.8}{12 \times 5 \times 52} = \frac{16{,}000}{3{,}120} = 5.1 \text{ years}$$

125. C: While cybersecurity concerns can intersect with ESG goals, they are not considered part of sustainable design. Failing to plan for cybersecurity concerns can make an organization less resilient, however. The key elements of sustainable design are environmental impacts, ESG alliance, design for health and well-being, and use of sustainable architecture.

126. B: The percentage of outside supplied is calculated by:

$$\% \text{ Outside Air} = \frac{(\text{Return Temperature} - \text{Mixed Temperature})}{(\text{Return Temperature} - \text{Outside Temperature})} = \frac{(70 - 65)}{(70 - 50)} = 25\%$$

127. B: As the outside air temperature gets colder it is possible to raise the chilled water supply temperature and still maintain the same supply air temperature. Other indications that the chilled water supply temperature may be increased are a smaller chilled water supply and return differential, and valve positions that are not fully open.

128. A: The actual chiller load does not change since this is dependent upon the heat gains and temperature set-point within the building. The time of load on the chiller is changed by operating the chiller at a constant load at all times (load levelling) or shifting the load to off-peak times.

129. A: A building that has been commissioned previously should periodically be recommissioned to ensure systems are operating as they were designed to perform. An existing building that has never been commissioned would require retrocommissioning.

130. B: The power savings are:

$$\text{Savings (kW)} = \left(\frac{\text{HP} \times 0.746 \times \% \text{ Load}}{\text{Efficiency}}\right)_{\text{Original}} - \left(\frac{\text{HP} \times 0.746 \times \% \text{ Load}}{\text{Efficiency}}\right)_{\text{New}}$$

$$\text{Savings (kW)} = \frac{20 \times 0.746 \times 100\%}{91\%} - \frac{20 \times 0.746 \times 100\%}{93\%} = 16.40 - 16.04 = 0.36 \text{ kW}$$

The energy savings in kWh are: $0.36 \text{ kW} \times 7{,}000 \text{ hours} = 2{,}520 \text{ kWh}$.

131. B: The percentage of voltage imbalance is calculated by:

$$\% \, Imbalance = \frac{|V_{Max\,Diff} - V_{Average}|}{V_{Average}}$$

The average voltage across the three phases is $\frac{235 \text{ V} + 245 \text{ V} + 246 \text{ V}}{3} = 242 \text{ V}$.

$$\% \text{ Imbalance} = \frac{|235 \text{ V} - 242 \text{ V}|}{242 \text{ V}} = \frac{7 \text{ V}}{242 \text{ V}} = 2.9\%$$

132. B: There are a variety of electrical measurement meters, and a multimeter can measure voltage, current, power factor, watts, as well as other measurement functions. It is best to use a true RMS meter because many loads are non-linear and would distorts a pure sinusoidal AC waveform and makes measurements with devices that do not make true RMS measurements inaccurate.

133. A: The Room Cavity Ratio is calculated by:

$$RCR = \frac{2.5 \times h \times \text{Room Perimeter}}{\text{Room Area}}$$

Where h is the height (in feet) from the top of the work surface to the lamp, which in this case is $9 - 32 \times \frac{1 \text{ ft}}{12 \text{ in}} = 6.33$ ft.

$$RCR = \frac{2.5 \times 6.33 \times (40 + 40 + 50 + 50)}{(40 \times 50)} = 1.42$$

134. D: Infrared thermography can be utilized to find excessively hot or cold areas in electrical systems, mechanical equipment, and the building fabric.

135. A: Preventive maintenance is a scheduled maintenance program whereby maintenance occurs at pre-determined times. Condition-based assessments are used in predictive maintenance programs so maintenance is only carried out when it is determined that the equipment requires maintenance.

136. A: The existing level of illuminance is:

$$\text{Footcandles} = \frac{N \times \text{lumens} \times LLF \times CU}{Area} = \frac{(90 \times 2) \times 2{,}800 \times 0.7 \times 0.75}{5000} = 53$$

The number of lamps needed to achieve the same illuminance is:

$$N = \frac{\text{FC} \times \text{Area}}{\text{lumens} \times LLF \times CU} = \frac{53 \times 5000}{2{,}400 \times 0.85 \times 0.8} = 162$$

Therefore, only 162 lamps ÷ 2 lamps per fixture = 81 fixtures would be needed.

137. B: The present worth of the investment (P) is \$112,000 and the uniform series of savings (A) is \$20,000 over 10 years (n). Therefore, the interest rate should be chosen so that the uniform series present worth factor (P/A) is greater than \$112,000/\$20,000 = 5.6. The interest rate table with an interest factor in row n=10 that is the closest value greater than 5.6 is 12%, which has an interest factor of 5.65. At a rate of 12% the maximum investment they could make for the annual savings over 10 years to equal the initial investment, and therefore break even, is \$20,000 × 5.65 = \$113,000.

138. A: FERC does not have any regulatory responsibility for retail sales and local transmission of electricity or distribution of natural gas. FERC regulates the interstate transmission and wholesale sale of electricity as well as regulates the interstate transmission of natural gas. FERC will sometimes review the siting of electricity transmission projects but does not approve electricity generation facilities. However, FERC is responsible for approving the siting of interstate natural gas pipelines and storage facilities.

139. B: Measurement and verification are covered in depth in ASHRAE guideline 14-20xx. ASHRAE standard 211 defines the practices for conducting a consistent energy audit and for writing the energy audit report. ASHRAE 211 key components are detailing the steps for conducting an audit, defining a consistent approach for data collection, and listing guidelines to meet compliance and certification standards such as LEED and Energy Star.

140. A: A building that earns 40 to 49 points is eligible to become LEED Certified.

141. B: The simple payback is calculated by dividing the additional initial cost by the annual savings. In this case the extra cost for the high efficiency motor is \$1,300. The annual savings are 4,000 kWh × \$0.09/kWh = \$360. The simple payback is therefore $\frac{\$1{,}300}{\$360} = 3.6$ years.

142. B: A guaranteed savings ESPC requires the ESCO to cover any shortfall in savings. Often a provision is made whereby a portion of any excess savings can be set aside to help cover any future shortfalls.

143. B: The requirement to reduce energy use in federal buildings by 30% was in the Energy Independence and Security Act of 2007.

144. C: The minimum amount of outdoor air required is calculated by the ventilation rate procedure using:

$$\text{Outdoor Air (cfm)} = \text{No. People} \times \text{People Outdoor Rate} + \text{Area} \times \text{Area Outdoor Rate}$$

$$\text{Outdoor Air (cfm)} = 30 \times 5 + 5{,}000 \times 0.06 = 150 + 300 = 450 \text{ cfm}$$

The default values are used only when the occupancy is not known.

145. A: Heating degree-days are separate from cooling degree-days, and if there is a strong correlation between energy consumption and cooling degree-days is does not mean that there is either a correlation or no correlation with heating degree-days as well.

How to Overcome Test Anxiety

Just the thought of taking a test is enough to make most people a little nervous. A test is an important event that can have a long-term impact on your future, so it's important to take it seriously and it's natural to feel anxious about performing well. But just because anxiety is normal, that doesn't mean that it's helpful in test taking, or that you should simply accept it as part of your life. Anxiety can have a variety of effects. These effects can be mild, like making you feel slightly nervous, or severe, like blocking your ability to focus or remember even a simple detail.

If you experience test anxiety—whether severe or mild—it's important to know how to beat it. To discover this, first you need to understand what causes test anxiety.

Causes of Test Anxiety

While we often think of anxiety as an uncontrollable emotional state, it can actually be caused by simple, practical things. One of the most common causes of test anxiety is that a person does not feel adequately prepared for their test. This feeling can be the result of many different issues such as poor study habits or lack of organization, but the most common culprit is time management. Starting to study too late, failing to organize your study time to cover all of the material, or being distracted while you study will mean that you're not well prepared for the test. This may lead to cramming the night before, which will cause you to be physically and mentally exhausted for the test. Poor time management also contributes to feelings of stress, fear, and hopelessness as you realize you are not well prepared but don't know what to do about it.

Other times, test anxiety is not related to your preparation for the test but comes from unresolved fear. This may be a past failure on a test, or poor performance on tests in general. It may come from comparing yourself to others who seem to be performing better or from the stress of living up to expectations. Anxiety may be driven by fears of the future—how failure on this test would affect your educational and career goals. These fears are often completely irrational, but they can still negatively impact your test performance.

Elements of Test Anxiety

As mentioned earlier, test anxiety is considered to be an emotional state, but it has physical and mental components as well. Sometimes you may not even realize that you are suffering from test anxiety until you notice the physical symptoms. These can include trembling hands, rapid heartbeat, sweating, nausea, and tense muscles. Extreme anxiety may lead to fainting or vomiting. Obviously, any of these symptoms can have a negative impact on testing. It is important to recognize them as soon as they begin to occur so that you can address the problem before it damages your performance.

The mental components of test anxiety include trouble focusing and inability to remember learned information. During a test, your mind is on high alert, which can help you recall information and stay focused for an extended period of time. However, anxiety interferes with your mind's natural processes, causing you to blank out, even on the questions you know well. The strain of testing during anxiety makes it difficult to stay focused, especially on a test that may take several hours. Extreme anxiety can take a huge mental toll, making it difficult not only to recall test information but even to understand the test questions or pull your thoughts together.

Effects of Test Anxiety

Test anxiety is like a disease—if left untreated, it will get progressively worse. Anxiety leads to poor performance, and this reinforces the feelings of fear and failure, which in turn lead to poor performances on subsequent tests. It can grow from a mild nervousness to a crippling condition. If allowed to progress, test anxiety can have a big impact on your schooling, and consequently on your future.

Test anxiety can spread to other parts of your life. Anxiety on tests can become anxiety in any stressful situation, and blanking on a test can turn into panicking in a job situation. But fortunately, you don't have to let anxiety rule your testing and determine your grades. There are a number of relatively simple steps you can take to move past anxiety and function normally on a test and in the rest of life.

Physical Steps for Beating Test Anxiety

While test anxiety is a serious problem, the good news is that it can be overcome. It doesn't have to control your ability to think and remember information. While it may take time, you can begin taking steps today to beat anxiety.

Just as your first hint that you may be struggling with anxiety comes from the physical symptoms, the first step to treating it is also physical. Rest is crucial for having a clear, strong mind. If you are tired, it is much easier to give in to anxiety. But if you establish good sleep habits, your body and mind will be ready to perform optimally, without the strain of exhaustion. Additionally, sleeping well helps you to retain information better, so you're more likely to recall the answers when you see the test questions.

Getting good sleep means more than going to bed on time. It's important to allow your brain time to relax. Take study breaks from time to time so it doesn't get overworked, and don't study right before bed. Take time to rest your mind before trying to rest your body, or you may find it difficult to fall asleep.

Along with sleep, other aspects of physical health are important in preparing for a test. Good nutrition is vital for good brain function. Sugary foods and drinks may give a burst of energy but this burst is followed by a crash, both physically and emotionally. Instead, fuel your body with protein and vitamin-rich foods.

Also, drink plenty of water. Dehydration can lead to headaches and exhaustion, especially if your brain is already under stress from the rigors of the test. Particularly if your test is a long one, drink water during the breaks. And if possible, take an energy-boosting snack to eat between sections.

Along with sleep and diet, a third important part of physical health is exercise. Maintaining a steady workout schedule is helpful, but even taking 5-minute study breaks to walk can help get your blood pumping faster and clear your head. Exercise also releases endorphins, which contribute to a positive feeling and can help combat test anxiety.

When you nurture your physical health, you are also contributing to your mental health. If your body is healthy, your mind is much more likely to be healthy as well. So take time to rest, nourish your body with healthy food and water, and get moving as much as possible. Taking these physical steps will make you stronger and more able to take the mental steps necessary to overcome test anxiety.

Mental Steps for Beating Test Anxiety

Working on the mental side of test anxiety can be more challenging, but as with the physical side, there are clear steps you can take to overcome it. As mentioned earlier, test anxiety often stems from lack of preparation, so the obvious solution is to prepare for the test. Effective studying may be the most important weapon you have for beating test anxiety, but you can and should employ several other mental tools to combat fear.

First, boost your confidence by reminding yourself of past success—tests or projects that you aced. If you're putting as much effort into preparing for this test as you did for those, there's no reason you should expect to fail here. Work hard to prepare; then trust your preparation.

Second, surround yourself with encouraging people. It can be helpful to find a study group, but be sure that the people you're around will encourage a positive attitude. If you spend time with others who are anxious or cynical, this will only contribute to your own anxiety. Look for others who are motivated to study hard from a desire to succeed, not from a fear of failure.

Third, reward yourself. A test is physically and mentally tiring, even without anxiety, and it can be helpful to have something to look forward to. Plan an activity following the test, regardless of the outcome, such as going to a movie or getting ice cream.

When you are taking the test, if you find yourself beginning to feel anxious, remind yourself that you know the material. Visualize successfully completing the test. Then take a few deep, relaxing breaths and return to it. Work through the questions carefully but with confidence, knowing that you are capable of succeeding.

Developing a healthy mental approach to test taking will also aid in other areas of life. Test anxiety affects more than just the actual test—it can be damaging to your mental health and even contribute to depression. It's important to beat test anxiety before it becomes a problem for more than testing.

Study Strategy

Being prepared for the test is necessary to combat anxiety, but what does being prepared look like? You may study for hours on end and still not feel prepared. What you need is a strategy for test prep. The next few pages outline our recommended steps to help you plan out and conquer the challenge of preparation.

Step 1: Scope Out the Test

Learn everything you can about the format (multiple choice, essay, etc.) and what will be on the test. Gather any study materials, course outlines, or sample exams that may be available. Not only will this help you to prepare, but knowing what to expect can help to alleviate test anxiety.

Step 2: Map Out the Material

Look through the textbook or study guide and make note of how many chapters or sections it has. Then divide these over the time you have. For example, if a book has 15 chapters and you have five days to study, you need to cover three chapters each day. Even better, if you have the time, leave an extra day at the end for overall review after you have gone through the material in depth.

If time is limited, you may need to prioritize the material. Look through it and make note of which sections you think you already have a good grasp on, and which need review. While you are studying, skim quickly through the familiar sections and take more time on the challenging parts.

Write out your plan so you don't get lost as you go. Having a written plan also helps you feel more in control of the study, so anxiety is less likely to arise from feeling overwhelmed at the amount to cover.

Step 3: Gather Your Tools

Decide what study method works best for you. Do you prefer to highlight in the book as you study and then go back over the highlighted portions? Or do you type out notes of the important information? Or is it helpful to make flashcards that you can carry with you? Assemble the pens, index cards, highlighters, post-it notes, and any other materials you may need so you won't be distracted by getting up to find things while you study.

If you're having a hard time retaining the information or organizing your notes, experiment with different methods. For example, try color-coding by subject with colored pens, highlighters, or post-it notes. If you learn better by hearing, try recording yourself reading your notes so you can listen while in the car, working out, or simply sitting at your desk. Ask a friend to quiz you from your flashcards, or try teaching someone the material to solidify it in your mind.

Step 4: Create Your Environment

It's important to avoid distractions while you study. This includes both the obvious distractions like visitors and the subtle distractions like an uncomfortable chair (or a too-comfortable couch that makes you want to fall asleep). Set up the best study environment possible: good lighting and a comfortable work area. If background music helps you focus, you may want to turn it on, but otherwise keep the room quiet. If you are using a computer to take notes, be sure you don't have any other windows open, especially applications like social media, games, or anything else that could distract you. Silence your phone and turn off notifications. Be sure to keep water close by so you stay hydrated while you study (but avoid unhealthy drinks and snacks).

Also, take into account the best time of day to study. Are you freshest first thing in the morning? Try to set aside some time then to work through the material. Is your mind clearer in the afternoon or evening? Schedule your study session then. Another method is to study at the same time of day that you will take the test, so that your brain gets used to working on the material at that time and will be ready to focus at test time.

Step 5: Study!

Once you have done all the study preparation, it's time to settle into the actual studying. Sit down, take a few moments to settle your mind so you can focus, and begin to follow your study plan. Don't give in to distractions or let yourself procrastinate. This is your time to prepare so you'll be ready to fearlessly approach the test. Make the most of the time and stay focused.

Of course, you don't want to burn out. If you study too long you may find that you're not retaining the information very well. Take regular study breaks. For example, taking five minutes out of every hour to walk briskly, breathing deeply and swinging your arms, can help your mind stay fresh.

As you get to the end of each chapter or section, it's a good idea to do a quick review. Remind yourself of what you learned and work on any difficult parts. When you feel that you've mastered the material, move on to the next part. At the end of your study session, briefly skim through your notes again.

But while review is helpful, cramming last minute is NOT. If at all possible, work ahead so that you won't need to fit all your study into the last day. Cramming overloads your brain with more information than it can process and retain, and your tired mind may struggle to recall even previously learned information when it is overwhelmed with last-minute study. Also, the urgent nature of cramming and the stress placed on your brain contribute to anxiety. You'll be more likely to go to the test feeling unprepared and having trouble thinking clearly.

So don't cram, and don't stay up late before the test, even just to review your notes at a leisurely pace. Your brain needs rest more than it needs to go over the information again. In fact, plan to finish your studies by noon or early afternoon the day before the test. Give your brain the rest of the day to relax or focus on other things, and get a good night's sleep. Then you will be fresh for the test and better able to recall what you've studied.

Step 6: Take a Practice Test

Many courses offer sample tests, either online or in the study materials. This is an excellent resource to check whether you have mastered the material, as well as to prepare for the test format and environment.

Check the test format ahead of time: the number of questions, the type (multiple choice, free response, etc.), and the time limit. Then create a plan for working through them. For example, if you have 30 minutes to take a 60-question test, your limit is 30 seconds per question. Spend less time on the questions you know well so that you can take more time on the difficult ones.

If you have time to take several practice tests, take the first one open book, with no time limit. Work through the questions at your own pace and make sure you fully understand them. Gradually work up to taking a test under test conditions: sit at a desk with all study materials put away and set a timer. Pace yourself to make sure you finish the test with time to spare and go back to check your answers if you have time.

After each test, check your answers. On the questions you missed, be sure you understand why you missed them. Did you misread the question (tests can use tricky wording)? Did you forget the information? Or was it something you hadn't learned? Go back and study any shaky areas that the practice tests reveal.

Taking these tests not only helps with your grade, but also aids in combating test anxiety. If you're already used to the test conditions, you're less likely to worry about it, and working through tests until you're scoring well gives you a confidence boost. Go through the practice tests until you feel comfortable, and then you can go into the test knowing that you're ready for it.

Test Tips

On test day, you should be confident, knowing that you've prepared well and are ready to answer the questions. But aside from preparation, there are several test day strategies you can employ to maximize your performance.

First, as stated before, get a good night's sleep the night before the test (and for several nights before that, if possible). Go into the test with a fresh, alert mind rather than staying up late to study.

Try not to change too much about your normal routine on the day of the test. It's important to eat a nutritious breakfast, but if you normally don't eat breakfast at all, consider eating just a protein bar. If you're a coffee drinker, go ahead and have your normal coffee. Just make sure you time it so that the caffeine doesn't wear off right in the middle of your test. Avoid sugary beverages, and drink enough water to stay hydrated but not so much that you need a restroom break 10 minutes into the test. If your test isn't first thing in the morning, consider going for a walk or doing a light workout before the test to get your blood flowing.

Allow yourself enough time to get ready, and leave for the test with plenty of time to spare so you won't have the anxiety of scrambling to arrive in time. Another reason to be early is to select a good seat. It's helpful to sit away from doors and windows, which can be distracting. Find a good seat, get out your supplies, and settle your mind before the test begins.

When the test begins, start by going over the instructions carefully, even if you already know what to expect. Make sure you avoid any careless mistakes by following the directions.

Then begin working through the questions, pacing yourself as you've practiced. If you're not sure on an answer, don't spend too much time on it, and don't let it shake your confidence. Either skip it and come back later, or eliminate as many wrong answers as possible and guess among the remaining ones. Don't dwell on these questions as you continue—put them out of your mind and focus on what lies ahead.

Be sure to read all of the answer choices, even if you're sure the first one is the right answer. Sometimes you'll find a better one if you keep reading. But don't second-guess yourself if you do immediately know the answer. Your gut instinct is usually right. Don't let test anxiety rob you of the information you know.

If you have time at the end of the test (and if the test format allows), go back and review your answers. Be cautious about changing any, since your first instinct tends to be correct, but make sure you didn't misread any of the questions or accidentally mark the wrong answer choice. Look over any you skipped and make an educated guess.

At the end, leave the test feeling confident. You've done your best, so don't waste time worrying about your performance or wishing you could change anything. Instead, celebrate the successful completion of this test. And finally, use this test to learn how to deal with anxiety even better next time.

Review Video: Test Anxiety
Visit mometrix.com/academy and enter code: 100340

Important Qualification

Not all anxiety is created equal. If your test anxiety is causing major issues in your life beyond the classroom or testing center, or if you are experiencing troubling physical symptoms related to your anxiety, it may be a sign of a serious physiological or psychological condition. If this sounds like your situation, we strongly encourage you to seek professional help.

Online Resources

Due to our efforts to try to keep this book to a manageable length, we've created a link that will give you access to all of your online resources:

mometrix.com/resources719/energymanager

It's Your Moment, Let's Celebrate It!

Share your story @mometrixtestpreparation